DIDEROT AND STERNE

DIDEROT
AND
STERNE

ALICE GREEN FREDMAN

OCTAGON BOOKS

A DIVISION OF FARRAR, STRAUS AND GIROUX

New York   1973

Reprinted 1973
by special arrangement with Columbia University Press

OCTAGON BOOKS
A DIVISION OF FARRAR, STRAUS & GIROUX, INC.
19 Union Square West
New York, N. Y. 10003

LIBRARY OF CONGRESS CATALOG CARD NUMBER: 72-13743

ISBN 0-374-92884-3

Printed in USA by
Thomson-Shore, Inc.
Dexter, Michigan

CLARKE F. ANSLEY AWARD

This study was selected by a committee of the Faculty of Philosophy, Columbia University, to receive the Clarke F. Ansley Award for 1953. Three such awards are given by Columbia University Press for outstanding dissertations submitted in candidacy for the degree of Doctor of Philosophy in the three Graduate Faculties of the University.

For Midge — with love and gratitude

ACKNOWLEDGMENTS

IT is a pleasure to record here my gratitude to the persons responsible for what may be found meritorious in this study: to Professor James L. Clifford, for carefully reading the manuscript and for offering spirited cooperation; to Professor Otis E. Fellows, for providing the initial spark and for continuing to guide the work through its various stages; to Professor Marjorie H. Nicolson, for suggesting additions and emendations and for contributing subtle support; to Professor Norman L. Torrey, for sharing his knowledge of the eighteenth century and the history of ideas and for generously applying his wise counsel; and to my husband, for criticizing with acuteness and for encouraging with compassion.

Grateful acknowledgment is also made to the Clarendon Press, Oxford, and to Mr. Lewis Perry Curtis for permission to quote from *The Letters of Laurence Sterne;* and to the Librairie Gallimard, Paris, for permission to quote from Diderot's *Lettres à Sophie Volland.*

CONTENTS

DIDEROT AND STERNE

CONFRONTATIONS

I N the year 1713, in Langres, France, and in Clonmel, Ireland, two men were born who were destined to have a lively posthumous relationship. In their own lifetimes, Denis Diderot and Laurence Sterne did not confront each other until they were mature men—forty-nine, to be exact. By that time, each had decided on the means by which he would make his mark in the world. Sterne had already achieved his goal of becoming a famous author and had just finished the fifth and sixth volumes of *Tristram Shandy*. Diderot had set aside his ambition to write plays and was entering the last period of his duties as editor of the *Encyclopédie*. A half dozen years later, Sterne died before he could savor his greatest vogue, and Diderot, having discharged his most monumental obligation to posterity, was free to apply himself to other interests. To be sure, in the six years between their mutual introduction and Sterne's death they did not meet each other steadily. Sterne made a point of stopping in Paris on his way to and from the Continent, but in all he visited the city only four times. While he certainly never failed to see the *philosophes,* he also appeared in circles of the Parisian social world which Diderot did not frequent.

Yet, starting with Diderot's own admission of copying a paragraph from *Tristram Shandy* [1] for *Jacques le fataliste,* Diderot's and Sterne's names have been coupled by critics from the eighteenth to the twentieth century.[2] The general tendency of most of the criticism has been to see *Jacques* as a fairly weak imitation of *Tristram*. In their efforts to prove that Sterne's influence is not to Diderot's credit, critics have suggested a variety of reasons: Diderot lacks ideas, Diderot is graceless, he does not even know *how* to copy from Sterne, he is more obscene than Sterne, his style is heavy-handed, he cannot create characters, he lacks Sterne's humanity, he has no sense of humor—to note a few. Underlying much of the condemnation is probably the tacit agreement among critics that since Sterne presumably "did it first," Diderot should not be allowed to escape unreproved. In the twentieth century, some attempts have been made to balance the judgment: Baldwin and Cru both work in the direction of minimizing the influence of Sterne; Green reverses Barton's procedure and attacks Sterne while praising Diderot; and Loy develops the most extensive exoneration yet to appear.

Actually, neither plagiarism nor its related practice, ghostwriting, was wholeheartedly decried in the eighteenth century. A recent critic of Sterne has pointed out that the practice of pillaging and copying was common among members of the English clergy and was recommended for inexperienced preachers.[3] Even Dr. Johnson wrote some forty sermons for various clerics to pass off as their own, although his sense of ethics forbade him to tell Boswell how to recover them.[4] Pope's opinion was that, in matters literary, writers "should repay with something of their own what they take from others." [5] Neither Diderot nor Sterne regarded it a crime to use the works of others. Diderot himself stated in the *Salon* of 1765, "I want a painter, a poet, to improve himself, grow warm, draw his inspiration from another; and this borrowing of light and inspiration is no plagiarism." [6] Both men were adept at taking the writings of someone else as a point of departure and creating from these something entirely their own. In the transposition and improvisation that form an integral part of their use of other writers' material, both Diderot and Sterne have always repaid their creditors more than adequately. The tantalizing problem is not that Diderot helped himself to a few Shandean ideas for a work that represents only a small part of his total writings, but that there must have been something about the Anglican clergyman's work and thought which attracted the Parisian *philosophe*.

It was early in the year 1762 that Diderot met the man, Sterne. Sterne had left London so precipitately that he had neglected to apply for a passport, and Baron d'Holbach was one of the Frenchmen who guaranteed security for Sterne's conduct in France. By the thirty-first of January, Sterne was proudly reporting to Garrick that in the two weeks he had spent in Paris he had been as much lionized as in London. He added that D'Holbach, "the great protector of wits, and the Scavans who are no wits," entertained him at his open house and welcomed him into the family circle.[7] A most intimate friend of the family was Diderot, who rarely missed an opportunity to attend the baron's biweekly salons at the rue Royale-Saint-Roch or to relax at Grandval, the baron's country seat. The "Scavans," who at first bored Sterne as they bored Walpole, constituted the core of the *philosophes;* two years later D'Holbach was to tell another British visitor, David Hume, that of the eighteen men Hume saw at D'Holbach's table, fifteen were atheists and three had not quite made up their minds.

Apparently Sterne found no difficulty in adjusting himself to the anticlerical group. By March seventeenth, he was speaking French "fast and fluent" and had spent a month more in

Paris than he had planned. By the middle of April, he was reading, at Diderot's request, a rough translation of the *Fils naturel,* because Diderot was considering sending it to Garrick for an English production and wanted Sterne's opinion. What Sterne told the *philosophe* is not recorded, but he wrote Garrick that it was too sentimental, wordy, and didactic for his taste.[8] This judgment did not prevent him from completing the favor. In May he recommended the play to Thomas Becket, who had taken over the publishing of *Tristram* with volumes five and six. Becket, in turn, must have handed it over to Sterne's earlier publisher, for it was printed by Dodsley as *Dorval, or the Test of Virtue,* in 1767 and received favorable notices in both the *London Magazine*[9] and the *Monthly Review.*[10]

Sterne's good offices did not stop there. In the same letter to his publisher he gave further indication of his affection for Diderot by enclosing a list of books for Becket to send from England:

All the Works of Pope—the neatest & cheapest Edition—(therefore I suppose not Warburtons)
The Dramatick Works of Cibber—& Cibber's Life—
Chaucer
Tillotson's Sermons—the small edition—
All Lock's [sic] works.
the 6 Vols. of Shandy—NB. These place to my Acct) for they are for a present to him—and all the works of (Vide Card)[11]

One would indeed like to "see the card," for this constituted a list in Diderot's own hand which Sterne was unable to decipher. Meanwhile, Sterne was forming other friendships. He had closed an agreement with Crébillon *fils* for the publication of mutual "expostulatory letters" on the authors' respective indecorums, "the copy to be sold, and the money equally divided," [12] and was basking in the glory afforded him by his French admirers. The early reference to the "Scavans who are no wits" never reappears. In subsequent years it is replaced by "my best respects to my worthy Baron D'Holbach and all that society," or "my most grateful respects to the worthy Baron D'Holbach"; "If you see Baron D'Holbach and Diderot, present my respects to them," "my comps to Foley to Baron Holbach—Diderot." In 1765 he is looking forward to enjoying himself "a week or ten days at Paris with my friends, particularly the Baron d'Holbach, and the rest of the joyous sett."

The friendship was by no means one-sided. The *philosophes* reciprocated not only by welcoming Sterne each time he passed through Paris but also by attending a sermon Sterne preached in Paris in May, 1764: Hume, Diderot and D'Holbach were reported to be among the "concourse of all nations, and religions too" which attended. Moreover, the names of Diderot, D'Holbach and Voltaire appeared on the list of subscribers to the third and fourth volumes of Sterne's sermons.

June, 1766, was the last time the "joyous sett" was to see Sterne as he stopped over in Paris on his way to England, but Diderot may have rendered his English friend another posthumous service in addition to proclaiming his regard for M. Sterne in *Jacques*. When the Abbé Raynal's *Histoire des deux Indes* was reviewed in the *Correspondance littéraire* of June, 1781,[13] an effusive "Eloge d'Eliza Draper" which appeared in the second part of the *Histoire* was attributed to Diderot. There is no certainty that Diderot was the author. Among his manuscripts it was bound in the same notebook as the *Eloge de Richardson,* definitely written by Diderot, and an *Eloge de Lycurgue,* which bears no evidence of Diderot's authorship.[14] Diderot's son-in-law, Caroillon de Vandeul, listed it as "éloge d'Eliza Draper p. l'abbé Raynal" without indicating whether it was "par" or "pour," but Diderot himself explicitly attributed "l'oraison funèbre d'Eliza Draper" to the abbé in the "Lettre apologétique de l'abbé Raynal à M. Grimm." [15] One can merely speculate on the evidence that as a fitting conclusion to his friendship for Sterne, the aging *philosophe* penned an elegy for Sterne's Eliza.

And there were, indeed, very good reasons for a friendship to develop between the English clergyman and the French encyclopedist. Certainly so far as Sterne's acclaim by the *philosophes* was concerned, the anglomania of the D'Holbach circle was an important factor. While the French *haut monde* of the mid-eighteenth century was setting the fashion of aping English taste, French intellectuals since the Edict of Nantes had been looking to England as the symbol of political, civil, and religious liberty and eventually outdid their models in free-thinking.

Diderot was among the foremost enthusiasts for England, and fortunately he was not dependent on French translations. As a matter of fact, he had contributed to their number early in his career with his translations of Temple Stanyan's *The Grecian History,* James's *Medicinal Dictionary,* probably several unidentified works, and his translation-adaptation of one of his great interests, Shaftesbury. In his *Prospectus,* he emphasized the encyclopedists' respect for Bacon, clearly established in D'Alembert's *Discours préliminaire.* He entitled his *Pensées sur l'interprétation de la nature* after Bacon's work [16] and dwelt on his more personal admiration for Bacon in his discussion of the chancellor's genius in the article "Encyclopédie." Grimm was to use many of these passages to draw a flattering parallel between the English genius and his eighteenth-century French counterpart, Denis Diderot,[17] who,

Grimm claimed, had done more than any other man of his century to popularize the works of his great predecessor. Newton, Locke, and Hume all received the *philosophe's* warm approbation, and although he was rather wary of Hobbes, he eventually developed much admiration for the treatise on *Human Nature.* Diderot, who had glorified the spirit of experiment in a passage of the *Bijoux indiscrets* in 1748, certainly drew much light and inspiration from the English writers of the empirical tradition. He was, in addition, one of the few in eighteenth-century France to appreciate Shakespeare intelligently, and he fully realized the difficulty of introducing Shakespearean drama to an audience schooled in the tradition of Racine and Corneille. But he also wanted to reform the French theatre, which he believed had degenerated into stiffly acted imitations of a genre that had reached its climax a hundred years before. He found authority for his *drame bourgeois* in the domestic tragedy and prose works for the theatre in England. A half dozen years before he met Garrick, he was using him as an illustration of the natural acting and pantomime so necessary for improving the stage.[18] And if he sought precedent for his theatrical reforms in England, he responded with equal enthusiasm to the "new fiction" of Fielding and Richardson [19] and, later, Sterne. There is much evidence to support M. Legros' contention that it would be hard to find a period in the *philosophe's* life when he did not have an English book in his hand.[20]

Diderot was not, however, completely uncritical of all things English. His unflattering comparative study of English and French manners in the *Bijoux indiscrets* concludes with the implication that neither London nor Paris high society has much to recommend it. In his "Réflexions sur Térence," he appreciates the vitality of the Restoration dramatists but accuses them of sacrificing taste and simple realism for false animation. Dorval, in the *Second Entretien sur le Fils naturel,* is rather embarrassed to be reminded that he used to be "mad about those people. You used to look on their country as the asylum of liberty, the land of virtue, invention, originality." [21] In the *Salon* of 1765, as later in *Jacques,* Diderot comments that while the French have a tendency to go into ecstasies over all English productions, the English generally deprecate French works. And in October, 1765, after D'Holbach had returned, thoroughly disenchanted, from England, Diderot gives Sophie Volland a critical report on English political, economic, and social institutions. These comments do not mean that Diderot shared the baron's disillusionment or ceased to recognize his debt to the independent spirit and the innovations that attracted him to England. He simply developed more perspective and was replacing a somewhat uncritical enthusiasm with more tempered judgments.

Though Diderot probably would have been unsuccessful in eliciting from Sterne any objective analysis of England, Sterne shared Diderot's distaste for the monotony of French polite society. At first, the Englishman was delighted to claim that *Tristram* was almost as well known in Paris as in London—technically, this was true; it was "known" through a review, but it was not widely read—and was pleased to report that the French assured him he was making remarkable progress in their language. Yet in two months he had perceived and was describing with patronizing amusement that

here every thing is hyperbolized—and if a woman is but simply pleased—'tis *Je suis charmée*—and if she is charmed 'tis nothing less, than that she is *ravi*-sh'd—and when ravi-sh'd (which may happen) there is nothing left for her but to fly to the other world for a metaphor, and swear, qu'elle étoit toute *extasiée*—which mode of speaking, is, by the bye, here creeping into use, and there is scarce a woman who understands the *bon ton,* but is seven times in a day in downright extasy—that is, the devil's in her—by a small mistake of one world for the other—[22]

Increasingly, he was to remark on the French emphasis on appearance at all cost, on the wearisome civility, artificiality, and insipidity of French character. His most succinct expression on this subject was the famous metaphor of the coins worn smooth by circulation,[23] a comment that met the approval not only of Diderot, who repeated the figure in *Jacques* and in his *Réfutation suivie de l'ouvrage d'Helvétius intitulé "L'Homme,"* but also of their mutual friend, Garrick, who echoed the sentiment by advising a friend that such was the nature of French *politesse* that "when you have seen half a dozen French men and women you have seen the whole." [24]

As his experience of France widened, Sterne was to comment on more pernicious abuses, but his major criticism always returned to the insincerity and affectation of the social world. Sterne was no Smelfungus, however, and somewhat archly prided himself on equaling the French at their own game. If he protested in *Tristram* and the *Sentimental Journey* his incredulity at the notion of making love by sentiments, in actuality he conducted his own *affaires d'amour* in the same manner; and while his chapter on Paris in the *Sentimental Journey* is a witty exposé of the "children of art," it was doubtless by using their own methods that he was able to talk a lady into postponing her epoch of deism for two years. For the man who started out as an obscure Yorkshire parson became a master of *marivaudage.* This was a talent that Diderot had neither the requisites nor the incentive for developing. He confided to Sophie Volland in 1760 that he had often wondered why, with his affable and easy temper, his indulgent nature, his good humor and learning, he was so little made for high society. It was impossible, he explained, for him to act according to those standards with his friends, and he was totally ignorant of that "reserved" and "senseless" language one spoke to indifferent people. "I am either silent or indiscreet," was his conclusion.[25]

Fortunately, Sterne was also indiscreet and doubtless set aside the *bon ton* while relaxing with the D'Holbach group, because Diderot singled him out as an Englishman for whom he had particular esteem. They had in common certain traits of personality that were to encourage a pleasant relationship. Both men were noted for their sensibility and good will as well as for enjoying buffoonery, for brilliantly impetuous conversation and the uninhibited expression of their feelings. Recently, a critic has said of Sterne "that if the whim struck him, he veered about like a weathercock in a blustery wind," [26] but in 1759 the son of the Langres cutler had told Sophie Volland that the head of a Langrois sits on his shoulders like a weathercock on top of a steeple. Indeed, repeated references to their volatility have done Sterne and Diderot considerable disservice by grossly exaggerating their mental and artistic "chaos." The self-imposed disciplines of each have not been recognized until fairly recently.

Although affinities of temperament may well have supplied a partial basis for friendship, Diderot and Sterne found that they had further reasons for mutual attraction. Sterne was not Diderot's intellectual equal, but he was by no means a British provincial totally indifferent to French literature. There is no way of determining when Sterne collected his library—he increased it greatly by his purchase of seven hundred books "dog cheap" in 1761—but a reproduction of the catalogue printed in 1768 indicates that French writers, including the precursors and authors of the enlightenment, were well represented. Bayle, Saint-Evremond, Fontenelle, Fénelon, Montesquieu, and Voltaire appear in company with Rabelais, Montaigne, La Bruyère, Boileau, La Fontaine, Scarron, Le Sage, and the three great dramatists of the French classic theatre. These readings would certainly have constituted a good background for a conversation with Diderot, who would also have been gratified to learn that there were a number of Latin editions of Horace in Sterne's possession. Sterne added, perhaps as they came out, the works of Rousseau, Gessner, and Marmontel, so that along with Prévost's *Le Doyen de Killerine* and *Cléveland* he had a fair sampling of moral and sentimental tales.

And if the *philosophe* was pleased that Sterne was able to discuss French authors with him, one can imagine Sterne's reactions to the keen interest and appreciation Diderot had for English writers. Sterne may not have studied Locke with the intellectual penetration of Diderot and Condillac, but he read him intelligently and often. Included in his library were some half dozen editions of Locke's works. Newton was represented by two volumes and several commentaries. He could recall any of his three editions of Shaftesbury's *Characteristics* in case Diderot turned the subject to his earlier enthusiasm, and both men could exchange opinions on Hutcheson's theories of beauty and virtue. They could compare notes on Bacon, Hume, and Hobbes, or the mathematical writings of Saunderson, who figured in the *Lettre sur les aveugles* which had served as pretext for Diderot's imprisonment in 1749. They could turn the discussion to Milton, whose *Paradise Lost* had occupied Diderot during his confinement at Vincennes, to Swift or Shakespeare. In short, their mutual interests extend beyond boisterous toasts to their Cervantes or Rabelais. Sterne could find in Diderot a man who was not merely conversant with English literature and philosophy, but who was, more than any Frenchman of his century, deeply oriented in English thinking. R. Loyalty Cru has justifiably entitled his study of Diderot's relations with England, *Diderot as a Disciple of English Thought.*

F. C. Green has developed the thesis that the mental climates of England and France in the eighteenth century were so fundamentally different that it was impossible for mutual influences to penetrate deeply. His argument is that the English attitudes were formed in the tradition of Bacon and Shakespeare, the French in the tradition of Descartes and Racine, and that these divergent currents prevented any truly common understanding. Yet Diderot does not seem to fit into the pattern contrived for his contemporaries. He was to confide to Grimm that he felt like an "hors d'œuvre" in his own time: "I was not made for this world, nor this world for me." His mind was too restless and explorative to remain contentedly within the confines of his cultural inheritance. It darted across the Channel to study and carry further the achievements of some of Sterne's countrymen. It deliberately sidestepped *à priori* reasoning—"Incredulity is the first step toward philosophy," was Diderot's final comment—and it used experimental and inductive methods to examine anew all it met. "I would rather raise clouds than scatter them," he said; "I prefer suspending judgments to making them"; and his mind busied itself with anticipations and suggestions of theories and practices that were not to be fully explored until the nineteenth and twentieth centuries.

Sterne's mind was not so deeply rebellious as Diderot's, but he, too, must have regarded various elements of the contemporary cultural and social scene with the view that he did not "belong." As Diderot frequently turned to England for a springboard, so Sterne was attracted to the writings of Rabelais, Montaigne, Scarron, Le Sage, for these men represented to him, as well as to Diderot, refreshing individuality, freedom, and vigor. Far from misunderstanding each other, Diderot and Sterne were qualified by taste and temperament to enjoy a significant kinship in the literary history of the eighteenth century. A study of their resemblances, and of the directions in which their common traits developed, will indicate to what extent Diderot and Sterne may be regarded in a comparative position and will illuminate the transition from the eighteenth to the nineteenth century.

This investigation deals with the efforts, both conscious and unconscious, of two English and French contemporaries of the eighteenth century to break with vestiges of the neoclassical spirit and to arrive at modes of literary creation and expression that led to romanticism and the modern era. For the Englishman it was not a great struggle, because neoclassicism in England had been more of a vogue than a deeprooted institution, and it was being superseded by the school of "common sense." There was a natural empirical tradition in English thought that remained constant. In literature, there was a tradition of freer, individual expression—notable even in a neoclassic like Swift—which did not bow to strict formulae. For the Frenchman it involved a much more conscious effort. An earlier literary tradition of a broad, free scope had yielded to a predominant taste conditioned by the classicism of the seventeenth and the neoclassicism of the eighteenth century. Empiricism was in general foreign to the spirit of both Thomists and Cartesians.

Both Sterne and Diderot were sufficiently aware of cultural environments to realize that they were consciously differing from many of the practices and attitudes of their contemporaries. During their sessions at D'Holbach's table, the bond between them was undoubtedly strengthened as each man learned that the other had been developing ideas similar to his own. Despite the later misleading cries of plagiarism, the interaction of their theories was to be of minor importance for their literary achievements because in their approach to literature, Diderot and Sterne, independently, were working in a parallel fashion. The parallel is indicated not only in their practices but also by the coincidence of certain ideas to which they attach great importance. They both place a marked emphasis on originality and experiment. They consciously reject the inhibitions that the neoclassical influence places on literary form and on the free expression of the individual. They stress the personal, even intimate characteristics of human beings, for they are interested in the particular. Not man, the abstraction, but the individual, specific person is the proper study of mankind, they would say, and they would also insist that one must be free from all kinds of restraint to achieve this goal. They study, liberate, restore, and glorify the true, whole being. It is the man within rather than the composite, established representative who draws their attention.

Had they investigated the sources of their ideas, they would have discovered that those ideas frequently stemmed from common bases. They would have found that the empirical tradition, particularly their respective interpretations of Locke, determined in large measure the plane of their parallel thought. It is true that Diderot's interpretations owed much to the discussions he had with Condillac; moreover, he carried his researches farther than either Locke or Condillac; but all this does not alter the fact that Locke was a source that both he and Sterne used.

Locke holds that the objects of sensible reality have two distinct characteristics: primary and secondary. The primary characteristics are objective and inherent in the object; the secondary characteristics are qualities that depend on perception alone. These latter are not within the object itself, although the object has the power to evoke them; they exist only in the mind of the perceiver and so are more subjective than primary characteristics. They are also much more dynamic than primary characteristics: no one will deny that an orange has a certain extension, figure, solidity, but what has more possibilities for drawing one's attention is the fact that an orange is perceived as having a certain color, taste, smell, moistness.

Diderot and Sterne, both interested in sensible reality, are more fascinated by the secondary characteristics. Neither would reject the notion of an objective reality, but each is attracted by the study of the ways in which reality impresses people and of people's reactions to reality. Diderot the scientist could observe and discuss natural history, biology, physiology, at the same time that Diderot the psychologist and artist could tell Sophie Volland that "things in themselves are nothing, they have no real sweetness or bitterness; our mind is what makes them what they are." [27] Now Diderot knew very well that from a strictly scientific point of view things in themselves are not "nothing," but he was always intrigued by man's interpretation of things: it not only reveals man, but it also illuminates reality. The most important consideration to keep in mind, Diderot writes, is that if one banishes man or the thinking and contemplating being from the face of the earth, this affecting and sublime spectacle of nature is nothing but a mute and mournful scene; the universe becomes silent, mastered by stillness and night. Everything changes in a vast loneliness where the unobserved phenomena pass away in a deaf and gloomy fashion. It is the presence of man that renders interesting the existences of beings.[28] Sterne did not trouble himself with speculations. From personal experience, he simply proved to his readers that each man's world was what he made it.

Diderot and Sterne's curiosity about how man responds to sensible reality can also be traced to Locke. Locke divides the sources of all ideas into sensation and reflection: the immediate reception of sense impressions and the activity of the mind in perceiving its own operations on the impressions. Once again, it is the latter phenomenon that particularly appeals to Diderot and Sterne. Going beyond the superficial realities, they become preoccupied with that mental reflective life of a person which heightens and truly establishes his very individuality. For this is the tempting mystery to be solved in plumbing the man within.

Using their common literary and philosophical interests as a springboard, Sterne and Diderot were to add another dimension to fiction. But as one studies their concurrent development, one notes that it takes on individual directions for each writer because of his personality, intellect, and cultural heritage. All is not black and white; transitional figures, precisely because of their intermediary positions, do not represent a clean break with their backgrounds. In examining the relationship of Diderot and Sterne, I have selected three basic aspects of their work which illuminate these parallels and divergences. A study of their treatments of sensibility, humor, literary procedures and style makes it possible to reevaluate a connection that has attracted critical attention for over one and a half centuries.

CHAPTER II

SENSIBILITY

DURING 1767, Sterne, when he was not presumably weeping over Eliza's departure, was writing and revising the *Sentimental Journey*—a new work that was gauged to please all readers possessing tender sentiments. It was also intended to encourage an appreciation of the author's own delicate emotions. This, at least, was the excuse that Sterne gave out for the benefit of public consumption; but Sterne was a wily and elusive writer and rarely revealed his full intentions. Perhaps nowhere was he more evasive than in his treatment of sensibility, and while it may be too extreme to suggest that he was secretly laughing *all* the time, one should not overlook the possibility that he may have had his tongue in his cheek *part* of the time.[1]

In the same year, in his *Salon* of 1767, Diderot was approaching a culmination of his intellectual trend against sensibility which was to result in a strong denunciation of the highly-touted man of feeling. Yet Sterne and Diderot had not always been at odds on this popular subject. To see the background for what appears to be their eventual disagreement, one should turn to a tradition which received great impetus in England in the years following the Restoration.

The major impulse of this tradition was a reaction against Thomas Hobbes, whose writings constituted "the most potent stimulant to English thought in the last half of the seventeenth, and even during the first half of the eighteenth century in England." [2] Characteristic of the response to Hobbes was that of the Latitudinarian churchmen who were advancing such notions as the natural goodness of man, the rehabilitation of the passions, admiration of the man of sensibility.[3] They included among their *bêtes noires* the pessimistic views of the Calvinist Puritans; the doctrine of "stoical insensibility," which distrusted and denied "natural affections" and bodily passions; and, particularly, the unpleasant opinion of Hobbes that a forceful government was the only means of preventing man's naturally bad passions from regressing into their initial state of war. Equally opposed to the author of the *Leviathan* and the treatise on *Human Nature* were the Cambridge Platonists, who formed a smaller group within the Latitudinarian framework.[4]

Consequently, a movement developed in which a newer emphasis became apparent. The passions *per se* were regarded as being in a sense neutral; they therefore could be put to virtuous uses and achieve a positive value. Virtue itself was held to be universal benevolence; tender feeling was the mark of the true Christian, who is moved emotionally before he lends a helping, charitable hand. A later summation of this manifold virtue was published in *The Prompter* for 17 June 1753:

When strongly *impress'd* on the *Mind*, [Humanity, in its first and general Acceptation] assumes a *higher* and nobler Character, and is not satisfy'd with good-*natured* Actions alone, but *feels* the *Misery* of others with *inward Pain*. It is then deservedly named *Sensibility*, and is considerably increased in its intrinsick Worth. . . .[5]

Locke's interests found an important place in this mainstream of post-Restoration thought, and he added further incentive to the trend toward benevolence. He, too, was concerned with conduct, as the purposes of his political writings and his *Essay Concerning Human Understanding* demonstrate. But he was also at pains to counteract Hobbes. Contrary to the latter's views, Locke argued that it was man's natural goodness and sociability that inspired his social compact. As Professor L. J. Thielemann has pointed out,

Locke's vindication of the unwritten and eternal laws of nature, and his insistence upon the sovereign's responsibility to these natural laws did much both to reestablish man's good opinion of himself and to challenge Hobbes' allegation that human depravity could be controlled only by complete political subjection.[6]

Moreover, Locke's emphasis on sensation encouraged the rehabilitation of the passions, which were increasingly regarded as natural and useful phenomena. Since man moves toward his own happiness, it is logical for him to search for pleasant sensations. The concept of the will itself is involved in the process: the understanding, passive until it can get to work on material furnished by the senses, is activated by the basic principle of uneasiness, the desire for whatever is lacking to attain enjoyment. Yet the pleasure principle was not immediately to result, in England,[7] in sensuality. The third earl of Shaftesbury explicitly announced "how much the social pleasures are superior to any other."[8] Professor Kenneth MacLean's explanation is that sensation "was most probably greatly diverted into the mild channels of sensibility. . . ."[9] Whether this would have been so had Hobbes—who before Locke had cited sensation as the source of knowledge, and desire as the basis of will—held the field unopposed, is open to some speculation.

The apogee of the "gentle" or "benevolent" school of human nature came with Shaftesbury, whose popular *Character-*

istics had a very strong effect on French as well as English deism. Also of great significance was another result of this work, summed up by Professor Thielemann's statement that the *Characteristics* "helped considerably to prejudice French readers against Hobbes." [10] This anti-Hobbes stand is not surprising when one considers that Shaftesbury's education was supervised by Locke and that his first publication was an edition of sermons by Whichcote, a Latitudinarian churchman and Cambridge Platonist. [11] Shaftesbury gathered together many of the doctrines of his predecessors and further integrated the movement, which was gaining increasing popularity. He concluded that the natural state of man was not only good but also sociable; that because benevolence is the true frame of man's mind, his virtue lies in the notion of public interest. Disagreeing with his famous tutor, [12] Shaftesbury argued that man has a natural sense of right and wrong even before he has any apprehension of a deity; and as befits such an instinctively virtuous creature, "To have the natural, kindly or generous affections strong and powerful towards the good of the public, is to have the chief means and power of self-enjoyment." [13]

In keeping with the tradition, Shaftesbury vigorously supported the passions, including enthusiasm, which, when rightly understood, is a high and noble passion raising man above himself. Having distinguished between true and false enthusiasm—thereby safely placing himself on the side of Locke—in "A Letter Concerning Enthusiasm," Shaftesbury viewed "proper" enthusiasm as a kind of divine inspiration. He praised it in "The Moralist" as "the transports of poets, the sublime of orators, the rapture of musicians, the high strains of virtuosi. . . . Even learning itself, the love of arts and curiosities, the spirit of travellers and adventurers, gallantry, war, heroism." [14] And in his "Review of Enthusiasm" he commented that it was required for "the gallant sentiments, the elegant fancies, the belles passions." [15] After such encomiums, no one who prided himself on being a man of feeling could take issue with the necessity of passions.

Certainly in his early period, Diderot would have been the last man to argue against either Shaftesbury or his forerunners. While Sterne was penning those tender letters to Elizabeth Lumley which have been described as "studies in emotion, possessing the harmony and cadence of phrase and sentiment that were to distinguish, a quarter-century later, the *Sentimental Journey* from all other English books," [16] Diderot was toying with deism, on the way to producing his adaptation of *An Inquiry Concerning Virtue and Merit*.

With his conception of a dynamic universe and man's part in it, with his intense desire to restore man's true personality, Diderot could be expected to seize those aspects of philosophical currents which would liberate the man within and exalt human nature. His knowledge of the Latitudinarians' writings may have been indirect for the most part, but he was familiar with the works of three of their leading apologists: Clarke, Wollaston, and Tillotson. [17] For Locke, of course, the grounds are more positive. His emphasis on the psychology of man, his investigations of the source and process of the individual's mental activity, the conclusions to be drawn about man's relationship to sensible reality, all appealed to Diderot. Locke's utilitarian intent, "to our concerns as human beings," [18] also commended itself to the *philosophe*. And while the subject of the *Essay* encompasses man generically, its approach is a study of specifics; its result, Locke hoped, would be to keep men from meddling in things exceeding their comprehension. Diderot was hardly one to "sit down in quiet ignorance," but he could appreciate Locke's stand against speculations and abstractions. Furthermore, if Locke somewhat unwittingly had given the man of passion his declaration of rights, as Paul Hazard has stated,[19] Diderot was quick to investigate this aspect.

Shaftesbury had gone even farther than Locke in promoting the release of the "natural" man by emphasizing the efficacy of the passions. His insistence on virtue as social benevolence harmonized both with Diderot's efforts to improve man's conduct and Diderot's belief that man is a social being. Sterne, too, was in complete agreement with both Shaftesbury and Diderot on these points, but it will become evident that while Sterne was always ready to *discuss* social virtue, Diderot was largely concerned with putting it into practice. It was not mere concidence that in his adaptation of the *Inquiry Concerning Virtue and Merit* Diderot noted Shaftesbury's advocacy of the exercise of social affections as a recipe for one's ill-humor;[20] he frequently echoed this opinion in his own correspondence. Typically, in his "Abrégé du code de la nature" from D'Holbach's *Système de la nature*,[21] he says that man cannot be happy alone, that he derives his own pleasure from contributing to the pleasure of others. There is no reason to doubt his sincerity when he tells Rameau's nephew that for his part he would sooner be remembered for having rehabilitated the Calas family than for having written *Mahomet*. Not only Diderot's letters but also the reports of witnesses and friends attest to his lifelong activity in the interests of others.

Shaftesbury's praise of enthusiasm appealed to the iconoclast in Diderot, who rebelled against restrictive customs and inhibitions. Enthusiasm, a liberating force, was a natural compulsion responsible for man's best works. Sterne was to write it off as fanaticism or as a stubborn "hobbyhorse"—his special term for a man's ruling passion [22]—for he favored the negative argument. But Diderot, as Franco Venturi has indicated, found in this doctrine a twofold advantage: the exaltation of the moral value of a concrete, living experience as opposed to abstract schemes, and the positive benefit offered by abandonment to the most intimate and profound side of man's nature.[23]

For several years, the combined influences of the English movement inspired Diderot to a glorification of the passions—principally enunciated in the *Pensées philosophiques* of 1746—a hearty approval of the man of feeling, and a belief in the basic goodness of man, as opposed both to Spinozist and Cartesian distrust of emotions and to Pascalian asceticism. They also inspired a lifelong enthusiasm for virtue that amounted to an almost religious fervor. Sterne soon gave notice that he embraced these sentiments, though without the profounder insights of Diderot; yet even though "Parson Yorick" emerged as a champion of "dear sensibility," he could not equal Diderot's ardor. With characteristic vigor, the *philosophe* embarked on a period that was often highlighted by strong preromantic flashes.

Until new material is uncovered, the *Essai sur le mérite et la vertu* of 1745 and the *Pensées philosophiques* of the following year must be taken as the earliest evidence of Diderot's indebtedness to Shaftesbury and the benevolent tradition. For more than a decade, many of his pronouncements were to bear this stamp. In all probability he wrote some pages for Rousseau's *Second Discourse* in 1754, extolling, if not the completely noble savage, at least the nobler one in contrast to civilized man.[24] He also argued that uncivilized man is filled with the natural sentiment of humanity because pity is a basic law of nature.[25] Many years later—in the *Entretien d'un père avec ses enfants*—he looked back on the impetuous Diderot of the fifties and characterized him as an impulsive believer in the natural goodness of man, upholding the superiority of natural law and conscience over man-made law. He even gave himself tacit leave to break the laws of society in favor of the higher justice established by nature.[26] Following the requirements for the man of sensibility, he weeps over a scene in the *Fils naturel* and comments that he surely must be good to be so afflicted. Ten years later, in 1767, Sterne uses the same argument as he sobs with Maria in the *Sentimental Journey* and sees in his tears conclusive evidence that he has a soul.[27] Both the *Fils naturel* and the *Père de famille,* as well as Diderot's novel, *La Religieuse,* are lacrymose attempts to encourage the audience to weep its way to virtue. Sterne could well write to Garrick that "The Natural Son, or, the Triumph of Virtue" had "too much sentiment in it" and "would not do for your stage," [28] because the actor-owner of the Drury Lane Theatre was trying to reform the English taste for "la comédie larmoyante." [29] Even admitting that the elegiac style, as Diderot interpreted it, might demand a high degree of enthusiasm, one cannot doubt that a large part of Diderot's admiration for Richardson in the *Eloge* stemmed from the *philosophe*'s warm reaction to an emotional appeal to virtue.

His most extensive aesthetic formulations of this period appear in his *Entretiens sur le Fils naturel*. Enthusiasm is everything, and Dorval glorifies the passions as the *sine qua non* of great art.[30] Sensibility, not judgment or reflection, is the quality absolutely essential for stirring, moving productions; judgment itself requires a close connection and dependence on feeling.[31] In good romantic fashion, Dorval is depicted as a brooding, melancholy figure who is frequently overcome by emotion or possessed by the daemon of his inspiration. Even the settings appropriately reflect the moods of the protagonists, for Diderot utilizes the pathetic fallacy.

Emotional performers like Dorval and, a few years later, the Nephew, have a distressing tendency to emerge from their transports thoroughly exhausted, without any recollection of what has happened. Yet in 1757 Diderot approvingly passed over his hero's trances—they are evidence that Dorval practices what he preaches—whereas in 1761 he keenly delineated the disorganized personality of the Nephew, who cannot achieve the genius he seeks.[32] This contrast and its aesthetic implications are of fundamental importance in the development of Diderot's thought. In the change in his attitude from the beginning to the end of that four-year span, he anticipated the *Paradoxe sur le comédien* and its distinction between the *fou* (the man who gives free course to his passions and emotions) and the *sage* (the self-controlled philosopher, dispassionate and observing).[33] Indeed, in relation to the Nephew, the *fou,* Diderot acts consistently as the *sage.*

Unlike Sterne, whose thinking generally followed a consecutive pattern, Diderot was not averse to changing his opinion. It is not unusual to find him gradually winning himself over to what had commenced as a kind of minority argument. He treated the problem of the passions and sensibility in this fashion, moving from acceptance to increasing distrust of the tradition on which he and Sterne, it would seem, had initially agreed. This divergence underlies the difference in their attitudes in 1767, but Diderot's defection is not basically illogical.

There is a minor pattern in Diderot's thinking which constitutes an antithesis to the themes that reflect the major lines of the tradition. In 1751, in the *Lettre sur les sourds et muets,* he warned that people most sensitive to harmony are not the best judges of expression: "They are almost always too far beyond that calm emotional state in which feeling does not harm comparison."[34] Conveniently forgetting Dorval's strictures of 1757, Diderot in 1758 strongly disagreed with Helvétius' statement in *De l'esprit* that judging and feeling are the same.[35] He also attempted to straighten him out on other misinterpretations of materials found in Locke. He did not share Helvétius' behavioristic contention that because all men commence with equal endowments, it is their education and not the organization of the human mechanism which differentiates them. Adhering to his earlier ties with Shaftesbury, he rejected Helvétius' belief that the principal and only aim of the passions is physical pleasure. In a letter of 11 November 1760, he provided Sophie Volland with a very neutral, even objective conception of sensibility as the "sharp effect on our feelings of an infinity of delicate observations which we bring together." He adds, "This quality, whose source is given to us by nature, suffocates or revives according to age, experience, reflection."[36] Seven years later, Sterne contributed a significantly different description. In characteristic fashion, he wrote: "Dear sensibility! source inexhausted of all that's precious in our joys, or costly in our sorrows! thou chainest thy martyr down upon his bed of straw—and 'tis thou who lift'st him up to Heaven. . . ."[37]

As Sterne strove to play up to the vogue, so Diderot sought to curb the role of sensibility and correspondingly modified many of his earlier enthusiasms. It has been suggested that during the first five years of the sixties, he went through a crisis of pessimism in the course of which his beliefs in the natural goodness of man, the goodness of nature, the perfectibility of man were all severely shaken.[38] It seems more likely that he was actually outgrowing his rather youthful impetuosity. Perhaps one could say that in about fifteen years, from 1745 to 1760, Diderot passed through a period which France later took more than an entire generation to experience—the Romantic Movement. His attitudes became more critical as he relied on increasing observation and gained more acute perceptions. There is no indication for any extended period of time that Diderot seriously considered giving up his efforts to make the world a better place to live in. Those notes of despair which Professor May stresses are really the somewhat belated "growing pains" of an idealistic *philosophe* as he moves on to the realistic ground necessary for fuller growth, taking stock of himself along the way.[39] When he wrote to Sophie Volland in 1759, "It is true that I am naturally inclined to pass over faults and to be enraptured by excellencies. I am moved more by the beauties of virtue than by the ugliness of vice," [40] he anticipated a self-knowledge characteristic of his augmented capacity for detachment.

Diderot's interest in man continued, but the emphasis was changed from the deist's concept of naturally good man to a very practical and constructive attitude. Instead of blindly following a popularized doctrine or nostalgically longing for the noble savage, Diderot increasingly regarded human nature as being neither essentially good nor essentially bad; the essential point was that man is modifiable, and Diderot directed all his efforts toward modifying him.[41] Rather than trust to the activities of a beneficent deity, man must accept his own responsibility for his improvement. That is why Diderot reasserted, in his *Réfutation suivie de l'ouvrage d'Helvétius intitulé "L'Homme"* (1773–74), his disagreement with Helvétius, who refused to separate judgment from feeling. It is because reason and judgment are not overpowered by the senses that man can better himself, just as, aesthetically, it is the *sage* who is the critic, not the emotional *fou*. The importance of education is to encourage or discourage man's "natural disposition"—which is not to be confused with "basic nature"—toward good or bad.[42] Diderot reached these conclusions by observing what exists, not by embracing illusions of what he wanted to exist.

It was also through observation that he became aware of the corruption implicit in the fashionable cult of the man of feeling. He foresaw the possibility of a distortion through misplaced emphasis that Rousseau—and, perhaps, Sterne— was not to avoid. Even before Diderot broke with Rousseau, he was demonstrating by his relations with others that virtue, for him, was a social phenomenon.[43] If he had had the opportunity to reply to the article in *The Prompter*,[44] he would have reversed its meaning to stress the importance of "good-natured *Actions,*" for these actions constituted the test of virtuous feelings. Speaking through Bordeu in the *Rêve de d'Alembert* (1769), he was to insist that virtue is not an abstraction: it is the concept of *doing good* and requires a pragmatic application. With biting sarcasm, he remarks in the *Salon* of 1767:

At the account of a noble deed, our emotions get entangled, our heart is aroused, our voice fails, our tears fall. What eloquence! what praise! Our admiration has been stirred. Our feeling has been put into play; we show this feeling; it is such a precious quality! We strongly urge others to be noble; we are so concerned! We would rather tell of a lofty deed than read it alone to ourselves. The tears it wrings from our eyes fall on the cold pages of a book; they exhort no one; they recommend us to no one; we need living witnesses. How many hidden and complex motives there are in our blame and praise! [45]

He concludes this attack on the man of feeling by hinting at the nature of sensibility itself in terms hardly calculated to increase its charms: "Our habits are established so early that they are called natural, innate; but there is nothing natural, nothing innate other than nerves, more flexible, or more rigid, more or less mobile, more or less disposed to vibrate." [46]

It is quite fitting that these comments challenging Diderot's earlier stand in favor of emotions should be found in the *Salons*. As he began to reconsider more carefully the aesthetic importance of sensibility, he was stimulated not only by self-judgment but also by his experience in examining the work of others. The most fully developed summation of Diderot's aesthetic preoccupations during the sixties—if one excepts the *Neveu de Rameau* and the D'Alembert sequence, which deal with a more extensive variety of subjects—is the *Salon* of 1767. It is here that he clearly enunciates the principle of the ideal model, conceived by the imagination of the genius. The model is not a direct reproduction or copy, but it is drawn from nature, improves on it, and represents the basis for the most sublime productions of art.[47] Diderot was to emphasize this principle later in the *Paradoxe,* which he began outlining in 1769, but it was the result of considerations he had been developing in the earlier *Salons*.[48]

In the *Salon* of 1761, he says that there are some passions which are most difficult to render because they are almost never observed in nature. Where is the model for them? he asks.[49] In the *Salon* of 1763, he tries a different approach: the artist's sensibility is not by itself sufficient for producing great art. Furthermore, how does the artist, constantly approaching and moving back from his canvas to achieve perspective, manage to preserve warmth of feeling during the long process of creating a picture? [50] By 1765, he is wondering by what means an artist who seems to transcend himself just once to produce a masterpiece could be brought to sustain this flight, and in the *Essai sur la peinture* he finds that a rigorous balance of enthusiasm and judgment is necessary, otherwise the artist will be either too wild or too cold.[51] He even suggests that reserved men, austere and calm observers of nature, often understand best the delicate chords one must strike; they can make enthusiasts without being so.[52] The examples, drawn from Diderot's experience, are found in the *Salon* of 1767. La Grenée, "man of ice, artist of marble," violates the obligation of art to move the spectator emotionally. La Tour, on the other hand, paints with cold reserve; Diderot has watched him work and concludes that nothing La Tour produces is the result of warmth. Yet his paintings evoke strong feelings in the spectator; La Tour acts like a "man of ice," but his art does not have that effect.

The resolution of these related considerations is found in the *Paradoxe sur le comédien,* completed in 1773. Sensibility, as Diderot had pointed out in the *Rêve de d'Alembert,* is the quality of second-rate people, immature fools who are ever at the mercies of their emotions and who are consequently unable to attain self-control, judgment, greatness. Sensibility is the extreme mobility of certain fibres of the nervous system; instead of the mind dominating, it is the diaphragm that rules. The great artist may experience feeling, but his productions are not the direct result of it. Utilizing his knowledge, he constructs an ideal model, bases his performance on that, and passes it off as the real thing on the man of feeling who accepts the clever copy as the authentic emotions of the artist. It is thus, by avoiding dependence on the first rush of passion, which will subsequently weaken, by using judgment to analyze and reproduce feeling, that the truly great artist can sustain an even excellence. Physical distance, discussed in the *Salon* of 1763 as a requirement for good technique, has developed into psychic distance, the quality essential for great art.

In the twenty-five years since Diderot's adaptation of Shaftesbury, he had diverged from the path that he and Sterne had at first followed. Unqualified approbation of enthusiasm and the other passions, naive transports over gratifying doctrines, have given way to more tempered judgment, to more sharply critical and even self-critical perceptions. The Diderot of 1757, who commended Dorval's insistence on sensibility, is very different from the Diderot of 1773, who characterized himself as a mediocre fool, a man of feeling, or the Diderot who laughed at himself in 1774 for being a cry-baby, or who told Grimm, with detachment, that in the present society he felt like a dog trying to walk on two legs. He has reached the period, mentioned in the *Paradoxe* as the one most favorable for great artistry,[53] that comes after long experience, when the ardor of the passions has been modified, when the head is calm and the emotions are controlled. He presents, objectively, in the *Paradoxe* two aspects of his nature: the one emotional, as he sobs out his admiration to Sedaine; the other reserved, as he vanquishes an opponent by self-restraint and cool calculation. His natural warmth has not atrophied. He still repeats to Sophie Volland in the late sixties, "Happy is he who has received from nature feeling and mobile emotions"[54]—but he can say this with the assurance that he knows himself and is capable of objective analysis. He is even able to reevaluate Hobbes, the "villain" of the tradition which Diderot had earlier espoused, and to comment that Hobbes' treatise on *Human Nature* has taught him more than either Locke or Helvétius.

Diderot's final stand in opposition to a movement in which many of his attitudes began is evidence of a major evolution in his thought from 1749.[55] This evolution consists in developing with increasing clarity the distinction between order and disorder in the category of feeling, in analyzing and praising the roles of reason and judgment, in questioning the values of that school which had elevated the passions and the man of feeling. The *Paradoxe,* as Professor Yvon Belaval has demonstrated, is not really a paradox but a logical culmination. It is part of a coherent, intellectual development that forced Diderot to review and alter many of his former beliefs. His ultimate position is a natural outgrowth of a minority argument which he could not ignore, even in the years of his most impassioned support of the philosophers of sensibility.

Sterne, who did not admit being troubled by minority arguments, presumably did not cease to follow these writers, although significantly his published reactions lack Diderot's vehemence. Partially because he did not appear to share Diderot's intensity, he may have been unaware of the pitfalls the *philosophe* discovered. Partially because he was not a person of serious stamp like Diderot, he did not bother to examine the full implications of philosophical matters. Sterne, it should be pointed out, cannot be written off as a man devoid of intellectual curiosity, but he does seem to have been a disillusioned man. It may well be that where Diderot chose to delve into subjects deeply, Sterne refused to do so *not* because he was mentally incapable of it but simply because he did not really care. It will become apparent, for example, that all along Sterne was successfully practicing—with very few theoretical side remarks—certain features of the theory which marked the climax of the change in Diderot's attitude.

Like Diderot, he was attracted by temperament to any measures granting the individual free indulgence of his natural feelings and propensities. Emphasis on such restraining qualities as caution and discretion—highly regarded by Richardson, as Cross has noted—found little sympathy with Sterne because "they are always intruding upon a man's conduct to prevent free and spontaneous expression of his real selfhood." [56] Sterne was prompted by personal as well as financial reasons to use a subjective approach in his fiction. Locke, whose common sense in all matters appealed to him, gave Sterne further authority for centering his attention on sensation. It was a kind of intellectual justification for his own consumptive state of health. Moreover, though Sterne may have been a cynic, he was not essentially an embittered man. His personality responded to the principles of the Latitudinarian tradition, just as his mind was oriented by their teachings. Universal benevolence, tender charity, a view of human nature as being basically good, a Beneficent Providence, the desirability of gentle passions—all found full approval in a man whose "world of good nature" and whose refusal to use his wit "to alarm or wound his neighbour" commended themselves to the critical Mrs. Montagu. Despite the fact that success had turned his head, he was "full of the milk of human kindness, harmless as a child," she wrote to her sister in 1765. [57]

In his correspondence, his Shandean philosophy, genial, sympathetic and crack-brained, allowed much latitude for the gamut of gentle emotions which he carried into his fiction:

I laugh 'till I cry, and in the same tender moments *cry 'till I laugh*. I Shandy it more than ever, and verily do believe, that by mere Shandeism sublimated by a laughter-loving people, I fence as much against infirmities, as I do by benefit of air and climate. [58]

He enjoys passing a sentimental afternoon with a person of sensibility,[59] and takes pains to stress the necessary distinction between, on the one hand, sensibility and its pleasures and, on the other, "gross" sensuality.[60] Consequently, Eliza is notified—with a paradoxical lack of delicacy—that her friend, "with all his sensibilities," is "suffering the Chastisement of the grossest Sensualist—" [61]

In keeping with Sterne's penchant for tender feelings, his sermons are invariably fashioned as an emotional appeal, for he, as well as Diderot, recognized the force of this approach. His best examples are achieved through a visually dramatized situation or character. He begs leave, in his sermon on "The House of Feasting and the House of Mourning," "to recall both of them for a moment, to your imaginations, that from thence I may appeal to your hearts. . . ." [62] In "Job's Expostulation," he disapproves of those "moral writers of antiquity" for the reason that "as what they said proceeded more from the head than the heart, 'twas generally more calculated to silence a man in his troubles, than to convince, and teach him how to bear them." [63] Sterne's design was to teach and convince by way of the feelings. The story of the Levite and his concubine is "a story on which the heart cannot be at a loss for what to say." [64] St. Peter's character is vindicated— somewhat sophistically—on the basis of those very qualities which led him to renounce Jesus: "The tenderness and sensibility of his soul." [65]

What Sterne taught may not have dealt much with heaven and hell, as Walter Bagehot objected,[66] and possibly it could have been preached "in a synagogue or mosque without offense," according to the Reverend Henry Venn.[67] Sterne kept in line, however—despite Thackeray's and Bagehot's accusation that he had no Christian sentiments [68]—and a very popular line it was. "The prevalence of the theme of conduct in all Sterne's religious writings," says Professor MacLean, "proves that he was professing the new science [morality as the proper study of man] established by Locke's *Essay*." [69] But the "new science" was propagated by leading Latitudinarians from whom Sterne pillaged regularly. [70]

His sermons are permeated with appeals to humaneness, charity, man's obligations to society and his instinctive goodness. Taking his stand against Hobbes, Sterne says in "The Vindication of Human Nature":

Surely, 'tis one step towards acting well, to think worthily of our nature; and, as in common life the way to make a man honest, is, to suppose him so, and treat him as such;—so here, to set some value upon ourselves, enables us to support the character, and even inspires and adds sentiments of generosity and virtue to those which we have already preconceived. [71]

But while Sterne unquestioningly repeats his masters in commending the social virtues, there is a distinction between his ready acceptance of their teachings and Diderot's efforts to clarify by limiting virtue itself to a purely social phenomenon. Sterne agrees with Diderot that solitude is unnatural for man and voices the tenets of the sociability school in "The Levite and his Concubine":

. . . in the midst of the loudest vauntings of philosophy, Nature will have her yearnings for society and friendship;— . . . let me be wise and religious—but let me be Man: wherever thy Providence places me, or whatever be the road I take to get to thee— give me some companion for my journey. [72]

Yet he would never make the emphatic statement, full of overtones, that Diderot included in his *Fils naturel:* "L'homme seul est l'homme méchant"—for Sterne's whole approach to the teachings of the Latitudinarians was one of easy-going superficiality. Despite the fact that he favored the "natural passions" and owned three copies of the *Characteristics,* he gave no evidence anywhere of interpreting enthusiasm in any but its narrow sense, that "most wild and unintelligible institution." This was, to be sure, a perfectly acceptable practice; "fanatick" supporters of religious enthusiasm were popular objects of denunciation and Sterne was following other satirical masters like Swift and Pope. But Sterne's carelessness does indicate certain shortcomings. His indifference to, or refusal to grapple with, some of the topics that he shared with Diderot is evidence of a basic difference between the two men's attitudes. Largely through Sterne's efforts, the very term "sentimental" became a catchword, handy but inexact, with emphasis on the feelings, for all the admirable qualities advocated by the Latitudinarians.[73]

Consequently, it is not surprising that Sterne's fiction should appear to idealize that Christian gentleman, the man of sensibility. In *Tristram,* it is Toby and Trim who fill the role of the natural, unspoiled man of tender feeling. Their ready tears and compassion fortify the popular theory that a soft heart and a wet eye bespeak goodness. "The heart, both of the master and the man, were alike subject to sudden overflowings." [74] In contrast to Walter's thorny intellect, Trim goes "straight forwards as nature could lead him, to the heart." [75] Yorick, while capable of more detachment than his friends, agrees with them on this point. He suffers "unspeakable torments" in composing a sermon because "I was delivered of it at the wrong end of me—it came from my head instead of my heart." [76] Even Walter readily capitulates and shows moist regret after an impatient remark.

The *Sentimental Journey* appears to be a thoroughgoing effort to show the superiority of heart over head—though the author maintains such a delicate balance here that one cannot completely discount the critics who suggest that he may be laughing. But certainly on the surface Sterne carefully stressed those fashionable qualities which made the book an immediate success. "I told you my design in it was to teach us to love the world and our fellow creatures better than we do—so it runs most upon those *gentler passions and affections,* which aid so much to it." [77] Scattered among Yorick's tender emotions are various statements reasserting the principles that were currently in vogue. Praising the "sweet pliability of man's spirit," Sterne agreed with Diderot that "I was never able to conquer any one single bad sensation in my heart so decisively, as by beating up as fast as I could for some kindly and gentle sensation, to fight it upon its own ground." [78]

Unfortunately, he does not state that he plans to conclude the fight by some concrete act of good will, and one is left with the suspicion that Sterne, in company with the contributor to *The Prompter* and Rousseau, was quite content merely with having good intentions. He asks those whose "clay-cold heads and lukewarm hearts can argue down or mask your passions," to tell him "what trespass it that a man should have them?" and calls on the great governor of nature to "whip me such stoics." [79] He rhapsodizes about that "eternal fountain of our feelings" which enables him to experience "some generous joys and generous cares beyond myself." [80] He exclaims that "Surely—surely, man! it is not good for thee to sit alone—thou wast made for social intercourse and gentle greetings, and this improvement of our natures from it, I appeal to, as my evidence." [81]

In all this, Sterne is in accord with the prevailing attitude of his sermons. There is only one drawback: our tendency to smile at his characters' humanity as well as to laugh at their antics makes us wonder if perhaps Sterne did, too. The majority of the audience of the sentimental vogue probably was not too concerned whether the material which moved it to pleasant tears reflected the author's sincere feelings. It doubtless imputed good will to any writer who produced satisfactory results, for this was a largely pragmatic business: so long as it worked, the reader did not care. We do, however. For the author of *Tristram Shandy* to state in the *Sentimental Journey* that he is ever one to blush at indelicacies, and to say it, moreover, when he includes in the same work such insinuations as Madame de Rambouliet's fountain, Bevoriskius' sparrows, and the equivocal adventure which closes the book, impresses the modern reader as rank falsehood—or perhaps as a great hoax.

There are other examples that present themselves to the skeptic. In *Tristram*, Yorick's death is relieved of its pathos by the inscription on his tombstone and the black page of mourning. Sterne's "apostrophe" to Toby's kindness sounds more like a mock invocation, and there is something ridiculous about Toby's generous conclusion that the world has room for both him and flies. The celebrated story of Le Fever mitigates the purely sentimental twice. In the first place, Le Fever's wife is killed in a rather awkward situation; typical of Toby's chasteness, he does not exactly recall all the circumstances.[82] In the second place, the on-and-off fluttering of Le Fever's dying pulse-beats is typical of a seesaw pattern of alternating actions that Sterne uses for comedy.[83] Sentimentalists may have been too blinded by their tears to suspect Sterne's "Shall I go on?—No"; but, as Ernest Dilworth has commented, "The pathos is completely in the hands of Sterne and his hands are cool."[84] Once Sterne has decided to stop the flutters, he cheerfully and briefly concludes the aftermath. His description of that "poor, hapless damsel" Maria, piping away in gentle idiocy, is overdone for us, and quite probably for Sterne, too. Struck by Maria's apparent endeavors to compare him to her goat, Sterne chides his untoward mirth, burlesques the entire incident, and goes off to his "excellent inn at Moulins!"

It may seem to some that in the *Sentimental Journey* Sterne was trying too hard to exonerate himself of charges of previous indecency, but it does not follow that his stress on feeling thereby became completely shoddy or simulated. Without fully abandoning the tradition which Diderot in large measure outgrew, Sterne put into practice, in both *Tristram* and the *Sentimental Journey,* a theory which Diderot explained in the *Paradoxe.*

The *Paradoxe* raises a crucial question for all artists: which is more successful, the true feeling or the imitated one, reality or illusion? It answers a problem posed by Condillac's discussion of enthusiasm in the *Essai sur l'origine des connaissances humaines* in 1746: "Conserving one's composure, one could imitate enthusiasm if one were in the habit of analyzing the beautiful pieces poets owe to it; but would the copy always be equal to the original?" [85] Yes, says Diderot, strongly favoring the illusion, provided that the artist produces a successful counterfeit. The artist must use his powers of analysis and judgment to recreate experienced emotion and convince the audience of its validity. If there is no feeling in his works, the audience is disappointed and the artistry suffers; Diderot has criticized Saint-Lambert, Thomas, and La Grenée for this deficiency. But while the artist is engaged in his task, even while he is utilizing inspiration, he should not be undergoing an uncontrolled emotional upheaval.[86] To *be feeling* is one thing, *to feel* is another; the first has to do with emotions, the second with judgment.[87] Diderot may have wept over Mlle de La Chaux, but he was not weeping when he wrote about her in *Ceci n'est pas un conte;* he was calculating the effect on his audience. He was surely contrite about his lack of filiality, but he was not sobbing during the composition of his *Voyage à Bourbonne*. Instead, the overdone eloquence and the rhetorical tone, the contrived stylistic gasps make one suspect that, like Sterne, he enjoys savoring tender emotions and is not above conforming to fashion: "Let me stop and again yield myself a moment to the most delightful emotional state. . . . I do not know what troubles me. I do not know what I feel. I should like to cry . . . O my parents, it is doubtless a tender memory of you that touches me." [88]

Sterne, too, was a feeling man, but when he delineated the emotional vicissitudes of Yorick, he "felt" in the sense of Diderot's *Paradoxe:* he analyzed, selected, reconstructed. Professor Rufus Putney has made the point: "To call Sterne a sentimentalist is to ignore the hard core of comic irony that made him critical of the emotional vagaries of his own life and of his imagined characters." [89] This sharpens the tantalizing mystery of Sterne and emphasizes a secret that he deliberately may have sought to conceal. Did he really experience the feelings he delineates, or was he joking all the time and entering into a consummate hoax? One can never be absolutely sure, for Sterne was too much the artist—artful in the extreme—to tell. It is very likely, however, that in the very places where Sterne has been accused of showing himself the most *dishonest,* he is really at his most *honest*—at least with himself. For while Sterne was indeed subject to his peculiar emotional vagaries, he did not fail to see the comedy of his own situation. Sterne's genius lies in his humor, and

Sterne is not the man to avoid self-exploitation, even when he does not profess to be humorous.

In the *Sentimental Journey* he notes that "men of a certain turn of mind" take interest "in their own sensations." [90] Sterne observes his with detachment and frankness. Frequently he is amused by his own inconsistency, which does not speak well for the dedicated man of feeling:

—Now, was I a King of France, cried I—what a moment for an orphan to have begg'd his father's portmanteau of me! I had scarce utter'd these words, when a poor monk of the order St. Francis came into the room to beg something for his convent. No man cares to have his virtues the sport of contingencies—[91]

and Sterne promptly refuses to give alms. Later, he desires to commence a liaison with an attractive lady and quite honestly admits that he is considering how to counteract the bad impression of him she may have received from his behavior toward the monk. He indicates, in a leading statement, that he regards his sensations *analytically:* "I write not to apologise for the weaknesses of my heart in this tour,—but to give an account of them." [92]

Sterne is, in fact, a clever exhibitionist. He wrote his intimate *Journal* with one eye cocked on the public; he asks the audience of the *Sentimental Journey* not to laugh but to pity him, for he is as weak as a woman. But this appeal for sympathy is misleading. His second work is no more than *Tristram* the immediate result of emotional mobility. It is a piece of composite artistry based on materials from two trips' worth of notes, a *Journal,* and some borrowings. Furthermore, it is clear from Sterne's remarks that the *Sentimental Journey* is the work of a man of lesser profundity than Diderot but, possibly, of more artistic skill, who has intellect enough to utilize an argument of the *Paradoxe.* Although

Sterne never read it, of course, and seems to have hit on the process intuitively—he certainly did justice by Diderot's conception of the *sage* and turned his feelings into sustained art.[93] To this extent, in 1767, Diderot and Sterne remained in agreement, and it was an agreement which did not harmonize with the notion of the purely instinctive sentimentalist.

There were, however, important differences in their approach. Diderot's was based not only on self-examination but on examination of how reality affects and is treated by others. Sterne worked within a more contained frame of reference. Diderot could analyze the inner drama of Rameau's nephew, or the results of Jacques' subjective interpretation of external events, or the mysterious manner by which illusion becomes emotionally experienced reality, but Sterne could not go beyond himself. He objectified his natural, subjective feelings —racing back and forth from laughter to tears—just as he objectified the Shandys' eccentricities and projected them into a Shandean universe. He had the capacity for "perception at the pitch of passion," [94] but the meaning he attached to passion itself was incomplete. Sterne enjoyed and was often amused by the caprices of feeling, but he did not sufficiently comprehend *deep* feelings to distrust or reject the man of sensibility. While both Diderot and Sterne regard man as a sentient being and recognize the connection between emotional and physical reactions, Sterne contents himself with pleasant blushes and cheerful vibrations. Diderot always goes beyond what is immediately apparent to seek its implications.

A few passages emphasize the contrast. In 1765, Sterne said:

. . . I myself must ever have some dulcinea in my head—it harmonizes the soul—and in those cases I first endeavour to make the lady believe so, *or rather I begin first to make myself believe* that

I am in love—but I carry on my affairs quite in the French way, sentimentally—"L'amour" (say they) "n'est rien sans sentiment." [95]

In September 1767, shortly after he discontinued his *Journal,* he wrote: " 'You can feel!' Aye, so can my cat, when he hears a female caterwauling on the house top—but caterwauling disgusts me. I had rather raise a gentle flame, than have a different one raised in me." [96] These remarks show acute self-knowledge, but they also show Sterne's limitations. He enjoys flirtations, harmless little entanglements which really skirt passion. The objects of his affections exist merely as a series of unattainable dulcineas, illusory loves, infatuations. They may be erotic, but they are not lustful, nor are they demanding. Sterne wants to raise and control the gentle flame in preference to becoming a *fou,* as Diderot would say, a victim of unmasterable forces. Caterwauling is too gross, perhaps too dangerous; Sterne needs refinement. One cannot imagine his voicing Diderot's "il y a un peu de testicule au fond de nos sentiments les plus sublimes et de notre tendresse la plus épurée," any more than his indulging in Diderot's gluttony. He has not Diderot's healthy animal reactions or Diderot's matter-of-fact sense of sex.

Partially, Sterne's personality—his disillusionment, perhaps —and his precarious health are to blame for his limitations. But his cultural heritage should also be regarded as a determining factor. The English do not seem to manifest strongly that tradition of the *moraliste* which is so dominant a part of French thinking. The *moraliste* is interested in the ways of man, in what constitutes his mores. His central purpose is not to pass moral judgments—to condemn or approve—but to observe, analyze, and describe the different facets of human nature. He is psychologist and sociologist rather than moralizer. While Sterne had read the works of Montaigne, La Bruyère, La Rochfoucauld, Racine, La Fontaine, Molière, the common trait they shared was possibly not one that he could easily take over. At any rate, he did not choose to immerse himself in their spirit, to undertake profound studies of the actions of deep feelings. Even a Francophile like Chesterfield examined character with a significantly different motivation from that of a Madame de Sévigné.

Now Diderot was, to be sure, a moralizer, or a moralist in the English sense; but he was also a *moraliste* as is shown in the *Supplément au voyage de Bougainville* [97] and in aspects of his other works. Like his predecessors in this tradition, he had a serious and at times clinical interest in the workings of man's personality, in analyzing the emotions and their effects. He could perceive and accept the role of sensuality in sensation. Passion, including sexual passion, has for Diderot an elemental strength that is not included in Sterne's interpretation of the term. In October, 1760, he wrote to Sophie Volland that when a man becomes enamored of a woman, he should be distraught with love. Answering a question, he says:

"Does it suit me always to be loved madly?" It doesn't suit me to love and always to be loved in any other way but that. You know very well that all these petty affected passions make me wretched. I believe I've told you why. Merely add that they demand as much as great passions and give practically nothing in return.[98]

Diderot was capable of infatuations, but he generally thought of them in terms of physical consummation. Even as an old man, attracted by the sight of a serving girl in Riga, he made up a poem which is both questionable in taste and unquestionably earthy. He did not manifest any of the inhibitions to which Sterne, though trying to break them down, was still subject.

Both men could find in sensibility a release for natural emotions, but their interpretations of "natural emotions" are obviously quite different. Sensibility for the English school was restricted to gentle, noble or delicate shades of feeling. For Diderot in the early years it was already something more violent, suggesting far-reaching results; it was not a passing flicker. Because he conceived of the passions as a life force, he sought the origin of feeling in the individual and, as a good sensationalist, decided that it lay in some sense organ. Consequently, he arrived at his conclusion that the diaphragm was the basis of feeling. The vague phrase, "delicate feelings"—which reflects a rather disembodied view—is replaced by a very specific and scientific investigation of the physiological source of emotion. Actually, Diderot is a more literal Lockean than the English, for their tender nuances become somewhat divorced from the material basis of sensation. Diderot "restores" them—and surpasses Locke—by a logical extension in accordance with his belief that everything has its inception in sensible reality.[99] By doing so, he does not inevitably destroy the pleasant mystery of sensibility. Understanding its mainsprings, he can recreate it with authenticity. Instead of depending largely on his own emotions, as does Sterne, he can penetrate and delineate the feelings of others.

When Sterne and Diderot first met in 1762, their common derivation from the tradition which had developed the man of feeling and their personal qualifications for the title of *homme sensible* probably constituted one of the bases of their friendship. Yet Diderot increasingly was to challenge the "new cult" and its aesthetic and ethical connotations. By the time Sterne died, in 1768, the stream of their initial agreement was turning into two widely diverse channels. Sterne and

Diderot may not consciously have appreciated the scope of this change, but in historical perspective its importance becomes marked.

In Locke's summary of the pleasure principle, he had stated that it was only natural for man to seek pleasing sensations; his disciple, Sterne, could therefore seek them with a clear conscience. It is true that Sterne concentrated on the "gentler passions," as did most of his English contemporaries, but the tendency he manifested pointed toward eventual corruption. Like Rousseau, by exalting the immediate sensation, whether of love or of virtue, he was more preoccupied with the enjoyment of the feeling than with the real object of his affections or with the actual practice of virtue. Sterne did realize that he was courting Dulcineas, yet he did not perceive the trend of his emotional promiscuity: that ultimately this course would lead to an abnormal and disproportionate dedication to feeling for its own sake. He failed to note that because a "sensation" of virtue without any overt social action could be satisfactory for him, he was confusing ends with means. The danger here, it should be emphasized, was hidden from Sterne by the personal and cultural barriers mentioned in the previous pages. Eventually, however, the path that the Anglican clergyman embarked upon was to end in complete abandonment to emotional and ethical hedonism.

Diderot, at first commending the rule of feeling and the surrender to the intimate, soon began to express qualms. Ferreting out the weaknesses of the sensibility school, he became aware of its proclivity to disorder—artistic, personal, and ethical. With a kind of classical precision, the man who rebelled against neoclassicism tried to pin down and limit the nature and role of sensibility.[100] He was working away from the direction anticipated by Sterne and was moving toward a notion of a more narrowly circumscribed and controlled natural order. The emotions and the subjective life did not cease to interest him, but he knew that to glorify these as the sole guide could end only in chaos. He therefore applied his efforts to keeping the human personality integrated and capable of fulfilling its best potentialities. Passion and reason, he says in the *Essai sur les règnes de Claude et Néron* of 1778–82, are not always contradictory; sometimes one commands what the other sanctions.[101] In the final stage of his intellectual development, Diderot saw the life of reason and the life of emotion as two complementary elements in human nature. In his *Réfutation suivie de l'ouvrage d'Helvétius intitulé "L'Homme,"* of 1773–74, he had found Lockean sensualism insufficient; in 1778 he added that reason without the passions would be almost like a king without subjects. It is on this note of balanced judgment that Diderot concluded his long researches on a theme which may have served to introduce him to Sterne some sixteen years earlier.

CHAPTER III

HUMOR

SOMETIME in August 1762, the first six volumes of *Tristram Shandy,* which Laurence Sterne had ordered for his friend, Denis Diderot, reached France.[1] Diderot was busy with other affairs, however; it was not until the twenty-sixth of September that he hastily concluded a letter to Sophie Volland with the remark that for the last few days he had been reading the "maddest, wisest, and gayest of all books." On October sixth, he repeated his judgment, with some additions:

This book, so mad, so wise and so gay, is the Rabelais of the English. It is entitled *The Life, the Memoirs and the Opinions of Tristram Shandi* [sic]. It is impossible to give any idea of it other than that of a universal satire. Mr. Stern [sic], its author, is also a priest.[2]

The fact that Sterne was, as Diderot noted, a member of the clergy doubtless added to the *philosophe*'s enjoyment of the book; Diderot could not fail to appreciate the incongruity. But it seems more likely that his positive reaction to *Tristram* was inspired by more profound considerations.

Diderot had developed a fairly definite notion of what satire was. While he was to add to it over the years, his readings and his own writings provided him with sufficient working materials by 1762. Diderot's understanding of satire, as will become evident, was based on two elements—form and content. As to form, he had in mind the Roman model—a loose, flexible structure suitable for the inclusion of a variety of topics. Content was concerned with the attitude of the writer toward his subject, an attitude which depended on the personality and principles of the individual humorist who used satire as his mode of expression.

When Diderot finally found time to open his present from Sterne, he was already familiar with the works of such men as Juvenal, Persius, and Horace and was well aware of the differences in their spirits. In addition, he had considered some of the problems relating to satire, written what he was later to term a "shocking satire" against convents, and completed most of his celebrated *Satire II,* the *Neveu de Rameau.* All these works manifested a degree of moral seriousness that was not echoed by the Rabelais of the English.

Yet Diderot obviously admired Sterne's book. Although the final pages of the *Neveu de Rameau* achieve a degree of universal satire with Diderot's reference to the *philosophe's* detached observation of the world pantomime, it was to be another decade before he tried his hand at an extended "universal satire," and the result was to differ perceptibly from the Shandy saga. What he saw in *Tristram* was, in all likelihood, something which he himself wanted to do. Here was a rollicking novel, unrestricted by form or formality. The "satire" was indeed universal, for Sterne set no limits to the subjects which raised his amusement. His genial attitude may well have reminded Diderot of his favorite, Horace, and his deliberate disregard of conventional structural niceties might have recalled the tradition of the Roman satirists. Sterne, it is true, did not endeavor to develop a theory of satire equal to Diderot's; and had he attempted to do so, he doubtless would not have stressed the moral strictures that the *philo-*

sophe considered so important—at least for himself. But this oversight in no way modified either the popular success of the book or Diderot's regard for Sterne; and it is quite possible that Diderot the *philosophe's* efforts to prescribe the conditions for laughter and satire may have been responsible for the critical reception that Diderot the humorist has been afforded.

No critic has ever suggested that Sterne's vocation as a clergyman interfered with his high spirits. Some, like Thackeray and Bagehot, argue on the contrary that the reverse is true. Yet criticism of Diderot extending even into the twentieth century is frequently prejudiced by the belief that because Diderot was a serious-minded *philosophe,* he was humorless. It is true that the attitude of Diderot the moralist often determined the manner with which he handled his subjects; that is a major point of distinction between him and Sterne. It is hard to believe, however, that a man whose correspondence and actions reveal such a zest for life and who responded so warmly to the writings of great humorists could be totally lacking in humor himself. Nevertheless, this is the charge that such writers as Morley, Ellis, Barton, and Reinach submit when discussing Diderot and Sterne. Since they cannot deny that Diderot admired *Tristram*—Diderot having said so himself—they conclude that he tried, unsuccessfully, to imitate Sterne's humor.

There was, of course, no necessity for this. Diderot, as he and his friends imply, had ample resources of his own. In many ways, they bore a striking similarity to Sterne's. If Diderot enjoyed the qualities he found in the English Rabelais, he also shared with Sterne an appreciation of Sterne's French "predecessor," for Le Sage, Scarron, Cervantes. Natural sensibility was one bond between the clergyman and the encyclopedist, but certainly humor was another, for if they knew how to weep, they also knew how to laugh. They were sociable men, and often sought in conviviality an escape from domestic and personal disappointments.

The "joyous sett," as Sterne called the D'Holbach circle, was the equivalent for Diderot of the Yorkshire demoniacs. Sterne found amusement and relaxation among the eccentrics gathered at Crazy Castle, exchanging tales, plundering the library of Hall-Stevenson. Diderot laughed until his sides nearly split, he told Sophie Volland, as he witnessed the antics of Mme d'Aine or guffawed over the droll stories of the abbé Galiani. Sterne's recreations included such active pleasures as running wild chariot races by the sea, ice-skating before his disapproving parishioners, attending assemblies and dances. Diderot's tastes were inclined to be more sedentary, but on one notable occasion the *philosophe* could not restrain himself and chased the swans at Grandval with such abandon that he wound up with a fall and an injured leg. Boisterous enthusiasm, eccentric geniality, buffoonery were mutual characteristics of Diderot and Sterne that are exhibited in their letters and attested to by their contemporaries. Mrs. Montagu's judgment of Sterne's "world of good-nature" is echoed by Grimm's reference to Diderot's "good nature which gives a singular and uncommon character to all his other qualities." [3]

And in point of fact, both men were "singular and uncommon." A large part of their natural humor is based on an appreciation of their own incongruity. Sterne cheerfully agreed with a correspondent that he was a "queer dog" and was fully aware that it might be considered inappropriate for a churchman to admit to the authorship of *Tristram*. Indeed, this may have stimulated him to appear in society, soberly garbed and readily announcing his ties with the ministry, while simultaneously he "Shandied away" with all the vigor at his command. Other people amused him, but he was particularly pleased to give humorous accounts of his own escapades and quirks. Diderot, too, could laugh at himself—at his expanding waistline, at his attempts to philosophize seriously in the midst of Mme d'Aine's bawdy interruptions and the witty baitings of others, at some mournful lines he had written on man's fate which were only, he later confessed, the result of indigestion. When approaching the age of sixty, he reported that he had received a public ovation at a theatre near Bourbonne: "You know me; you can imagine my embarrassment. I bowed, bowed, bowed in the box; I narrowly escaped getting lost, through modesty, under the petticoats of the ladies." [4]

If such conduct and reactions are not held to be exemplary for a member of the Church of England, they are hardly more fitting for a sober, dedicated encyclopedist. Diderot cannot very well be accused of modeling his personal characteristics on Sterne, and there seems to be little sense in accusing him of plagiarizing the written expression of these idiosyncrasies. Sterne's humor resides in his genial and spontaneous mingling of laughter and tears, a combination Diderot never attempted to reproduce—and very wisely, too. What constitutes one man's humor does not necessarily apply to another's. Indeed, it is quite probable that any attempt to insist that it does will end only in confusion. For a number of years, M. Louis Cazamian has been suggesting that humor itself cannot be defined because it is an original attitude toward life completely dependent on the personality of each humorist.[5] A humorist may share certain characteristics with other humorists, but the end product bears his personal

stamp. Voltaire, for instance, said that Swift was the first
English Rabelais and Sterne was the second, yet it is not
likely that one would argue that Sterne's humor is Swift's
and that Swift's is the same as that of Rabelais. Correspondingly, there is little point in examining Diderot's humor
within a purely Shandean context.

There are grounds, however, for comparing Diderot and
Sterne as humorists, for both men possessed a sense of humor,
they appreciated that trait in others, and they utilized humor
in their writings. Just as the role of sensibility in their work
operates against a common background of personal and intellectual elements, so a similar confluence furnishes the point
of departure for an investigation of their humor. In this case,
peculiarities of temperament and point of view are of special
importance, for these are the distinguishing marks which
set the humorist apart from his fellow man.

The world of sensible phenomena provides a starting point,
for whether an author uses his humor for satire or for
comedy, his material must be clearly related to reality. Taking their cue from Locke as well as from their own experience, Diderot and Sterne realized that there are two ways of
seeing things: as they are and as we interpret them. Consequently, a kind of double vision results. There is the so-called
"norm," on which everybody agrees. It is in a sense a general-
ity, an abstraction necessary for communication. There is also
the individualized, subjective manner of regarding and interpreting, which is determined by each man's temperament.

This double vision is really the basis for a paradox, and as
Diderot's Jacques admonishes his Master, just because something is paradoxical does not mean that it is not true. The
humorist is aware of the discrepancy between his personal
way of seeing things or of acting and the "normal" way; and

in his mind there is an implicit comparison which he exploits. His view of life, as Professor James R. Caldwell notes,[6] includes both the stable, normal focus, and the nonsensical, chaotic focus. Because order and intelligible purpose are characteristic of the one, while impulse, chance, disorder mark the other, the humorist deals simultaneously with the rational and the irrational.

Moreover, the humorist knows that if he is concerned with dramatizing the two interpretations of reality, one accepted and established, the other unusual and individual, he is dependent on originality as a tool. Sterne was consciously emphasizing a personal characteristic—and one that he knew would make him a success—when he told a friend in 1759 that the originality of his book must resemble that of its author. The thirty-eighth chapter of the *Bijoux indiscrets* of 1748 reflects Diderot's natural bent toward freshness of thought. In the interchanges between the pro-ancients Ricaric, "who had a most scrupulous attachment for the old rules which he was eternally citing," and the pro-moderns Selim, who demands, "What care I for rules, so long as the results are pleasing? Is there any rule other than the imitation of nature?" Diderot sides with Selim and Mirzoza, who declares, "I don't understand rules at all, much less those learned words by which they are expressed." [7] These few pages contain the germ of all his future arguments and illustrations in favor of originality. He could join Sterne—and Burton, whose remark it was that Sterne borrowed for his own plea for originality—in crying, "Shall we for ever make new books, as apothecaries make new mixtures, by pouring only out of one vessel into another?" [8]

He and Sterne also concurred in their efforts to point out

the discrepancy between things as they seem and things as they are. In both *Jacques* and *Tristram,* the authors are constantly indulging in deflation, which is based on the double vision. They innocently build up our anticipation of one viewpoint or one situation, and then at the moment of climax we find that our logical inferences and conclusions are suddenly replaced by something quite different. By slipping in a surprise, the humorist totally deflates the audience's expectations and jars its complacency. This does not flatter the reader, who has been fooled. As a matter of fact, it leads one to speculate that perhaps the indignation of some of Sterne's detractors, such as Thackeray or F. C. Green, has been aroused simply because they expect the sentimental mood to continue and are annoyed to find themselves hoodwinked by his final grin.[9]

Sterne applies deflation in a number of ways. Stylistically, for one instance, he will utilize it at the conclusion of a long and complicated legal document to explain, "In three words —'My Mother was to lay in, (if she chose it) in London'." His characters unwittingly deflate each other at every turn. Consider, as an example, the effect of Captain Shandy's remark when his two mentors have just about clinched their arguments in favor of the existence of child prodigies. Yorick cites the great Lipsius, "who composed a work the day he was born:—They should have wiped it up, said my uncle Toby, and said no more about it." In its most extended usage, it corroborates Sterne's thesis that nothing falls out according to the ordinary way in the Shandy world. By that odd fatality which dogs the family, a bend sinister instead of a bend dexter appears on the coat of arms, the last of the Shandy line is misnamed and on two occasions mangled, the Peace of

Utrecht abruptly halts Toby's campaigns, and the entire movement of both the captain's amours and the novel itself continually upsets normal planning.

Diderot's *Jacques* is equally unpredictable, as the Reader soon learns. Even the characters are constantly duped by the unexpected. Jacques shows admirable but misspent gallantry for Nicole, who turns out to be the Hostess' dog. His Master and, one suspects, Jacques as well are puzzled by the outcome of a compromising situation which has confronted the hero. Describing the scene, Jacques says that he and Denise had just put in place one of the garters he had bought for her when his sweetheart's mother unexpectedly entered the room. What an embarrassing visit, is the Master's logical comment. "Maybe yes, maybe no," says Jacques, noncommittally: "Instead of noticing our uneasiness, she saw only the garter that her daughter had in her hand. 'Now there's a pretty garter', she said, 'but where's the other one'?"

Sterne and Diderot both use this device for amusement, but it also serves more serious purposes when they turn it on the reader to undermine conventional notions of how novels should be written, how people should react, to overthrow expected rules and forced plots. With even more profound intentions, Diderot avails himself of deflation to imply a lesson: there is no predestination; there is only chance, which people mistakenly rationalize into a preordained scheme of "order."

Actually, the qualities of the humorist have a significance for Diderot and Sterne which further elucidates their attitudes and relationships with their contemporaries. Originality, the overturning of conventional expectations, exploitation of the double vision are all aspects of Diderot's and Sterne's reactions against the formalizing tendency of neoclassicism. In the interests of combatting restrictive and artificial rules, whether of conduct or of art, they would stress the contrast between inexact generalities and specific occurrences. They would find means to break down the barriers that abstraction puts in the way of individual expression and behavior. Neoclassicism, to a greater extent in France than in England, did raise those barriers.

In a study of French humor in the Middle Ages, M. Cazamian develops an argument which suggests the problems Diderot faced. He indicates that French humor was quite rich during the medieval period and that by the Renaissance, a definite tradition had emerged. But with the triumph of classicism, and later neoclassicism, a different attitude was introduced which was in part responsible for the defection of French literature from its native humor. The spirit of classicism, as he notes, chooses the general man in his abstract and universal quality. Humor, however, is eminently individual and thrives on concrete particularity.[10]

It would be a gross overstatement to say that French humor quietly disappeared with the advent of new literary tastes. Even though the precepts of the prevailing vogue ran counter to those of humor, the popularity of such novels as the *Roman comique* and *Gil Blas* was not restricted to Diderot, Sterne, and a handful of coterie readers.[11] But Diderot and Sterne did recognize, appreciate, and utilize those characteristics which have been cited as components of humor. Diderot, in fact, had defined humor as "an original facetiousness, of an uncommon and singular vein," and had proposed Swift's works as an example of the element of surprise and the completely unexpected. But Diderot did not lose sight of his own heritage; contradicting the then prevalent notion that humor was a characteristic only of the English, he contended that Rabelais and Cyrano have an equal claim to it.

Rabelais may also have emphasized for Sterne and Diderot the value of humor as an antirepressive device. Working in the interests of healthy reactions, it is, like sensibility, a release for man's impulses. Much of the irreverence and blasphemy in medieval humor, for example, was a natural outburst against restraints and taboos. Diderot and Sterne, who were not notoriously respectful in their attitudes toward cant and repression, welcomed opportunities to expose artificiality and rigidity of thought and conduct. They could find authority for their natural inclinations not only in literary models but also in as recent a critic as Shaftesbury, who established ridicule as a principal medium for the recognition of truth and who stressed the liberating properties of humor:

And thus the natural free spirits of ingenious men, if imprisoned and controlled, will find out other ways of motion to relieve themselves in their constraint; and whether it be in burlesque, mimicry, or buffoonery, they will be glad at any rate to vent themselves, and be revenged on their constrainers.[12]

But in order that humor may fulfill its potentialities, whatever the form it takes, certain conditions are necessary. Specifically, the writer must use detachment and control, judgment and carefully selected materials. He must, in fact, apply the thesis of Diderot's *Paradoxe*. If he utilizes the double vision, he must first be aware that he sees things differently from the general observer, and then he must deliberately expose the contrast. He must not only know himself; he must also know his audience, for his art depends on manipulating his readers' participation. Should he use deflation, he should be a studied *ingénu,* constructing with an air of innocence a pattern whose aim is to fool the audience. When the audience realizes the hoax—and Sterne's great art is that often one cannot be sure—it also realizes that instead of being an accomplice, it has been a dupe. It has become the victim of what the French call a *pince-sans-rire,* defined in the eighth edition of the French Academy's dictionary as "Celui qui raille et plaisante en restant froid et impassible." [13] The discipline of the humorist is like that of the great actor or artist; they both consciously simulate in order to achieve success. The actor cannot be overwhelmed by his emotions any more than the joker can be completely submerged in the joke. Each must have the capacity for dissociating a part of himself from the rest. Fontenelle, whose works were familiar to Diderot and Sterne, had said,

Nature, through comedy, has given us a marvelous faculty to prevent us from becoming the dupes of ourselves. How many times has it happened that while one part of us does something with ardor and earnestness, another part mocks it? And if there were need for it, one could find a third part which could mock the other two.[14]

Sterne and Diderot, as has been indicated in the previous chapter, had the ability for detachment to which Fontenelle refers. Through self-knowledge, they could feel and perceive simultaneously; through self-consciousness, they could exploit facets of their individual temperaments and choose appropriate means of presentation. If Sterne's humor is spontaneous, it is not because spontaneity itself is essential to humor; it is because Sterne, in company with all humorists, as M. Cazamian has remarked,[15] could make good use of a personal trait. Explaining an inappropriate sermon, he says, "that unlucky kind of fit seized me, which you know I can never resist," [16] yet he turned his "fits" to his advantage in *Tristram.* He told Hall-Stevenson that he copied the present train of emotions running through his brain; [17] consequently, it is no wonder that his sentimentalism should appear to be a blind for comedy.[18] Because of Sterne's emotional volatility, he was always scuttling back and forth from laughter to tears, and because of his artistry, he could base his Shandeism on sudden changes like these. They are not typical of humor; they are typical of Sterne, for as Coleridge has pointed out, humor "always more or less partakes of the character of the speaker."[19]

Coleridge's insight is equally applicable to Diderot, who was himself subject to fits of spontaneity. Of his fictional works, it is *Jacques* which best reflects Diderot's natural gaiety. But Diderot was also a *philosophe*. While his moral seriousness did not destroy his humor, quite frequently it tempered and conditioned his expression. Therefore it is quite logical that Diderot should utilize a personal trait differently from Sterne. Satire, a mode which Sterne early rejected, is almost always present in Diderot's humor, and it is a mode which is "seldom 'honest' in the sense of forthright expression of emotion or opinion. It has an aim, a preconceived purpose: to instill a given set of emotions or opinions into its readers."[20] By using it, Diderot, like Sterne, deals with the present train of his emotions mediately instead of immediately, but his humor is no more Sterne's than the Nephew's is Yorick's.

This is not to say that Diderot and Sterne have nothing in common beyond the capacity for humor. They are, as will be seen, in general agreement on the meaning and function of laughter; they make similar distinctions between two main types of satire; both try their hands at different outlets for humor; and, at least superficially, one parallels the other in presenting interpretations of reality which are at odds with the "normal" view. But their motivation cannot always be the same. A writer may be a serious moralist; he might then choose to utilize his capacity for humor in some form of satire. He may be of a lighter nature and decide to use it for sheer amusement. He may be adept at handling either, and the combination of his mood and his environment may condition his procedure at different times. Personality, conscious choice and its determining factors will underlie the immediate differences between Sterne and Diderot as humorists.

In his treatise on *Human Nature,* Thomas Hobbes had suggested that there was an element of brutality in man's laughter.[21] Shaftesbury had to concede that nothing is ridiculous except what is deformed, and he therefore advocated means for curbing the inherent cruelty.[22] This is the position that Diderot took, and it is in harmony with the opinion which Sterne eventually developed. Both men were to seek ways to modify the ruthlessness implied by Hobbes. In a dialogue written in 1760, the *philosophe* says:

It is always the idea of defect which excites laughter in us; defect in ideas, or in expression, or in the person who acts, speaks, or who is the subject of a discussion.

But if this is so, should not all physical and moral defect make one laugh?

Yes, any time that the idea of something harmful is not associated with it; for this idea stifles the laughter of all those who have reached the age of reason.[23]

Diderot's contention is that there has to be a certain state of mind for true laughter. Earlier, Shaftesbury had noted that the persecuting spirit would raise a bantering one, and if the individual were repressed enough, his efforts toward release would not stop merely at banter. Jean-François Rameau was to provide a dramatic illustration for both Shaftesbury's point and Diderot's belief that "to be accessible to laughter, the mind must be in a state of calm and equanimity." [24] Laughter, as he and Sterne agreed, attacks the ridiculous, and if one is to judge by their selections, they included in that category anything which is unnatural, artificial, unrealistic.

Yet Diderot, mindful of Palissot's scathing attack on the *philosophes,* is careful to qualify and limit his meaning. "Yes, the ridiculous of condition; but I find personal ridicule very disagreeable." [25] Ultimately, Sterne was to concur, although his first literary efforts are hardly consistent with his later attitude. Diderot's reluctance to harm anyone deliberately appears to be fairly consistent, however. It is perceptible in a little piece entitled "Résultat d'une conversation sur les égards qu'on doit aux rangs et aux dignités de la société," which was published in the *Correspondance littéraire* of 1776. He refuses to elaborate on some of his statements because, he says, he does not care to fall into personal satire.[26] In his article "Encyclopédie," published in 1755, he remarks that if one has business with dishonorable men it is preferable to avoid naming them. And if one is forced to identify them, it should be from a stand of moral indignation, revealing their vices to their everlasting shame, recalling them to their position and duties "with cutting strokes," pursuing them "with the bitterness of Persius and the rancor of Juvenal or Buchanan." [27]

By citing as a corrective the manner of Juvenal and Persius, Diderot indicates that true laughter has no place in this kind of ridicule; vicious people are not funny. Even the *Neveu de Rameau,* which includes a merciless exposé of a number of Diderot's contemporaries, may be seen as an example corroborating the statements in the article "Encyclopédie." While it certainly does contain some of the bitterest personal invective in French literature of the eighteenth century, Diderot's treatment of his satire was consistent with the sentiments he expressed earlier. He never published it and, as far as scholars can ascertain, he did not even mention its existence to his closest friends or colleagues. The manuscript lay hidden until all its personages had died and posterity could render a more balanced judgment. To a twentieth-century audience, the motivation of the satire does not appear to be essentially one of calumny and slander—which is the Nephew's attitude and, quite possibly, the early Sterne's. The attack seems to be intended to reveal and right abuses. Bertin, Palissot, Fréron, and their group are, after all, ephemeral figures; their vices, however, are not. They are common to human nature and should be exposed and condemned as a warning to mankind. The corrupt society which draws Diderot's censure is a fit subject for corrosive satire, not for comedy. He makes a clear distinction between these in the *Paradoxe.*

Satire, he says, is of *a* tartuffe; comedy is of *the* Tartuffe. Satire pursues a vicious person, while comedy pursues a vice. Had there been only one or two "précieuses ridicules," they would have been suitable for satire but not for comedy. For comedy, he infers, is guided by the same principle as the ideal model: it is a generalization based on specific examples. *The* Tartuffe is drawn from all the individual tartuffes, and because it typifies them, it cannot be broken down into a recognizable portrait of a particular man.[28] By exposing a vice, the ridiculous but not the personally ridiculous, comedy becomes depersonalized. "To laugh at things in the world," Fontenelle had written, "you need some way of getting outside, and comedy draws you out of it. Comedy presents everything like a spectacle, as though you had never participated."[29] It is perhaps here that the proper state of mind for laughter is to be found. When laughter does occur in a satire like the *Neveu de Rameau,* it is the cruel, unregulated mockery that is based on a flaw: onlookers ridicule the Nephew, the Nephew ridicules Bertin; but this is not the laughter of calm and equanimity.

Diderot did not, however, regard all satire as an attack stemming from the mode of Juvenal. His personal preference was Horace, and it would appear from Diderot's references to the more caustic satirists that he was cognizant of the distinction between them and the genial observer of human foibles.[30] In his own work, he was to utilize both types of satire at significantly different stages of his development. And he was also to show that he applied satire to form as well as to content. Structurally, the *Neveu de Rameau* derives from classic satire, a genre which could include personal attack but which, originally, was a kind of hodge-podge where the author could throw odds and ends which defied more formal classification. The *Neveu de Rameau* is thus related to Diderot's *Satire à la manière de Perse* and to his *Satire sur les mots de caractère*.[31] Insofar as it pursues vices and vicious people, it is also a satire in content, partaking, despite its motto from Horace, of the spirit of Juvenal.

He clearly distinguishes between these two spirits of satire in reviewing his own work. Submitting a manuscript to Meister in 1780, he explains: "It is the counterpart of *Jacques le fataliste*. . . . I am quite sure that it will afflict your readers even more than *Jacques* made them laugh. . . . It is entitled *La Religieuse,* and I don't believe that anyone has ever written a more shocking satire of convents."[32] It is interesting that Diderot so well perceived the difference in attitude and intention that marked his first and last serious fictional endeavors. Had he wished to extend his comments, he might also have cited *Jacques* as the counterpart of another work written during the period of *La Religieuse* and resembling it in the sharp, corrosive satire which excluded good-natured laughter.

For if the comic satire of *Jacques* balances the frightening exposé in *La Religieuse,* the handling of Diderot's hero's dilemma is juxtaposed to the treatment of a similar philosophical problem in the *Neveu de Rameau.* Both satires demonstrate concern for the same question: what happens to vice and virtue in a mechanistic system under which responsibility for everything is attributed to the workings of fate? Despite Diderot's refusal to agree with the Nephew's excuse that "it is in the stars," despite his contention that the *philosophe* is the only man who can mount Mercury's epicycle and observe the world pantomime from without, Diderot finds the general picture quite sobering. He is deeply disturbed by the Nephew's "reasoning," and he does not regard with amusement the standards and activities of the Nephew's society. In *Jacques,* on the other hand, the major spokesman for fatalism is a harmless, good-natured fellow who is no more a thoroughgoing embodiment of his philosophy than he is a victim of social conditioning. Diderot emphasizes his own detachment from the start. With an air of superior mastery, he ridicules to absurdity Jacques' philosophic system and derives as much entertainment from his audience as from his protagonists. "I amuse myself by writing your follies under borrowed names," he tells the Reader; "your follies make me laugh."

Assuredly, human nature as Diderot understood it had not altered perceptibly between 1760 and 1773 or 1774. But certain conditions directly affecting Diderot had changed, and his own emotional and intellectual faculties had undergone a development toward fuller realization. That persecuting spirit to which Shaftesbury had referred must have been all too evi-

dent to the editor of the *Encyclopédie* in the years surround-
ing the composition of *La Religieuse* and the *Neveu de
Rameau*. In 1758, the Longchamp case, which had provided
the excuse for the *Préface Annexe* of *La Religieuse* had come
to a climax, intensifying Diderot's antipathy toward the
Church. The year 1759 had been crucial for the *philosophes,*
what with the revocation of the privilege for the *Encyclopédie,* D'Alembert's final break, the condemnation of Helvétius, the accusation of Diderot as author of the *Mémoire
pour Abraham Chaumeix*. In 1760, the side of reaction and
repression found further expression in Palissot's *Les Philosophes*. Moreover, Diderot's personal talents had, he supposed,
been thwarted. His ambitions to reform the theatre and to
introduce virtue through the medium of the *drame bourgeois* received a blow with the poor reception of his *Père de
famille* in 1761. At first, he even believed that his play had
failed because actors of the anti-*philosophe* group were in the
cast. The entire experience must have been a cruel setback
for a man who was to claim later that he had spent his best
years on a task for which he was unsuited and had written
only two plays. Reviewing the events of those years, saddened
by the death of his father in 1759, Diderot could have concluded, very understandably, that he was not in the mood for
producing comic satire; *La Religieuse* and the *Neveu de
Rameau* indicate as much.

But during the sixties, Diderot had brought to a close the
editorial duties which had preoccupied him for twenty years,
and in 1772 he finished revising the *planches*. Although Le
Breton's knavery took some of the edge off Diderot's victory,
the completion of the *Encyclopédie* was nonetheless a great
triumph for the *philosophes*. Equally important for Diderot
was the development discussed in the previous chapter. His

revised conception of sensibility would aid him in mounting Mercury's epicycle, enabling him to create so detached a self-portrait as M. Hardouin in *Est-il bon? Est-il méchant?* He had not withdrawn from the crusade of the *philosophes,* his arguments were not to be diminished in force, but he had become more patient and experienced, less emotionally involved. And when, in *Jacques,* he turned to the subjects of his earlier satires, he regarded the world pantomime with detachment and self-confidence.

Fatalism and its result in the *Neveu de Rameau* are frightening and serious as the Nephew exploits an immoral rationale to justify his actions. Fatalism in *Jacques* does not have a harmful effect on its inconsistent exponent; actually, it is an absurd farce, as Diderot readily implies. After the Master has raised the initial issue of cause and effect—was Jacques' benefactor cuckolded because it was "written up there," or was it "written up there" because Jacques was going to cuckold his benefactor—Jacques explains that both alternatives appeared on the great scroll, inscribed simultaneously one beside the other. The superior commentator promptly interrupts his two theologians who argue "without understanding each other, as it can happen in theology":

You understand, Reader, how far I could push this conversation about a subject on which so much has been said and written for two thousand years, without advancing one step further.[33]

The same alteration in attitude applies to the passages representing the true counterpart of *La Religieuse.* The supposed practices and institutions of the Church were revealed by a "shocking satire" in the earlier novel. Diderot's opinion has not changed in *Jacques,* but the tone is lighter than the grim account of Suzanne's tortured existence. He uses ridicule for his attack on the clergy and monastic life. People like Richard, whose parents had objected to his taking vows, escape easily from monasteries; others, like Père Hudson, Frère Jean, and Père Ange, exploit the Church for their own purposes. Substituting amused mockery for savagery, Diderot presents petty fools and shrewd charlatans instead of abnormal monsters. When Jacques asks his Master why it is that monks are so bad, Diderot does not belabor the point. The Master replies simply, "I suppose it's because they're monks."

Would it have been possible for Diderot in 1760 to handle these topics as he did in the 1770s? Very likely not; circumstances as well as his personal development combined to produce a more mellow, even a stoical attitude. In his last work of fiction, he demonstrates this evolution and composes his own universal satire with that state of mind conducive to laughter.

Instead of waiting over a decade, Sterne was less than a year in adopting the tone for that Rabelaisian book which Diderot so admired. Sterne's forte was comedy, and he established himself in this vein in his first major work. Yet it was not until after his first endeavors as an author that he altered his initial approach, changing from satire to comedy. Before he wrote *Tristram,* he had utilized effectively a cruel, harmful sort of laughter which was consciously based on defect.[34]

In 1741, the obscure parson was employed by his uncle to write for the Whigs in the *Yorkshire Gazetteer.*[35] The examples which remain indicate that Sterne was employing sarcasm and irony to humiliate the opposition in a series of hostile encounters. His sallies are generally of a personal, sometimes scurrilous nature: in one broadside, Sterne compares his opponent to a "certain nasty Animal in Egypt," whose only means of defense is to shower his attackers with excrement.[36] This letter has a Swiftian ring about it—perhaps to balance the passages from Pope that were used against Sterne—as Sterne ridicules his attacker with compact, corrosive satire.

He handles the mode with even more mastery in a belittling onslaught, decidedly lacking in geniality, which constitutes his *Political Romance* or *The History of a Good Warm Watchcoat* (1759). While the allegory lacks Swift's savage intensity and is considerably less complicated, it is reminiscent of *The Tale of a Tub*—and Sterne knew his Swift well. The *Romance,* as Cross has said, is "a clever elaboration of Swift's cruel and humorous philosophy. Reduce men to pygmies, and they at once become in character and conduct ludicrous and contemptible." [37] It seems doubtful that Sterne was impelled by the moral principles Diderot insisted on when using personal attack. There certainly is little to suggest that he was restrained by them or by the inscription on the title page, which implied that the *Romance* had no satiric intent. Topham, the "villain" of the satire, was to reappear as Didius and Phutatorius in *Tristram,* but the abusive treatment he receives in the *Romance* has a much crueler edge than the later buffoonery. Sterne himself must have realized that the earlier attack was too strong. In his will of 28 December 1761, he asked Mrs. Sterne to refrain from publishing the *Romance* because Fontayne, whose cause he had championed, had turned out to be unworthy of Sterne's efforts, and because "I hav hung up Dr Topham, in the romance—in a ridiculous light—wch, upon my Soul I now doubt, whether he deserves it—" [38]

With the exception of the portrait of Dr. Burton as Slop, Sterne's later works do not include this particular kind of "ridiculous light." Occasionally, he even denounces it. He

forewarns a correspondent: ". . . such Satyre & sarcasm—
scoffing & flouting—rallying & reparteeing of it,—thrusting &
parrying in one dark corner or another. There wd be nothing but mischief." [39] He mentions with distaste "a pelting
kind of thersitical satire, as black as the very ink 'tis wrote
with." Referring to Captain Shandy's campaigns, Walter
remarks that in the hands of anyone else, they would be
regarded as a satire of Louis XIV's conduct of war. "But 'tis
not my brother Toby's nature, kind soul! my father would
add, to insult any one." [40]

Apparently, Sterne liked to believe that it was not *his*
nature, either. Ridicule he would, with much buffoonery
and farce, but he did not care for rancor or raillery. He says
so in a frequently cited passage which resembles both
Shaftesbury's plea for controlled laughter and Diderot's distinction between satire and comedy:

This leads me to the observation of a fourth cruel inlet into this
evil, and that is, the desire of being thought men of wit and parts,
and the vain expectation of coming honestly by the title, by shrewd
and sarcastic reflections upon the broken stock of other people's
failings,—perhaps their misfortunes. . . .

He adds that this "has helped to give wit a bad name, as if
the main essence of it was satire; certainly there is a difference between Bitterness and Saltness": bitterness is "void
of humanity," whereas saltness is "so pure and abstracted
from persons, that it willingly hurts no man." [41] Although
Sterne's detractors may have denied that he kept his word,
he did promise, in 1759, that he would try to curb a tendency
to sport too much with his wit.[42] His proposed intentions, he
told Dodsley, were for *Tristram* to encompass not just the
weaknesses of the sciences, wherein lies the "true point of
Ridicule," but everything else which Sterne, "in my way,"

found *laughable*. Laughter and ridicule, saltness rather than bitterness, are Sterne's choice, and they are based on the personality of the humorist; he will include what strikes *him* as being funny, just as Diderot reserved that right for himself in *Jacques*.

Having censured bitterness, Sterne, for the most part, specified what he meant when he referred to satire. Unless he added a "theresitical" or "sarcastic" tag, he understood it to be laughing and good-humored.[43] He frankly acknowledged a major model for his treatment of laughter: "—but in general I am perswaded that the happiness of the Cervantic humour arises from this very thing—of describing silly and trifling Events, with the Circumstantial Pomp of Great ones—."[44] The attitude is that of the "pince sans rire," working through high burlesque, and had Sterne wished to admit it, he could have cited Fielding as a contemporary following the same vein.

Sterne's preference for Cervantic humor, which he associates with laughter and comedy, is decidedly evident. He tells the witty widow Fenton, "know then, that I think there is more laughable humour,—[in the third volume of *Tristram*] with equal degree of Cervantik Satyr—if not more than in the last—."[45] He even considered making a Cervantic comedy of *Tristram* for the stage. Because of the numerous references in both his letters and *Tristram,* it seems clear that rather than Cervantes the self-conscious narrator,[46] it was Cervantes the humorist who influenced him more strongly. If Cervantes hoped to make the melancholy smile and the merry laugh, Sterne announced directly that he was writing *Tristram* for "the laughing part of the world." He was pleased with his own "vile errantry," and declared in his will that he held "humanity and good nature" above all else.

Moreover, Sterne was quite aware that his nature was not fit for seriousness. Beginning with his avowal in 1759 that "a meditation upon Death" was more appropriate for his calling, "but then it Could not have been set on by Me," [47] he maintained a pretty determined optimism until just before his death. He may have been particularly attracted to Cervantes and Scarron because he associated his own refusal to give in to his illness with their cheerful fortitude. "—Tell me the reason, why Cervantes could write so fine and humourous a Satyre, in the melancholly regions of a damp prison— or why Scarron in bodily pain—" he asks Mrs. Montagu in the same letter in which he tells her that he wishes to die joking. "I am ill—very ill—," he adds, "Yet I feel my Existence Strongly, and something like revelation along with it, which tells, I shall not dye—but live—& yet any other man wd set his house in order—." [48]

But Sterne, as he took care to emphasize, was not like "any other man." His grief over Eliza could not prevent his emerging from a lacrymose session with the *Journal* to write merry letters to others. Death and illness are topics for jokes, not meditations. Although the *Sentimental Journey* is more subdued than *Tristram,* part of its tone, as Sterne's "redemption" book, necessarily results from the author's decision to exploit the new vogue. Enough of the agreeably eccentric humorist remains to suggest that Sterne was not consciously publicizing whatever intimations of his mortality he may have had.

It seems therefore safe to conclude that Sterne's temperament, which he understood quite well, was oriented toward optimism and good humor, and that he cultivated it accordingly. He was not meant to be a Swift or a Hamlet. The *Political Romance* proves that he was capable, artistically, of the Swiftian vein, yet shortly thereafter he said that he was tired of employing his brains for other people—a reference both to the *Romance* and to his earlier contributions for the Whigs. Sterne wanted to write for his own advantage, and the major reason for his change from "bitterness" to "saltness" was, very probably, his preference for following his own inclinations.

Out of this preference Shandeism grew, and it must be remembered that Shandeism is a very personal "philosophy," strictly derived from Sterne's way of seeing and reacting to life. He had found it extremely useful as a protection against what he called "poverty of the spirit." Sterne's ability to maintain high spirits was what kept him going, as he knew,[49] and he believed that Shandeism was a fitting philosophy to incorporate into a book which purported to amuse and please. He tells Pitt, in his dedication, that in his efforts to "fence against the infirmities of ill health, and other evils of life," he has become convinced that laughter "adds something to this Fragment of life." In answer to the readers' speculations, he denies that his book is written against anything but spleen; he is certain of the beneficial effects of laughter; he advocates a "kingdom of hearty laughing subjects." *Tristram* is deliberately written, he points out, as "a careless kind of civil, nonsensical, good-humoured Shandean book, which will do all your hearts good—. . . ." He does not forget to add, "And all your heads too,—provided you understand it,"[50] but many of his readers regarded this as an irrelevant afterthought. Sterne was evidently quite annoyed by their oversight, for he assumed the role of the injured author in a letter written a month before his death:

In *Tristram Shandy,* the handle is taken which suits their passions, their ignorance or sensibility. There is so little true feeling in the *herd* of the *world,* that I wish I could have got an act of parliament, when the books first appear'd, "that none but wise men should look into them." It is too much to write books and find heads to understand them.[51]

Although he characteristically cheered up in his next sentence by noting that "The world, however, seems to come into a better temper about them," he seems to have been genuinely, if somewhat naively, disappointed that his efforts to satisfy everyone were not completely successful.

Sterne's attitude is understandable, for while Shandeism was a natural bent, it was also a choice. He consciously carried himself toward the reader in a "fanciful guise of careless disport" because he wanted fame and fortune, and realized that good humor suited his ends as well as his nature. Later on, when his own feelings were becoming even more sensitized by ill-health and Eliza's departure, he was shrewd enough to realize that sensibility was also more attractive to his readers. Subjective he was, but not so lacking in detachment as people have believed. Like Diderot, he had the capacity Fontenelle mentions of watching himself and, as has been suggested in the previous chapter, he made capital out of it with an eye toward the vagaries of the reading public's taste.

Now it is no easy matter to please everyone all the time—Sterne finally had to admit it himself. A more thoughtful man would perceive the obstacles to this goal; a more serious man might hesitate to modify his stand in the interests of mass appeal. Diderot knew from the start that he would antagonize certain elements in the reading audience. As a dedicated *philosophe,* he could not and would not choose to avoid it. Therefore, for practical purposes, he deliberately withheld some of his work, and left to posterity the final judgment of his achievements. Sterne, though he was not a fool, did tend to

rush in blithely where others might fear to tread. If his treatment of humor lacks Diderot's more serious overtones, it is
because Sterne's aim is to entertain everyone. With the same
rather careless disregard that marked his "investigations" of
sensibility, Sterne makes his distinction between comedy and
and satire, and leaves it at that. His intellectual curiosity is
not stimulated by more complex problems relating to laughter
—questions that did interest Diderot—once he has selected the
mode most appropriate for his own humor. And that mode is
comic rather than satirical.

It is often difficult, as David Worcester has indicated, to
distinguish between the comic and satirical modes. Both
comedy and satire may use the same tools, such as burlesque
or irony; both require the writer's detachment as he contrives
to work on the reader. But satire has more unity of objective
and emphasis; comedy has less intensity and containment of
focus. Satire is directed toward a more defined and preconceived end, while comedy is less purposeful in that it is a kind
of laughter for laughter's sake.[52] It is the latter which attracts
Sterne, and by taking up anything which he finds laughable,
he naturally becomes quite diffuse. Even when he ridicules
a specific subject, like the abuses of learning, he has so many
things to laugh at that the result lacks the concentration and
direction of satire.

This distinction between the two modes—a difference
which sets *Tristram* apart from the earlier *Political Romance*
—is even more sharply defined by the contrast between Walter
Shandy's mental gymnastics and a source, *The Memoirs of
Martinus Scriblerus*. Cornelius Scriblerus, like Walter Shandy,
serves to ridicule the follies of learned men. He shares with
Walter certain odd notions such as his extended plan for Martin's education, his emphasis on the proper conditions for

geniture, his devotion to pet theories. Both fathers are eccentrics given over to intellectual extravagances of a specu-
lative nature; they insist on applying these speculations to
their sons' upbringing; they both suffer severe trials on christening day. But the Scriblerians directed their attacks against
the excessive admiration of the ancients, whence all Cornelius'
theories stemmed. Walter's mind is much messier than his
predecessor's because it is more eclectic. He is, very likely,
a broader conception than Cornelius; his theories and quirks
are more widespread. As a consequence, however, the "satire"
is more general and lacks force; the subjects keep switching,
new topics intrude, for Sterne is not interested in pursuing
a limited line of attack.

Both the Scriblerians and Diderot had more specific and
serious motivation. In *La Religieuse* and the *Neveu de Rameau,* Diderot was not even writing about anything he
thought was funny: his occasional amusement at the Nephew
is always tempered or interrupted by his disagreement with
the Nephew's *morale.* In *Jacques,* where the over-all tone is
changed, the satire itself is very clear. Within his comedy of
human nature are included pointed satirical attacks, often
totally exclusive of laughter. The moral Diderot appends to
the story of Mme de La Pommeraye, for example, is written
earnestly and gravely. Even in his amusement, Diderot maintains a sharper edge than Sterne. Taking firm mastery, he
refuses to cajole the Reader or audience. He is more out-
spoken, and seizes every opportunity to draw a moral, to
make his lesson very clear. He agrees that he should be amusing, but he will not subordinate himself to the Reader. Indeed,
he makes it quite evident that the Reader is the "goat" and
that the author is passing judgment on him. As Diderot says,
he wants to entertain his audience, but he also wants to enter-

tain himself, often at the audience's expense. If the occasion arises—and Diderot usually makes sure that it does—he castigates the Reader for assorted hypocrisies and faults. Moreover, he is anything but subtle: if the Reader pretends that he is shocked by certain words, Diderot screeches them at him; if the Reader has a double standard, Diderot upbraids him for it; if the Reader expects one thing and gets another, Diderot gloats and teases him. Not satisfied to burlesque love stories and conventional novels, Diderot stops outright to criticize the Reader's taste. When he has no other means of drawing a moral, he interpolates a story to emphasize the point he wants to make.

Sterne is never so frank and never so serious. He cannot be too obviously amused by his readers' follies or he will lose his public. Therefore, his manner is joking and often deferential. He resorts to subterfuge and equivocation, suggesting and hinting where Diderot speaks out directly. There is more subtlety in Sterne's humor, but there is less focus and honesty, for Sterne cannot afford to alienate people and he does not care to insult. He is also conditioned by another factor which has already been seen operating in a different sphere of his work.

It is significant that when Sterne and Diderot turn to a humorous consideration of sex, their attitudes are consistent with their reactions to its role in sensibility. The subject of both Diderot's and Sterne's indelicacies has always incited argument. Diderot himself vigorously defended his right to provide forthright discussions of all matters pertaining to human conduct and human functions. Sterne, however, had qualms; early during the composition of *Tristram,* he promised a correspondent that he would keep a due distance from Swift who, he added, had kept a due distance from Rabelais.

He doubtless thought that by acting like a genial crackbrain he would give less offense, but that he was even concerned over offending is a pointed commentary on the differences between Diderot's and Sterne's attitudes.

Whether one agrees with Professor Dieckmann that certain passages in *Jacques* are vile and salacious or with Professor Green that Sterne is sniggering and lascivious is largely a question of personal tastes and judgments. The fact remains that Diderot regards the sexual urge as a very important aspect of human nature, whereas Sterne is either apprehensive of it or thinks that it is funny—and somewhat improper. When Diderot chooses the comic view—and this is not prevalent throughout his writings—he handles his material with his usual candor, deriving lusty amusement from the wholesome, if unrestrained instincts of his characters. For the most part, Sterne's characters do not display these elemental instincts; indeed, the Shandy males appear reluctant to face the problem at all. While Sterne's insinuations are quite clear, his use of a thinly veiled approach coupled with suggestions of indecorum would seem to reflect the author's inhibitions. Furthermore, the topics that amuse him the most generally are not, in themselves, cause for hilarity. Sterne's preoccupation with impotency, sterility, castration has encouraged at least one critic to conclude that his "obsession by the obstetrical," as Professor Green terms it, is symptomatic of more than perverse humor.[53]

Whatever else it suggests, this obsession is a striking example of Sterne's personal sense of incongruity and bears significantly on the differences between his and Diderot's treatment of humor. For in this realm, Sterne is essentially a comedian —a "humorist" rather than a "man of humour," to use Coleridge's distinction. He derives his effect from the presence of his own oddity, even though he denies that he is Tristram or Yorick. Diderot uses a different approach. When he imposes his personality on his satire in the *Neveu de Rameau* and *Jacques,* his role is pointedly limited. He considers himself a *philosophe;* he is impelled by moral seriousness unknown to Sterne. His delightful self-portrait of M. Hardouin and his dilemmas is a variation on the theme of vice and virtue: is he good? is he bad? While Diderot certainly enjoys joking, he does not seek to raise a laugh in everything; he is more satirist than humorist. Even in *Jacques* he makes his superiority over the Reader clear; he maintains an air of dignity. This is because for Diderot, even in relaxation, there are certain subjects and attitudes which require serious praise or blame. It is doubtful whether even in his lightest mood he would ridicule virtue or nature, or miss a chance to aim a dart at current abuse or hypocrisy.

By contrast, there is a familiarity about Sterne which puts him on the same level (or even a lower level) than that of his readers. For Sterne, nothing is sacred and anything may be the stuff of comedy; there seem to be no bounds other than his strictures on insults and bitterness. This is because Sterne thought that laughter alone was sufficiently constructive, whereas Diderot, the moralist, always saw to it that the lesson was clearly pointed out. As a more profound thinker, he was aware that true laughter needs certain conditions. For Sterne, provided something amused him, it needed no conditions. He did not analyze laughter any more than he analyzed sensibility.

Ultimately, a consideration of Diderot's and Sterne's humor returns to the basic question of two individual minds pitted against empirical reality. Sterne's inclination to laugh at anything and Diderot's tendency to select and control his satire are reflections of something fundamentally different in their natures and in their thought. Diderot, despite his occasional doubts, really believed in the possibility of human progress and devoted the greater part of his energies to trying to make it come closer to a reality. Sterne, however, was more disillusioned and probably did not share Diderot's belief. Instead, he agreed with that school of thought in England which was centered not on human institutions but on the individual. And with appropriate precision, Sterne was to make this emphasis even clearer by stressing not just the individual but the self. His indiscriminate amusement suggests that, like the final implications of his attitude toward sensibility, he is leaning toward a state where no rules or regulating forces exist. If, in his novels, unexpected situations arise, if odd and presumably improper subjects entertain him, it is not that Sterne is unaware of propriety and order. It is simply that what constitutes good church talk [54] is quite distinct from what constitutes Sterne's own interpretation of life. And in discarding an intelligible and fixed cosmos for the universe of *Tristram* and the *Sentimental Journey,* Sterne does not substitute any other measure which could act as a stabilizing influence. His frame of reference is subjective, his guides are strictly personal.

The selectivity and compactness of Diderot's satire suggest that he believed in the efficacy of valid restraints. His interests and investigations as a *philosophe* usually acted as guides for his humor; they did not so much interfere with it as give it further depth. While Diderot had no use for artificial order, he was also opposed to the other extreme, disorder. He no more advocated the false systematizings of Jacques than he approved the personal disintegration of the Nephew. He did, however, feel the need for some guiding standards of human conduct and some basic coherence in nature. If appearances are invariably deceiving in *Jacques,* for example, that is because the audience has been misled by erroneous assumptions; it is not because there is no reason for those caprices which the Reader would call chance and which Jacques would attribute to fate. Instead of relying on the "pure designation" of a "superintending power" or on the dictates of subjective judgment, Diderot finds an objective explanation in the workings of the laws of nature. The flexibility of nature provides freedom from contrived design, and its basic laws guard against completely arbitrary criteria.

As a result of his search for integration, Diderot arrives at a standard or limit which naturally acts as a modifying agent on his humor, just as it guards against excesses of sensibility. In both instances, Diderot has sought to temper extremes by exercising controls. Sterne's humor *is* more abandoned, but if one considers that Diderot was not prompted to emulate it, then there seems little justification for invidious comparisons. Because the humorist's way of regarding life determines what he will do with his vision of reality, there is no basis for arguing that Diderot unsuccessfully tried to ape Sterne. They certainly had in common a great relish for depicting some of the more incongruous, comically absurd manifestations of human nature. But the *philosophe*'s treatment of humor results in intellectual satire; the parson's, in farce-comedy.

CHAPTER IV

FICTIONAL THEORIES AND PRACTICES

THE AUTHOR'S ATTITUDE TOWARD HIS WORK

IN 1765, Diderot and Sterne each posted to a correspondent a letter typical of their respective attitudes toward their writing. Sophie Volland learned, not to her surprise, that Diderot's vanity did not require a popular reward; indeed, he was even rather indifferent to his friends' appreciation of him. He would be quite satisfied, he told her, if there were, in the whole world, but one man, esteemed by him, who knew what he was worth.[1] Foley, Sterne's banker in Paris, was advised that the celebrated author of *Tristram Shandy* sought honor rather than wealth.[2] Both writers were telling the truth—in their own way. Diderot had already informed the small audience of the *Salon* of 1763 that he was writing for his friend,[3] not for the public. Sterne had asserted shortly after the first publication of *Tristram* that he wrote "not to be *fed,* but to be famous,"[4] a sentiment he was to repeat frequently in subsequent letters.

Yet Foley must have smiled at Sterne's protestation, for it is quite evident in the letters he received from his client that wealth was a necessary corollary of honor. In franker moments, Sterne himself had no illusions about one of his purposes in writing fiction: "That I proposed laying the world under contribution when I set pen to paper—is what I own, and I suppose I may be allow'd to have that view in my head in common with every other writer, to make my labour of advantage to myself." [5] As a matter of fact, for a man who was pleased to refer to "the contempt of money which *ma façon* [sic] *de penser* has ever impress'd on me," Sterne went to considerable pains to assure himself of a popular reward in the fullest sense of the term.

Despite his hasty and unpremeditated descent on London in March, 1760, he remembered to take along some sermons and promptly arranged for their publication. The next month, in the midst of a most gratifying social whirl, he managed to combine publicity and profits: "There is a fine print going to be done of me—so I shall make the most of myself, & sell both inside & out." [6] Once he had gained entry to influential circles, he did not hesitate to apply, through an intermediary, to one of the leading artists of the day for "ten strokes of *Howgarth's* [sic; Sterne's italics] witty Chissel, to clap at the Front of my next Edition of Shandy." After Hogarth had obliged with a frontispiece for Volumes III and IV as well as one for a new edition of Volumes I and II, Sterne noted with satisfaction that although *Tristram* had as many detractors as admirers, everyone was buying it. He was very conscientious in building up the sales of his books, and would press into service anyone from a lord to an ex-slave to solicit names for subscription lists.

Diderot did not manage his affairs in this fashion. He was prodigal of his time and his talents, always giving freely of himself to others. It is quite probable that had not his more practical-minded friends negotiated the sale of his library to Catherine II, the *philosophe* would have been hard put to raise sufficient funds for his own daughter's dowry. While it is true that his early incursions into fiction were prompted by the demands of Mme Puisieux on his pocketbook, he shortly abandoned the intellectualized licentious tales which he had imitated, and by 1761 in the *Neveu de Rameau* he suggested that Crébillon *fils* was passé. He never confessed to the authorship of *L'Oiseau blanc,* and Naigeon reported that Diderot later deeply regretted having written the *Bijoux indiscrets.*

Actually, he had a low opinion of most contemporary fiction. Although the works of Crébillon *fils* constituted one of the models for the *Bijoux indiscrets,* Diderot made sure to parody him in the thirty-ninth chapter. He even anticipated a distinction he was to make emphatically in his last novel by having one of his characters announce that he would not fail to describe the most frightening tempest to be found in any novel were he not telling a "history." Perhaps the very facility with which one could compose "any novel"—that is, the popular, conventional novel—increased Diderot's disdain for a genre that brazenly flouted the question of virtue and other fitting preoccupations. He constantly and derisively repeats in *Jacques* that nothing is easier than writing ordinary novels.

Nevertheless, Diderot was to alter his judgment of fiction and was to add to the field a number of innovations of his own in little more than a decade after his earliest productions. With his usual skepticism, he first had to be convinced that there was something worth-while in a mode he was prepared to reject completely.

Sterne, to the contrary, needed no urging. Hardly had the smoke cleared from the débris of his suppressed *Political Romance* when he began writing *Tristram* in January, 1759. His motives were obvious and uncomplicated. He was forty-six years old and had been singularly unsuccessful—in proportion to his efforts—in improving his position. The facts that he had some local notoriety as a wit and eccentric, that he was often called on to preach at the York Minster, that he had a yearly income of about £200 which was considered, according to his neighbor, John Croft, "a very decent one," and which had recently been implemented by the commissaryship of Pickering and Pocklington, made little difference to Sterne. He had spent twenty years in futile quest of advancement and was not inclined to follow a friend's suggestion to get his preferment first and then write: ". . . suppose preferment is long acoming (& for aught I know I may not be preferr'd till the Resurrection of the Just) and am all that time in labour—how must I bear my pains?" [7] With the appearance of the London edition of Volumes I and II of *Tristram,* Sterne had "arrived," and for the rest of his life he reveled in it. His letters abound with gleeful references to lionizing and descriptions of social triumphs.

While the Yorkshire parson was savoring the first results of his bid for fame and fortune, the Parisian *philosophe* was continuing to reject current literary vogues and was deep in a plot that would conclude in a very different kind of fiction. The most determining factor in Diderot's altered attitude toward fiction occurred in the fifties, when he enthusiastically discovered the English school.[8] Here was proof that fiction could serve a significant purpose that was worthy even of a *philosophe*. It could display and analyze the fight against social and moral corruption. In 1758, he wrote in *De la poésie dramatique* that the novels of Prévost moved him to tears over the trials of virtue. His *Analyse d'un petit roman* (1760) included the statement that literature should serve a useful end, that he admired *Le Paysan parvenu* and *Joseph Andrews* for this reason.

But he also admired them for another element which he found to be generally lacking in contemporary writers. It was not only immorality in literature which he condemned but also artificiality. "All literary work should have a model existing in nature. It is the imitation of nature. *Le Paysan parvenu* is a picture of our customs; *Joseph Andrews,* a picture of English customs." [9] A summary of his initial response to the new possibilities afforded by fiction appeared in the *Eloge de Richardson* of 1761. Richardson had strikingly proven that novels need be neither trifling fancies nor morally corrupting, and Diderot lavishly praised him for so realistically portraying the temptations and triumphs of virtue. Indeed, it was largely through Richardson that Diderot discovered that the very realism of fiction could make one arrive at a more forceful illusion of the truth. Instead of "novels," he preferred to call Richardson's works "moral dramas."

His belief that fiction could be useful doubtless is largely responsible for *La Religieuse,* the first novel he wrote after he had read Richardson, and for much of the rest of his fiction. In 1758, he had said that he preferred plays to novels because the dramatic form was more challenging. He had aspirations to be a dramatist, yet his plays, which seek to reproduce moral and social conditions, are weak testimonials to his dramatic theory. Diderot could hardly have been unaware of this with the disappointing reception of his *Père de famille.* On the other hand, he had become increasingly aware of the opportunities the novel offered to the perceptive analyst of human nature. It therefore seems quite logical that when confronted by material teeming with sociological and moral implications he would attempt a moral drama of his own, utilizing both the realistic and utilitarian elements he admired in the "new fiction."

Simply because Diderot revised his opinions and took a more positive attitude toward fiction in no way lessened his scorn for offenders. His aversion probably was intensified once he had found contrasting models. In 1762, he advised Sophie Volland, who apparently had had some reservations about Richardson, that above all, she should forget the ridiculous formula of contemporary novels. As he continued to investigate new possibilities, he found more facets to be exploited not only by the *philosophe,* but also by the experimenter and aesthetic theorist. Combining both roles in the early seventies, he wrote a novel in which both form and content flagrantly mock those ridiculous formulae he so detested. And in doing so, he produced a work that bears striking parallels to Sterne's first novel.

For despite the fact that Diderot and Sterne were attracted to fiction for different reasons—the one for philosophic and aesthetic purposes, the other for more worldly considerations—they both were to admire, introduce, and utilize a number of remarkably similar techniques. And even though Sterne admittedly turned to fiction as his last hope for social prestige and material security, perhaps it cannot be said that Diderot's motives were altogether selfless. It is true that he claimed he was indifferent to contemporary literary fame, and certainly after 1760 he restricted his efforts—with the exception of two stories of the seventies—to a very limited audience or none at all. Yet, in a more patient temper than Sterne, he, too, may have been equally concerned with the relationship between literary merit and his reputation. In 1766, with the manuscript of the *Neveu de Rameau* safely hidden in his study, the manuscript of *Jacques* yet to be produced, and the manuscript of

La Religieuse awaiting considerable revision, he wrote to Falconet:

There was a time when an author, anxious for the perfection of his work, preserved it in his portfolio twenty or thirty years. Meanwhile, an ideal joy replaced the real joy which he had deprived himself of. He lived in the hope of leaving after him an immortal work, an immortal name. If this man is mad, all my ideas of wisdom are overturned.[10]

Though throughout his life Diderot would express doubts as to his own ability to achieve immortality, there were moments when he felt confident that his emphasis of values would be recognized by posterity. In the field of creative writing, it would seem that he brought into particular relief certain aspects which may be profitably compared to Sterne's fictional approaches. In their respective treatment of the illusion of reality, characterization, new fictional directions, and form and structure, one again sees the meeting and parting of parson and *philosophe*.

THE ILLUSION OF REALITY

When Diderot and Sterne began writing their first important works of fiction, they were both concerned with the same problem: they wanted to produce the illusion of reality. The achievement of this goal did not depend on a photographic reproduction of life; they sought to go beyond this and to create a three-dimensional effect. As their writings increased, it became evident that the quality of depth was, perhaps, the most significant. Sterne stated unequivocally, by using a quotation from Epictetus to preface his book, that he was interested not so much in deeds or actions but in what men think of them. Diderot eventually produced in *Jacques* a tour de force by demonstrating that conventional physical description was not necessary for the creation of credible characters.

What was necessary for the successful illusion was possibly not merely Diderot's and Sterne's natural endowments of observation and perception but also some further stimulus from their readings. Sterne's "sagacious Locke" had pointed out that a dual action occurred in the process of man's acquiring knowledge: that each object perceived had in itself the ability to evoke certain characteristics to be discovered by each perceiver, and that the individual perceiver's reflections on his own sensations were at least as important as the sensations themselves. This certainly would appeal to Sterne, "the most industrious of all Locke's literary disciples" in the eighteenth century,[11] and to Diderot. Why limit oneself to repeating neoclassic generalities and reproducing the same "norm"? If Diderot was not inclined to follow ridiculous formulae, Sterne had no intention, he said, of twisting and untwisting the same rope. The tantalizing aspect of reality was that everyone really saw it and reacted to it differently, and *that,* Diderot, and Sterne were agreed, was the point to stress in building their illusion.

In addition, Diderot thought he had already found a literary model in Richardson. The *Eloge* praises, among other accomplishments, Richardson's success in achieving the illusion of reality. He convinces the reader, Diderot says, by involving him in the story, and through the authenticity of quotidian detail,[12] he makes the audience hear the voice of passion and witness the action. Instead of exploiting the taste for the spectacular and fantastic, Richardson—like Fielding, Diderot could have added—applies his novel to the current scene. Moreover, he directly corroborated Diderot's perceptions about his realism. Aware that he should be convincing, he wrote in the preface to *Clarissa* that it was both natural and necessary for Clarissa to have some faults; and that he wanted the letters to have the quality of "instantaneous descriptions and reflections" to maintain the illusion of spontaneous reactions to real experience.[13]

This accomplishment was to have important significance for Diderot and Sterne. Admonishing the skeptical reader, Sterne found authority in one of the precursors of the Enlightenment: ". . . but remember, 'La Vraisemblance (as Bayle says in the affair of Liceti) n'est pas toujours du Cote [sic] de la Verite [sic]'." [14] Diderot went even further and provided some helpful directions. In his notes to the *Deux amis de Bourbonne,* he referred to the *conte historique,* which has complete truth as its object. Its author wants to fool the reader into believing him and requires eloquence and poetry for his necessary appeal to the audience's emotions. But eloquence, Diderot was quick to admit, is a kind of falsehood, and poetry, as Diderot interpreted it, distorts factual truth. They both exaggerate and amplify to the point of inspiring distrust. The problem, then, is to reconcile and fuse two inimical extremes. This can be done if the author scatters throughout his account little circumstances closely integrated with the main idea and introduces touches that are so simple, natural, and hard to imagine that the audience says to itself: it must be true; people do not make up things like that. In this way, the author escapes the dangers of eloquence and poetry, for the truth of nature hides the dissembling of art. The ideal model has its place, but not in the *conte historique.* One should deliberately add some representative blemish to construct the portrait of a specific, recognizable individual.[15]

Clearly, neither Diderot nor Sterne sought slavish and, Diderot would say, dull copies of reality. Truth and verisimilitude were not synonymous, and quite obviously both men favored verisimilitude. Their aim was a convincing approximation, and while they both have been acclaimed as forerunners of nineteenth- and twentieth-century realism, they would not deny that some artifice was involved. The great man, Diderot had said in the *Salon* in 1767, is not the one who tells the truth; he is the one·who can best reconcile truth with falsehood.[16] The *peu de mensonge* and any other appropriate touches for deceiving the reader were thoroughly acceptable to the two empiricists, provided that these measures served to heighten, not to destroy, the illusion of truth and authentic experience.

Diderot lost little time in putting into practice the lesson he claimed to have learned from Richardson. Some years later, he told Catherine II that if he found anything which suited his purpose in the writings of other authors, he used it.[17] In utilizing it, however, he generally transformed it. He vastly admired the "moral dramas" of Richardson, which he believed to be the drama of humanity, but when he wrote his own moral drama he was really producing a contemporary social polemic, and he took care to be specific. *La Religieuse* contains a vast amount of individualizing detail and is based on an actual case which received considerable publicity.[18]

In Diderot's description of Suzanne's experiences, he is careful to provide some initial details which he afterwards develops more fully. A brief but frightening glimpse of a deranged nun gives way to the fully documented portrayal of the Lesbian Superior's violent and accelerating insanity. The implication of cruelty suggested by the mad nun's appearance in chains is amplified and dramatized by minute accounts of the intense persecutions the heroine suffers. Avoiding the danger of isolated lists, Diderot anticipates his advice in the *Deux amis* that each circumstance be closely connected with the main threads of the story. He therefore makes the narration more graphic by describing Suzanne's tortures within the context of convent practices. The physical description of Suzanne herself heightens the tension between innocence and corruption, because the most extended portrait of the heroine is given by the Lesbian Superior.

Pursuing his search for relevant details, Diderot drew more directly from personal experience in the *Neveu de Rameau.* In one way, his problem was easier; presumably, people are more familiar with eccentrics than with convents and therefore do not require so many convincing little touches. Furthermore, instead of trying to dramatize virtue, Diderot was creating a specific character whom he knew. But the very fact that Diderot and others were acquainted with Jean-François Rameau and that Diderot was not limiting himself to a vignette made for complications. The Nephew could easily have been exaggerated out of credibility, or he could have degenerated into a mouthpiece for Diderot's aesthetic theories. By admitting from the start, however, that he is fantastic, by giving penetrating descriptions of his bizarre acts, by commenting from time to time on how odd and unbelievable he is, Diderot makes him genuine. Like the audience of the *conte historique,* the reader says he is incredible, but accepts his reality.

In the fiction of the seventies, sometimes using those piquant aspects of truth which, he said in *Jacques,* should be reserved for the genius, sometimes adding those touches from daily life which he approved in Richardson, Diderot continued to work for validity of experience. In the *Entretien d'un père avec ses enfants,* it lies in the realistic, homely detail of an informal, domestic scene. *Ceci n'est pas un conte* and

Sur l'inconséquence du jugement public include more dramatic situations: Mlle de La Chaux in a frightening seizure of hysterics, Mme de La Carlière melodramatically renouncing the speechless Desroches.

Jacques le fataliste is particularly dependent on convincing strokes to substantiate Diderot's contention that he is not writing a "novel" but is telling the truth. And these details require all the more accuracy not only because the picaresque nature of the book encompasses a variety of social strata and characters, but also because the two protagonists are rarely described. Nevertheless, one does not question the existence of Jacques and his Master, although Diderot deliberately withholds extended physical description and does not provide any motivation for their mysterious journey or even a specific geographical background.

What he has done here is to carry to a climax a tendency which was apparent in his previous fiction. "Tell me the events, convey the idle remarks, and I'll know whom I'm dealing with," says the hero of *Jacques,* and it was always an integral part of Diderot's concern for realism that the conversations ring true. According to Naigeon,[19] Diderot had spent an entire month on just one small detail for *La Religieuse.*[20] He was seeking an appropriate opening phrase for the Lesbian Superior's confession, and finally Mme d'Holbach gave him—through feminine intuition, Diderot always claimed—the perfect combination of words and accent: "Mon père, je suis damnée. . . ." Because the Nephew is a bombastic self-dramatizer, Diderot makes him burst out with: "I, Rameau! son of M. Rameau, apothecary, of Dijon, a worthy man who has never bent the knee before anyone! I, Rameau, nephew of him whom they call the great Rameau. . . . I who have composed pieces for the harpsichord. . . ."[21]

Didier Diderot, the cutler, genially tells his favorite, "My son, we've both made a noise in the world, but with this difference: the noise you've made with your tool deprived you of peace, while the noise I made with mine deprived others of peace." [22]

Diderot had noted in the *Eloge* that Richardson distinguished people by their ideas and expressions and tones, but this was hardly a new discovery. Talk had always fascinated him and he was a perceptive listener. The accents and shades of emotions that he sought but was not able to convey in his plays are recorded with accuracy in his fiction, just as he recreated for Sophie Volland the different whims and personalities that emerged from the conversations in the D'Holbach circle. Following Jacques's advice, in his last novel he manages to minimize direct physical description. Speech is the basic medium for portraying the personality of his hero, and it is invaluable for representing the varied attitudes and social levels of the other characters. Diderot could render with authenticity the furious stuttering of an enraged vicar, the smooth "line" of a scheming nobleman, the eager attentions of a peddler—indeed, the very intimacies and nuances of a bedroom scene.

And if speech was essential for the illusion of reality, certainly gesture was no less significant. As early as the *Lettre sur les sourds et muets* of 1751, Diderot had announced his interest in gesture as communication. He used to go to the theatre, he said, and cover his ears so that he could concentrate on the action. Carrying over into his fiction this preoccupation, he succeeded in expressing the moods and personalities of different nuns by their individual actions, just as he particularized the characters in *Jacques* by their "tics": the Master's constant applications to his snuffbox, watch, and handkerchief, Père Hudson's deceivingly grand manner, Richard's monkish deportment. The most brilliant example of Diderot's mastery of gesture is, of course, the *Neveu de Rameau.* If the Nephew acts out the satisfied slumbers of the great man or the scrapings of the hanger-on, Diderot describes his motions. Rameau, vindictive, shakes his head and points to the sky; Rameau, distraught, forgets his audience, sobs, and fiercely pummels his brow. Nowhere, apart from the *Salons,* is Diderot's demonstration of the importance of description so forcefully emphasized; and nowhere is Diderot's faith in pantomime so convincingly illustrated as in the Nephew's miming. And it is justified because of the concentrated, remarkably appropriate detail which seduces the reader into believing that the Nephew can really imitate a violinist, a harpsichordist, even a whole operatic performance. One is amazed not that he can do such incredible feats at all, but that he can perform them so well.

Such dependence on gesture points up the "local color" of specific individuals, but Diderot was also careful to emphasize the local color of environments. Each convent Suzanne enters has its own special setting and atmosphere. The upper-class milieux of the Master's grievous affair are sharply differentiated from the peasant scenes of Jacques's lusty triumphs. Contrasts in Parisian locales—the Café de la Régence, the dinners with the sycophants, the Palais Royal—are neatly delineated in the *Neveu de Rameau.* Diderot took care to avoid the charge of tedious details, which had been leveled at Richardson. In the *Premier Entretien sur le Fils naturel* (1757), he discussed the distinction between fictional and dramatic techniques. The verisimilitude of a novel, he wrote, rests on many small incidents, whereas the theatre demands selected detail which must contribute directly to specific ends.

When he came to write fiction, however, he utilized the selectivity of dramatic practices, marshaling his incidents and details to emphasize definite effects.

But Diderot was too good a psychologist and realist to limit these effects to a superficial illusion. Physical description, gesture, speech, local color—all extend beyond the primary level of experience to indicate something very personal and significant about the characters. They are indispensable for displaying the inner life of man and his personal and professional *idiotismes,* as Diderot was to point out in his *Satire I, Sur les caractères et les mots de caractère.* Diderot was just as interested in showing *why* people act as *how* they act. Of the two, he was perhaps more deeply concerned with the "why," for that truly reveals the individual nature of each man. Incidents of external life often seem less important in themselves than in providing stimuli to which the characters react. For this reason, in his attempt to present the whole personality in its total existence, Diderot is inclined to emphasize the equivalent of Locke's secondary characteristics and reflections.

The Nephew, for instance, is a supreme mime as well as a musician and often combines the two. Over a period of time, he has mercilessly disciplined himself to imitate anything, and Diderot shows this by increasingly effective illustrations. Yet the Nephew derives scant satisfaction from his accomplishment. As his gestures, tone of voice, expression indicate, he is consumed with frustration. He enters into his pantomime almost with fury; he emerges in a state of near-trance. His momentary act of creation has resulted in another step in his destruction, for he is so enraged by his failure to attain genius that he squanders his talent. Starting from a description of the actions of a man, Diderot has advanced to the psychological level of creating a character in the process of destroying himself. In the same way that the gestures and demeanor of different Mothers Superior become evidence of their respective mental states, each act of the Nephew is a symptom of his complex emotional turmoil.

The freak interruption of a chance occurrence in *Jacques* also reveals layers beneath the incident itself, and ultimately those layers become more essential than the initial happening. For Jacques, it has one meaning, peculiar to the character of the hero: it is proof of *le destin*. For the conventional Reader, it means something else: here is another contradiction of his conditioning, another affront to his set notions of how a novel should be written. And to Diderot, it illustrates still a third point: it is a further example to refute predestination as a mode of determining the future. Yet each interpretation, subjective though it may be, is equally meaningful and corroborates Diderot's contention that it is not so much things in themselves but what we think of them that makes them what they are.

Once the circle of reflection begins to widen, additional results occur. If a "tic," a gesture, becomes symptomatic of an individual's inner life, his entire account of a situation or milieu also takes on new levels of meaning. Just as the Nephew's recital of Bouret's rise to power indicates both the Nephew's intense admiration of Bouret and his anger at himself for not having conceived of such a trick, so his description of Bertin's gatherings carries a dual significance. For Diderot, there is only one interpretation: the farmer general's circle is an example of corrupt society. The Nephew's reactions, however, are more complex, for his attitude is far more ambiguous than the *philosophe's*. Even as he describes the setting and actions of the patron and his hangers-on, the tension within himself increases; he is reliving the scenes of both his triumph and defeat, and his reactions mingle envy and regret, scorn and hatred.

There is likewise a suggestion that the Master's account of his dealings with the usurer is heightened by reflection. He tells Jacques that when the dapper chevalier first took him to negotiate a loan, he was impressed by the unctuous, evil, foreboding atmosphere of the loan broker's dwelling. Yet his entire narration of his misfortune indicates that he was a most ingenuous, unobservant victim; Jacques guesses the outcome considerably before the tale is concluded. It is more likely that the Master appreciates the grim signs of warning simply because *now,* as he is telling it to Jacques, he is reflecting on this incident in the context of the complete experience and only in retrospect really recognizes it as being a significant part of the whole unsuccessful pattern.

This deeply personal relationship between a character and his environment naturally results in the intensification of the local color of both persons and places. As Professor Georges May, among others, has suggested, Diderot's décor becomes impressionistic because it owes so much of its existence to the reactions it inspires in the characters.[23] Yet, whether Diderot would agree that the realism is thereby modified,[24] is highly dubious. The fact that Suzanne, for example, describes a convent through her personal reactions to it makes both story and setting that much more convincing. If Diderot is concerned with presenting an account of a young girl, what could better convey its actuality than a method which presents the necessary evidence filtered through her own experience of it?

And as the locales in his fiction take on special significance because of the meaning they hold for the characters, the action also shifts its grounds to one of interior realism. Any external event—for Diderot never denies existence on the primary level—may provide a point of departure for Jacques's struggle with *le destin*. Yet the struggle itself takes place within Jacques; it is one of Jacques's own making, and whatever validity it has depends on this fact. The Nephew is eating himself up with a contorted picture of his uncle and of society and life. One sees him as the result of the destructive process, but the true drama, the basic conflict, goes on inside the Nephew himself. Not the least of the tension in Suzanne's recital derives from the antagonism within her as she reflects on her desperate situation and strives to maintain her courage. As she tells her story, she is not only reliving the conflict, but she is also caught up in its aftermath. At the end of her account, she admits that her experiences have changed her. She is subject to fits of trembling; when a church bell rings, she automatically falls to her knees. She realizes that these reflexes may give her away, she knows that she cannot restrain her unconscious actions, and this sets up a new pattern of inner conflict.

In each of these instances, Diderot has concentrated on specific reactions to realities that are reflected upon by a particular individual. His interests lie in making people and experiences he has known live again in an art form, in preference to creating imaginary inventions. In his search to produce a genuine illusion of man in relation to reality, he emphasizes the mysteriously personal nature of the relationship, for in this way both man and reality can become more meaningful and dynamic.

Even more than Diderot, Sterne was preoccupied with the question of how the interior life works and how it affects and is displayed by the conduct of exterior life. And precisely because of this concern, he could not afford to ignore things in themselves. If verisimilitude was a common aim of both writers, surely Sterne needed to pay special attention to it because the kind of men whose opinions he chose to delineate were very strange. As the word "Shandy" suggests, they are crackbrains. Unlike Diderot, who recreates experiences familiar to him, Sterne draws more heavily on his imagination and commences with a collection of zanies in a topsy-turvy world. What he must do is to lure his public into accepting this world on its own terms, even though the readers know it is fantastic. He must hold their interest and persuade them of the reality of something which appears to be vastly exaggerated and out of proportion.

It is not surprising, therefore, to find Sterne echoing Diderot's notes on the *conte historique* in an appropriately Shandean apostrophe:

How do the slight touches of the chisel, the pencil, the pen, the fiddle-stick, et caetera,—give the true swell, which gives the true pleasure!—O my countrymen;—be nice;—be cautious of your language;—and never, O! never let it be forgotten upon what small particles your eloquence and your fame depend.[25]

These small particles are carefully selected, despite Sterne's pretense of handling them in a casual fashion. Taken as themselves, the opinions and preoccupations of the characters are quite incredible. Indeed, nothing could be farther from the truth than the narrator's on-the-spot observations of incidents and conversations that take place in his early childhood or on or before the day of his birth. Yet his very air of the authoritative eyewitness supporting his statements with corroborative detail makes for verisimilitude, despite the fact, as Sterne hinted, that this is not aligned with the stark truth.

In September of 1717, for example, thirteen months before

his birth, Tristram's mother erroneously believed she was with child and posted to London for the lying-in. Tristram reconstructs, with an eye for minute facts, the stages of his father's exasperation on the return trip. Tristram was five years old when his unfortunate accident with the window sash occurred. Writing of the event thirty-eight years later—he says that it is August 10, 1761—he displays an uncommon memory. Although he was upstairs, howling vigorously, he also managed to witness a multitude of consequences including Susannah's flight, Dr. Slop's mismanagement and lack of professional ethics, Walter Shandy's researches downstairs on ancient circumcision rites, and Captain Shandy's practical suggestion that his nephew be exposed publicly to lay the rumors circulated by Dr. Slop.

Furthermore, the attitude of each person toward this occurrence is fittingly specific. As a man of learning, Walter Shandy should naturally turn to his books for solace, just as Toby, in keeping with his role of a simple-minded man of action, should offer a pragmatic solution. Sterne, like Diderot, was sensitive to those small details of speech and gesture which set apart one individual from another. If Toby, an unaffected, quiet man of kindness and humility, sees fit to break into his brother's discourse, he lays the end of his pipe on his brother's hand "in a kindly way of interruption," or he poses a question "laying his hand upon my father's knee, and looking up seriously into his face for an answer." Trim, a model of deference and respect, always touches his hat, bows, or intersperses his speech with "an' please your honour." A slave to intricate hypotheses and sonorous phrases, Walter believes that he imitates Socrates by commencing a philosophical harangue "holding fast his fore-finger between his finger and thumb." Even Walter's shadowy mate is observed "going very gingerly in the dark along the passage which led to the parlour" and pausing to eavesdrop when she hears the word "wife":

> . . . so laying the edge of her finger across her two lips—holding in her breath, and bending her head a little downwards, with a twist of her neck—(not towards the door, but away from it, by which means her ear was brought to the chink)—she listened with all her powers:—[26]

Eccentric as Sterne's accounts are, in all details relating to his characters he maintains a basic element of consistency. In his opinion, he tells the reader, "to write a book is for all the world like humming a song—be but in tune with yourself, madam, 'tis no matter how high or how low you take it." His characters always talk and act like themselves, reacting so appropriately to situations that the reader can anticipate fairly accurately what follows. Walter Shandy always carries off everything in the grand manner. His speech, though often hard to follow, is dignified and lofty. His theories and projects may be endlessly confused and impractical, but they are grandiose in scope. His actions, frequently ludicrous, are never inappropriate for the man. Toby remains simple, literal, and innocent. While Walter engages in a melodramatic demonstration of grief, Toby sits by his afflicted brother in compassionate silence, his handkerchief ready and his face resting on his crutch. When he unwittingly angers Walter by interrupting a discourse, he cannot fathom the reasons for his brother's fuming so continues to smoke "with unvaried composure."

In a book which is deliberately original and perplexing, it is very necessary to have certain aspects which remain the same. The activities of the characters may put a strain on one's credulity, but at least they can be counted on to follow the quirks initially established for them. If the Shandy world heaps confusion on confusion, its figures are constant, and because of this, one gradually begins to rely on them for some degree of stability and they become acceptable.

Sterne fortifies this advance in the direction of verisimilitude by introducing other seemingly trivial elements. The Shandy universe is all awry and so, for that matter, is the Shandy dwelling place. However, Shandy Hall still has the vestiges of any country house, although its inhabitants are not to be thanked for that. It has a small back parlor where the Shandy brothers like to sit by the fire, despite Walter's distress at the squeaking hinge on the door. There is a dark passage leading to the parlor, a front stairway with landings, a backstairs near the nursery, a kitchen where a scullion scours fish kettles. There even are windows, albeit they are not very dependable because Trim has removed weights and pulleys for the model siege. Outside there are walks, a large uncultivated commons near the river, a fish pond, a stable yard which leads into a narrow and sometimes muddy lane running along the garden wall. Toby's cottage is very near by, its windows also in need of repair, and its kitchen garden and bowling green, protected by a hedge, are dug up and cluttered by an intricate arrangement of small fortifications and besieged towns. Through the hedge and an adjoining arbor is the widow Wadman's house.

These details of local color act as welcome, familiar bits of reality. Were it not for the ravages the Shandys have made on their property, the scenes could belong to a normal world. A thread paper, a satin pin cushion are common objects, even though Walter Shandy uses the former for a bookmark in a mad treatise and bites the latter in two in a fit of impatience. There may be something of the affected poser in Walter's attitude of sorrow, but "an old set-stitched chair, valanced and fringed around the party-coloured worsted bobs," where Toby patiently sits by him is a very natural touch. Moreover, Sterne does not insist upon these strokes; one learns about them indirectly as they become related to the course of the action. Just as one has to *see* Rameau's nephew perform to believe that he is a remarkable mime, so one needs to visualize the acts of the Shandys against the background of their environment in order to accept them.

And the fact that the milieu and activities of the Shandys are characterized nonchalantly by presumably inconsequential details does not mean that Sterne was ignorant of the importance of his "small particles" and "slight touches." He, too, saw in them the possibilities for further exploitation which so fascinated Diderot. Fully aware of the mental equalitarianism implicit in Locke's theories, Sterne realized that it was very likely that trivia should loom as large in an individual consciousness as great events. It is all a matter of relativity. Taking his cue from Locke and Fontenelle, Sterne even wrote a series of fragments on this subject and successfully dramatized it by presenting the Shandys' singular reactions to sensible reality. A window suggests reflections of narrowly averted disaster to Tristram but conveys visions of catapults and drawbridges to Trim. A squeaking door hinge assumes gigantic proportions in the mental life of Walter Shandy, and when, in the course of an extended series of actions, he ignores this source of annoyance: "—My father thrust back his chair—rose up—put on his hat—took four long strides to the door—jerked it open—thrust his head half way out—shut the door again—took no notice of the bad hinge—" the reader realizes that something is seriously amiss in Walter's private world. Indeed, by systematically screening life through the hobby peculiar to each character, Sterne proves the wisdom of a later satirical humorist's warning that things are seldom what they seem. Consequently, Sterne makes seemingly unimportant things significant both for the character and the reader. As Professor James Foster has said, "It was his triumph to be able to interest readers in his demonstration of the importance of the little things in life." [27]

This impressionism is developed with particular effectiveness in the *Sentimental Journey*, where Sterne is careful to pinpoint individuals, localities, and incidents not so much for their own sake as for the way they appear to a sentimental traveler. Yorick, of *The Sermons of Mr. Yorick* fame, is the observer, and although he may still love a jest in his heart, he is perceptibly toned down. Sterne concentrated on selecting the details which impressed him the most, endeavoring to present them in such a light as to show a reformed Yorick —compassionate, kindly, delicate—who is not to be mistaken for one of the ribald associates of the Shandys. Everyone and everything, from a count or chambermaid to a green satin purse or a pair of gloves, owe their existence to Sterne's impressions of them. Although his reactions may be colored too frequently by the man of sensibility's protestations of good will, they do suggest that a subjective report of one's travels can be considerably more lively and arresting than the conventional accounts to be found in more formal guidebooks. Sterne had already indicated this with Book VII of *Tristram*.

Yet for all their impressionistic detail, neither Book VII nor the *Sentimental Journey* has the vitality of the other eight books of *Tristram*. Diderot's impressionism remains dynamic because when he deals with secondary levels of experience he takes care to move the conflict inside, too. Sterne, however, presents no inner conflict; he is perhaps too much in harmony with himself, and when he confronts the reader with the emotional states of a single character, he tends to be rather monotonous. It is only when an individual appears in conjunction with other equally important individuals that the experience becomes truly activated. For instead of locating the drama inside each character, Sterne turns it inside out, and the reflected reality appears to be extraverted. The fascination and dynamism of, say, Toby's world and Walter's world seem to lie in the fact that one can *see* the worlds of the two men not only projected into physical realities but also struggling and conflicting, resulting in impasses as well as temporary satisfactions.

And while Diderot and Sterne were both fascinated by creating the illusion of reality, realism in fiction did not mean precisely the same thing to each of them. For Diderot, it was both a moral and an aesthetic problem. His constant passion for virtue stimulated his appreciation of Richardson. As a matter of fact, his enthusiasm occasionally provides an excellent example of Locke's theory of reflection. Diderot tended to read into *Pamela* a good deal more social and moral significance than possibly even Richardson meant to include. "How meanly you regard the subject of *Pamela*," he told Sophie Volland, whose judgment seems quite acute to the twentieth-century reader,

It is a shame! No, mademoiselle, no; it's not the story of a chambermaid pestered by a young libertine. It's virtue, religion, chastity, truth, goodness, without power or force, debased, if it be possible, in all the circumstances imaginable, by dependence, abjection, poverty, in conflict with grandeur, opulence, vice, and all its infernal dominions.[28]

This might very likely be the kind of *Pamela* that the socially conscious *philosophe* would have written, but Richardson, whose social awareness was limited and who had no desire to alter the *status quo,* did not write it.

Had Sophie Volland pointed this out to Diderot, he probably would not have altered his opinion. The important discovery, for the *philosophe,* was that fiction need not be frivolous, that it could be an effective medium for putting morality into action. He had tried to do this with his plays, but unfortunately his concentration on conditions, instead of the psychological reality of his characters, resulted in abstractions. Diderot was not averse to trying another approach, however. In the *Eloge,* he writes: "A maxim is an abstract, general rule of conduct, the application of which is left to us. By itself, it does not impress any sensible image on our minds: but he who acts is seen, we put ourselves in his place or by his side, we grow excited for or against him." [29] His implication, of course, is that fiction can realistically apply a maxim, and that the justification of fiction, for a *philosophe,* lies in its achieving a convincing approximation of reality.

Consequently, the aesthetic element is of fundamental importance, because only by making the reader believe in the truth of what he reads can Diderot bring to bear the sociomoral slant which appears in all his works of fiction. For both experimental and utilitarian purposes, fiction must be accepted as real. Diderot deliberately chose to reproduce experience, and he constantly insists that it is valid. His assumption is that all this is true, and whatever tricks he employs are directed toward making the reader share this assumption.[30]

With this in mind, he differentiates between modes of fiction. Excepting Richardson's universal moral dramas, he says in *Jacques* that he does not care for "novels" and that he favors "history." Indeed, he frequently asserts that he is not writing a "novel," but that he is writing a "history," and that the "history" is true. Warning the Reader of the novelist's license for introducing wildly exaggerated incidents, he admonishes him, "Demeurons dans le vrai." This prejudice, so repeatedly enunciated in *Jacques,* was not a recent development. Diderot had initially marked the differences in 1748, and in *Pensées détachées sur la peinture,* he said, in passing, "All things being otherwise equal, I prefer history to fictions." What he does in *Jacques* is emphasize and clarify by example the tendency he displays in all his fiction to create stories based on contemporary people, incidents, and scenes. In separating the "history" from the "novel," he is, perhaps, anticipating the later distinctions between "novel" and "romance," to be made by Hawthorne in his prefaces to *The House of the Seven Gables* and *The Marble Faun,* and by Clara Reeve in the year following Diderot's death: "The Novel is a picture of real life and manners, and of the time in which it is written. The Romance, in lofty and elevated language, describes what never happened nor is likely to happen." [31]

Sterne made no such distinction and no such claims to truth, for he had no axe to grind. He did say, a year after the first appearance of *Tristram,* "But I beg I may add, that whatever views I had of that kind, I had other views—the first of which was, the hope of doing the world good, by ridiculing what I thought deserving of it—or of disservice to sound learning, &c." [32] But this letter was projected as an apologia, suitable for publication if the response to *Tristram* demanded it, and Sterne had previously qualified his statement by agreeing with a fellow clergyman and critic who "Made Answer Upon My saying I Would consider the colour of My Coat, as I corrected it—That that very Idea in My Head would render My Book not worth a groat—" [33] If Diderot's admitted penchant for introducing *un peu de philosophie* did not interfere with his creation of genuine people and experiences, certainly the versatile clergyman was equally adept at shifting around the ideas in his head.

Moreover, Sterne's premises were not the same as Diderot's. The Shandys and the Shandaic universe were largely products of Sterne's imagination, and his business was to make them acceptable. For this reason, his problem is predominantly an aesthetic one. People do not have to be convinced of the utter reality of something in order to laugh; the prerequisite is that they recognize there is a relationship to fact, and it is frequently the exaggeration of this factual basis which provides amusement—or any other emotion Sterne wishes to evoke. He is doubtless aware of his audience's suspicion that he is presenting human nature and human interests in one-sided extremes. Instead of insisting that this is a strictly true picture, Sterne contrives to make the audience recognize the common reality from which Shandean activities branch out so that he can achieve, where he needs it, what a later writer was to call "the willing suspension of disbelief."

Consequently, while the object they seek and the techniques they use are very similar, Sterne's and Diderot's interests in realism do not lead to the same conclusion. In adding to fiction a third dimension which was to bear fruitful results in succeeding centuries, both writers imply that obvious physical reality is of a secondary nature to the reality of mental existence—a reality which is brought to life by what physical details connote. But by an inverted reflection on reality, Diderot makes a sober, intellectual point: that the thing we see objectively has a strangely individual and subjective meaning to each of us. Sterne, on the other hand, by turning personal reflection inside out, seems to burlesque the entire notion

Diderot has raised and to emphasize the idea that this apparently frenetic level of existence is the truly valid one. He may start out by suspending his audience's disbelief, but he ends by suggesting that for him there is no real experience beyond the subjective.

Diderot could invest with vitality people of his acquaintance without confusing *his* experience of them with their own experience of reality. He could distinguish between the world of sense phenomena and his own reflections of it. Some of Diderot's most fascinating characters could not make this distinction, and, one suspects, Sterne went to no great trouble about it either. The eccentric Yorkshireman began by encouraging people to associate him with the narrator of *Tristram*. He lived to regret his impulsiveness: "The world has imagined, because I wrote Tristram Shandy, that I was myself more Shandean than I really ever was—," [34] although he was forced to make an admission which was significantly applicable to his own procedures, ". . . we are often painted in divers colours according to the ideas each one frames in his head." [35] Nevertheless, even as Sterne was voicing his complaint he was bringing to a close the first two volumes of a second novel which pointedly identified the author with the narrator. He could be remarkably perceptive about himself, but it seems dubious that in his fiction he could totally divorce the creator from the created. Shandean or sentimental, Sterne could not be an impersonal writer—and in his most honest moments, he knew that his success did not lie in that direction. It was *his* peculiar way of regarding reality which infused his books with life, and as he drew on himself for inspiration, so he reflected himself on his privately created universe. Diderot had said, "Every artist should draw his inspiration from both within and outside of himself; he should be sufficiently endowed to reflect both himself and the universe." [36] That the result, as demonstrated by Diderot's realism, is a more balanced reflection, there is no doubt; yet the fact that Sterne, while operating on only half of Diderot's advice, achieved an illusion that was highly successful within its more limited context, is ample testimony to his artistry.

CHARACTERIZATION

Early in the first book of *Tristram Shandy,* Sterne tells the reader, "if you should think me somewhat sparing of my narrative on my first setting out—bear with me." He might have been speaking for Diderot as well, because both writers put more emphasis on character than narration. Plot serves largely to reveal character, and characterization itself has a combination of functions. It is a most important element in the fictional realism of Sterne and Diderot, it is significant in its own right, and it further acts to underline the ulterior motives of each author.

Sterne, for instance, conceives of his characters as unwitting exponents and illustrations of Shandeism. This is one of their major functions, just as demonstrating sensibility is Yorick's primary activity in the *Sentimental Journey.* Shandeism itself involves two main characteristics: eccentricity, which can pick out the absurd, even in a presumably touching situation, and geniality, which can at any moment lead to tears of sympathy. Diderot, on the other hand, is at pains to create living scenes, peopled with living persons whose stories are familiar to him. An intent student of human nature, he cannot look at human beings without considering the influence of the society in which they move. Therefore, as they are examined from sociological, psychological, and moral standpoints, the function of the characters is not only to be authentic people but also to reveal their relationship to their environments. One would expect this to be the attitude of a socially conscious *philosophe* when he turns to fiction.

Despite the differences in their ultimate points of view, both writers frequently use similar means for portraying character. Their method, as indicated by their treatments of realism, is generally one of indirection. Jacques's strictures on portraiture [37] are faithfully executed by Diderot and Sterne, and Sterne himself provides a somewhat amplified statement of this process: ". . . see Monsieur le Duc's face first—observe what character is written in it—take notice in what posture he stands to hear you—mark the turns and expressions of his body and limbs—and for the tone—the first sound which comes from his lips will give it to you." [38] In addition, there are other practices which occur so repeatedly in Diderot's and Sterne's characterizations that they may be regarded as a basic method.

The socio-moral implications that underlie Diderot's fiction are enlivened and relieved of the danger of preachment by his use of foils and contrasts. These also sharpen and develop his characters. There is nothing strikingly new or original about this treatment. Diderot has been accused of borrowing it from Sterne for the delineation of Jacques and his Master, but he was utilizing it before he read *Tristram,* and it seems more likely that both Diderot and Sterne found precedent for it in earlier authors, such as Cervantes or Rabelais. It may well have impressed each of them as being an almost foolproof method for their purposes. It certainly is of great advantage to Diderot when he comes to dramatize, through his characters, his "peu de philosophie."

In *La Religieuse,* for example, the *philosophe's* interests are turned to the psychological results of a sociological problem.

Suzanne and the other important characters reflect his study of the effects of an unnatural life on natural emotions. Suzanne, whose own emotional life is to undergo marked changes, acts as the norm. She is set off against the three Mothers Superior. One represents an inspired mystic and unintentional spellcaster; another illustrates how petty hypocrisy can be diverted into sadistic and superstitious channels; and the third—the most frightening and most dramatically portrayed victim of what Diderot considers to be an unnatural institution—reveals complete perversion. The atmosphere of each convent is determined by the attitude of its Superior, and in this way Diderot can show how environment acts on both the psychology and the morality of the characters.

The *Neveu de Rameau* demonstrates the same method of characterization with the juxtaposition of "lui" and "moi." Diderot restrains himself here, remaining the sincere, dedicated *philosophe* while the Nephew dominates the dialogue. But Diderot deepens our insights into the Nephew's personality by his own comments, and his reactions emphasize certain striking characteristics of his companion. The result is so dynamic a masterpiece of characterization that the heroine of *La Religieuse* seems almost weak and incomplete in comparison. Admittedly, the Nephew is a more fascinating individual than Suzanne and affords Diderot material for marshaling the utmost of his artistry. But possibly there is another reason for the overwhelming success of his characterization. *La Religieuse* is quite evidently a *roman à thèse* and was the first fictional work Diderot wrote after his two plays. The characters in the plays did not come off because Diderot leaned too heavily toward abstractions, and sometimes Suzanne does not completely escape this. Occasionally she tends to be more of a personification of virtue than simply Suzanne Simonin, heroine of a story about a girl whom Diderot had never known. Perhaps *La Religieuse* may be regarded as showing traces of a transitional step between Diderot's earlier characterizations, which are subordinated to a thesis, and his later characterizations, which have a vitality all their own.

Certainly the fact that the Nephew figures in a satire that has many themes—and figures, moreover, as a type, the parasitic hanger-on—does not diminish his freshness. This may be because beyond the social type he represents another—the eccentric or original. And these terms say everything and nothing because each eccentric, according to his highly individualized personality, is completely different. That is why Diderot himself is intrigued by the Nephew; there is nothing hackneyed about him. Furthermore, the complexity of the character is a necessary part of this kind of satire. As the Nephew admonishes Diderot, he is a knave, not a fool. Consequently, he is absolutely essential for the discussions of drama, genius and talent, and related themes. It is true that the positive theories are Diderot's. A few years earlier, in the third *Entretien sur le Fils naturel,* he had worked out to a considerable degree his arguments about music. But Jean-François Rameau was actually a musician, and he thereby also illustrates a *third* type, according to the theory of professional deformation which Diderot develops in *Satire I*. Parasitic and eccentric he is, but in hearing and watching him, one would soon note that he has all the "tics," reflexes, jargon of the man professionally steeped in music. By keeping a relationship to fact and by making the Nephew's speech and actions—both conscious and unconscious—characteristic,

Diderot always maintains the illusions of the Nephew's words and thoughts. The character remains wholly itself even when it is functioning to some other purposes. This sharpens the moral condemnation, for one cannot possibly excuse the Nephew's abominable standards simply because he is a creature of his environment. He, as an individual, is as much to blame as the group whose code he adopts. In this respect, the moral polemic, though more subtly handled than in *La Religieuse,* is more emphatic. Virtue triumphant in his earlier work lacks the force of the spectacle of depravity afforded by the Nephew and his society.

The foils and contrasts in characterization serve a similar dual purpose in the fiction of the seventies. In 1772, Diderot wrote a penetrating little study of female psychology entitled *Sur les femmes. Ceci n'est pas un conte,* the story of Mme de La Pommeraye, and *Sur l'inconséquence du jugement public* all illustrate incisive comments he makes in his analysis of the relationship between a woman's emotional life and her role in eighteenth-century society.

The neatly balanced *Ceci n'est pas un conte* is organized as two contrasting stories: one the account of a good man and a bad woman, the other the account of a good woman and a bad man. Within this frame, Tanié is contrasted to Gardeil, and Mme Reymer is counterbalanced by Mlle de La Chaux. Mme Reymer represents the unscrupulous, dissembling woman Diderot mentions in *Sur les femmes,* while Mlle de La Chaux is a striking example of the transports of hysteria. Juxtaposed as they are, they both reveal different aspects of the "bête féroce," the contrast between extreme "froideur" and extreme "sensibilité."

The same distinction is worked out in further detail in the

more complex analyses of Mme de La Pommeraye in *Jacques,* and of Mme de La Carlière in *Sur l'inconséquence du jugement public.* Each woman is balanced against the man who she believes has wronged her, and each, in her own way, effects revenge—Mme de La Pommeraye, consciously, by cold reasoning, Mme de La Carlière, unconsciously, by an emotional lack of reason. The result in both cases is self-destruction, but unnatural though the protagonists seem, Diderot does not totally condemn them. Using the characters as a point of departure for further discussion, he makes the apology for Mme de La Pommeraye by stressing the relationship between her motivation and her character and position in society. The real villain of *Sur l'inconséquence du jugement public* is, as the unwieldy title suggests, society itself. Diderot concludes with the remark that he has his own theories about certain actions which, he says, are not so much the vices of individuals as they are the results of laws and customs. By hinting that he will clarify these ideas in the future, he invites one to consider the stories of the seventies in a new way: perhaps they may be seen as pendants to his *Supplément au voyage de Bougainville,* one of the culminations of Diderot's sociological investigations.

Even the *Entretien d'un père avec ses enfants* points to this. Inspired by Diderot's return to Langres, the *Entretien* appears to be an imaginary visit that he would have liked to have paid his father many years before. The dominating personality is Didier Diderot, but the theme is indicated by the subtitle: *Du danger de se mettre au-dessus des lois.* While the characterizations of the family circle are not slighted, Diderot uses them to show both the contrasts in personality and the contrasts of each person's response to the subject of the

Entretien. And although the Diderot who figures in the story does not agree with the subtitle, the Diderot who writes it does, for the theme anticipates an important argument in the *Supplément.*

Yet the procedure Diderot employs should not be interpreted as resulting in moral or social or philosophical judgments dressed up like human beings. To some extent, Diderot may have skirted this danger with Suzanne in *La Religieuse,* but none of his succeeding fiction, manifesting the interplay of characters and ideas, lies open to such criticism. Certainly of all his stories, *Jacques le fataliste,* with its central dialogue about fatalism, is peopled with vibrantly living characters, not marionettes. The core of its major philosophical theme depends on two men whose physical existence the audience briefly sees at rare intervals. Yet neither the Master, who presents conventional arguments in favor of free will, nor Jacques, who bows to *le destin* but whose instinctive reactions are those of a man with the illusion of free will, is a mechanical mouthpiece for Diderot. Their arguments derive force from their respective personalities, and the validity of their personalities is not diminished even when their arguments are reduced to absurdity. Jacques and his Master are set up as one another's foils. Jacques tells his Master that they are indispensable to each other, and in a larger sense, this is also true of their characterizations. Jacques's attitudes are revealed through his responses to his Master's questions, teasings, and interruptions, and the Master approaches humanity largely by his conversations with Jacques and by his reactions to Jacques's tales. When he consoles his companion about his captain's death, when he anxiously tells Jacques how to guide his erratic horse, when he is overwhelmed with concern for a situation that Jacques merely relates about his past, he is no longer the automaton Diderot has earlier suggested; he is a human being.

He also manifests certain peculiar characteristics which become distinguishing traits or "tics," as Diderot calls them in his satire *Sur les mots de caractère.* One can no more divorce the Master from his snuff-box and watch than one can separate the Nephew from his pantomime. But "tics," as previously suggested, achieve their fullest significance for characterization when Diderot uses them to explain the motivations of his characters' mental life. He will not emphasize the *idée fixe* to the extent that Sterne does, but he employs it to indicate an aspect of the forces underlying personality.

Each of the three Mothers Superior has her *idée fixe,* although she may not be aware of it. The Nephew's character derives a significant measure of its complexity from his futile struggle for genius. Jacques's personality is high-lighted by his devotion to a philosophical system which he has picked up second-hand and simplified for his own purposes. Both Mme de La Pommeraye and Mme de La Carlière are immovably centered superwomen, dedicated to one goal. Even Diderot is subject to his own "tic." If he tries to act like a detached spectator in the *Neveu de Rameau,* he is anything but cautious as the radical, hot-headed young *philosophe* in the *Entretien d'un père avec ses enfants.*

It should be noted, however, that Diderot's use of a dominating idea to individualize and elucidate character is not his exclusive method; it constitutes only a part of it. This is important, for although occasionally the characters become "monsters," as he would say—the Nephew, for instance, the two Mothers Superior, even Mme de La Pommeraye and Mme de La Carlière—Diderot does not deal with aberration

simply for its own sake. His purpose is to present men and
women in society, often as victims of society, and his interest
in abnormal psychology is oriented toward the achievement
of social progress.

Sterne's intentions are markedly different, for the "philosophy" his characters impart is quite distinct from the preoccupations of the *philosophe*. Consequently, when Sterne
avails himself of the *idée fixe* for delineating personality, he
gives it a central place. Shandeism stems from a fundamental
way of portraying character. Odd though the results seem,
it is apparent that Sterne had consciously developed a method.
In a letter of 30 January 1760, he explains his point of view:

. . . and reason and common sense tell me, that if the characters of
past ages and men are to be drawn at all, they are to be drawn like
themselves; that is, with their excellencies, and with their foibles
—and it is as much a piece of justice to the world, and to virtue
too, to do the one as the other.—The ruling passion, *et les egare-
mens du coeur,* are the very things which mark and distinguish
a man's character;—in which I would as soon leave out a man's
head as his hobbyhorse.[39]

He proposes, of course, to rely mainly on the ruling passions.

Locke begins his discussion of the theory of ruling passions
early in the first book of the *Essay Concerning Human Understanding*. The concept was to become very popular in the
eighteenth century and might be regarded as that period's
equivalent of today's interest in characterology. Locke, a believer in free will, would not grant reason a subordinate place;
but, as Professor MacLean has pointed out, a large number of
writers, including Pope, "overlooked Locke's common sense
and succumbed to this deterministic view that put men in
absolute subjection to their ruling passion." [40] Sterne accepts
Locke's hypothesis, altering the name, and indicates that be-

cause wise men of all eras have had their hobbyhorses, he finds no reason to object so long as the rider does not force others to mount his steed. He treats the hobby sympathetically because it has a peculiarly Shandean merit:

'Tis the sporting little filly-folly which carries you out for the present hour—a maggot, a butterfly, a picture, a fiddle-stick—an uncle Toby's siege—or an any thing, which a man makes a shift to get a-stride on, to canter it away from the cares and solicitudes of life—. . . .[41]

And in his famous pronouncement toward the end of the first book of *Tristram,* he determines to use it as a basis of characterization.

According to the psychology of his day, it is a sound basis, but it must be remembered that Sterne is writing a Shandean book. For the sake of amusement, he wants to account for and exploit eccentricity. It is here that the concept of ruling passions shows further advantage for Shandeism. Sterne was too devoted a follower of Locke to overlook his master's common sense and make man a slave to his passion.[42] He personally had no belief in a fatalistic, mechanistic universe and did not share the materialist views of his French friends. According to his report in the *Sentimental Journey,* a Parisian lady told Diderot and Morellet that Sterne had said more in half an hour for revealed religion than all the *Encyclopédie* had said against it. The comic possibilities attracted him, however, so that he fastened on hobbies as mental aberrations: "When a man gives himself up to the government of a ruling passion,—or, in other words, when his Hobby-Horse grows headstrong,—farewell cool reason and fair discretion!"[43]

Sterne is vastly diverted by the consequences of a natural psychological phenomenon pushed beyond the norm. He will not push it too far because then it becomes serious, like the frightening "humours" of Jonson and Molière. These would spoil Shandean geniality and they would detract from the commonplace humanity of his characters. The reader would then see an abstraction—a Tartuffe, an Alceste, a Mosca—instead of an engaging figure where something has gotten a little out of hand. What Sterne wants is an association whereby the audience recognizes its own mental habits in Walter or Trim or Toby but also realizes and enjoys the absurdity of these habits once they escape the control of reason.[44]

It is evident that the resultant single-mindedness of the characters impedes understanding. Diderot could show tragic effects as well, but Sterne preferred to stay within the bounds of comedy. In the fourth book of his *Essay,* Locke says that the ruling passions, among other obstacles, stand in the way of knowledge. The Shandy group is clearly blighted by this curse because their hobbies, at every turn, defeat any possibility of their separating illusion from reality. Walter Shandy, the self-appointed "master of one of the finest chains of reasoning in nature," is in the habit of forcing "every event in nature into a hypothesis, by which means never man crucified Truth at the rate he did." Carried away by plans for a defensive campaign, Toby plots a strategic retreat, "and having done that, corporal, we'll embark for England.—We are there, quoth the corporal, recollecting himself. Very true, said my uncle Toby," with, one suspects, a shade of regret.

In addition, integrally bound up with the ruling passion is an association of ideas which obliges the afflicted character to view everything in terms of his own hobby. Locke takes a negative view of association of ideas and believes it to be the source of the greatest number of mental errors. In his discussion in Book II of the *Essay,* he cites some results of what he considers a disease of the mind, and Sterne, recognizing the possibilities for the ludicrous, seized on this "disease." Well aware that everyone is subject to it,[45] he finds it hilarious as a mental disorder. The confusion that arises not only makes for accidental agreement and disagreement among the hobby riders, but it is also rife among the kitchen circle's reactions to Master Bobby's death and Trim's famous funeral oration.[46]

But while Sterne finds the key to personality in a man's hobby and therefore stresses the Shandean *idée fixe,* he joins Diderot in setting up his characters as foils to one another. The greatest incongruity of the Shandys lies in this very matter: their hobbies and mental associations both obscure general truth and destroy any meeting ground for the characters. Life is one of constant frustration through misunderstanding. Furthermore, the characters are usually blinded to the ridiculous in their own hobbies but take a dim view of their companions' respective quirks. Dr. Slop parodies Captain Shandy "though full as hobbyhorsical himself." Walter is generally amused, unless his theorizing is interrupted, by Toby's hobby, although his own literary tastes are equally curious. Poor Toby, utterly unable to comprehend Walter, is even moved to tears by what he considers to be mental unbalance in his brother.

The very dissimilarity of the characters themselves adds to the comedy. Sterne has Tristram declare that

. . . the hand of the supreme Maker and first Designer of all things never made or put a family together (in that period at least of it which I have sat down to write the story of)—where the characters of it were cast or contrasted with so dramatic a felicity as ours was, for this end; or in which the capacities of affording such exquisite scenes, and the powers of shifting them perpetually from morning to night, were lodged and intrusted with so unlimited a confidence, as in the Shandy Family.[47]

It is vitally necessary that he have some way of shifting his scenes and playing up contrasts. Even the hobbies, different though they are, need to be relieved by some device. The contrasts in personalities provide the required variety as well as the means of revealing other facets of the characters. Walter's natural aggressiveness suits him for Toby's military pursuits, while Toby's peaceful disposition might be more appropriate for philosophical speculations. The juxtaposition of a man and his hobby therefore helps Sterne to avoid monotony. And the fact that a character like Mrs. Shandy has no hobby at all provides further contrast. She is also the simple-minded foil to her hobby-dominated husband on another score. It is his fate to have such a submissive wife that he has no chance to indulge his love for argumentation or to explain theories to her with any guarantee that she will understand them. "—That she is not a woman of science, my father would say—is her misfortune—but she might ask a question." [48] Walter has forgotten that once his mate did ask a question, in the very first chapter of the novel, at a most unpropitious moment.

It becomes evident that when the foils and contrasts are not at work, the interest tends to flag. The character of Tristram, serving as a necessary thread of unity, does not emerge so dynamically as the others. This is fitting if Sterne wants to subordinate the narrator to his family, but when Sterne is forced to depend on him alone the novel becomes pallid. Although Tristram is a Shandy, he is not so fascinating as his relatives and their group. He is blighted by the assorted family curses, but even though he plays the eccentric, it is hardly with the same intensity as the others. Their delightful antics stem from their subjection to their hobbies and from their misunderstandings as each other's foils. In Book VII, Sterne has to rely on Tristram by himself. He has no foils or overwhelming hobbies, his quips and gasps are rather forced, and the novel thereby becomes monotonous.

In the *Sentimental Journey* one finds the same pallor. Yorick has undergone a transformation. Tristram's clergyman is amused by the hobbies of his neighbors, but he himself is afflicted by irresponsible levity, which qualifies him for a place in the Shandy circle. When he tours the continent, however, he is so busy being in sweet harmony with himself and all that he encounters, he is so dedicated to displaying the pleasures of dear sensibility, that his account comes dangerously near insipidity. It is all of an even tone, unalleviated by hobby or foil. Characters are duly met, briefly recorded, but there is no effort to search out their complexities or thoroughly unveil any personality except that of the one-sided author. Indeed, aside from the narrator, one finds no attempt at extended characterization. Sterne confines himself instead to brilliant little sketches.

Actually, Sterne's method of characterization is, at best, somewhat limited. Despite his foils and contrasts, his dependence on his major instrument—the hobby—makes the characters quite static. Of course, when the hobby cannot provide it, Sterne adds supplementary material directly: "I could not give the reader this stroke in my uncle Toby's picture, by the instrument with which I drew the other parts of it,—that taking in no more than the mere Hobby-Horsical likeness: —this is a part of his moral character." [49] He also seeks to build character further by that digressive-progressive fashion he discusses in his celebrated defense of digressions. [50] But although digressions are "incontestably the sunshine" and certainly help to familiarize the reader with a character, even Sterne will admit that the "great contours" derive from the hobby. Digressions substantiate the initial material, but they do not gradually reveal it because the essential strokes have already been established. The subsequent behavior of the character is basically the hobby in operation.

This is a telling difference from Diderot's procedures, for while he agrees with Sterne on the value of "tics," he will not base character on the *idée fixe*. It does not offer a sufficiently elaborate or valid explanation of real, complex personalities. The result is that although most of his characters do not show dramatic growth as do, say, some of the people in *Wuthering Heights* or the novels of Dostoyevski, they do not appear to be so static as Sterne's.[51]

Another reason that Diderot's characterizations appear less static than Sterne's is Diderot's preference for cumulative effects. Instead of portraying a character by his hobby and adding supplementary information by digression, Diderot works to reveal his characters gradually. One is aware that the third Mother Superior is unbalanced when she is first introduced, but it is only after Suzanne has copiously and innocently described her words and actions that the reader realizes the extent of her neurosis. The characterization of the Nephew is really not complete until his final, mocking "He who laughs last, laughs best." This procedure is perhaps most brilliantly effective in the portrayal of Mme de La Pommeraye. Unprepared for her diabolical measures, both the reader and Jacques watch with increasing apprehension her ruthless calculations for success. By the end of the story, one's sympathies have been turned away from her, largely because she has lost her attraction as a wronged woman. The fanaticism of her revenge as it unrolls makes her unnatural, abnormal, almost repulsive.

Moreover, the different purposes served by Diderot's and Sterne's characterizations bring out further divergences. Shandeism and sensibility do not necessarily demand a strict adherence to real models; but fiction that deals with the interaction of social and moral questions possibly does require a closer relationship to fact. In any case, that is probably the way that Diderot, with his interest in "histories" rather than "novels," saw it. Whenever it is possible, he says in his *Pensées détachées sur la peinture,* prefer real personages to symbolic beings,[52] and though his remark is addressed to painters, Diderot would doubtless extend it to writers as well.

There is no doubt that Sterne's fiction does draw on personal experiences of the author. Book VII of *Tristram* and the *Sentimental Journey* could not have been written if Sterne had not traveled abroad. He was indebted to Dr. John Burton for the inspiration for Dr. Slop; Yorkshire readers were to find local allusions in *Tristram* even though Sterne claimed to have excised many topical references; and Bishop Warburton was to be confronted by a somewhat undignified mention of himself. Sterne pointedly includes himself quite often, going so far as to seize the occasion for some advance publicity for the *Sermons of Mr. Yorick* by interpolating his own on "The Abuses of Conscience." [53] But Sterne so refined and altered his source material that, with the exception of himself, the relationship between created characters and contemporary personalities is quite tenuous for the modern reader. His triumph in characterization is to make imaginary figures live.

The ultimate success of Diderot's characterizations, however, probably rests on his ability to describe real people. He takes care to emphasize this by protesting that his stories are true and by working himself into his fiction. It is true that he does not figure in *La Religieuse,* but the novel includes material from his personal experience: he himself had spent a brief time under duress in a monastery; a sister of his had gone mad after becoming a nun; and he had followed the Longchamps case very closely. In the *Neveu de Rameau,* he includes references to his Bohemian days in Paris and he plays a role in the dialogue. While some critics have suggested that the Nephew is Diderot's *alter ego,* there is considerable evidence to show that the Nephew is quite faithfully drawn from Diderot's acquaintance, Jean-François Rameau.[54] The characterizations of the family group in the *Entretien d'un père avec ses enfants* are based on Diderot's own family, even including Diderot's self-portrait as a young *philosophe* of the 1750s. He plays himself as the author of *Jacques,* including remarks about his own idiosyncrasies—which he had previously mentioned to Sophie Volland—and weaving in an account of Mme d'Holbach's dog for the story of Nicole's devoted suitor. Indeed, he so often vouches for the truth of the stories in *Jacques* that critics have suspected the hero's exploits to be an echo of Diderot's provincial experiences. He also claims that he was an eyewitness to Desroches's tragedy, and he likewise asserts that neither the story of Mme Reymer nor the story of Mlle de La Chaux is a falsehood. Mme Reymer has apparently faded into oblivion, but the information Diderot divulges about Mlle de La Chaux is verified by factual evidence. Even the plays carry an autobiographical stamp. In *Le Père de famille* there are obvious hints of Diderot's encounters with Mme Champion and 'Toinette, and Clairet was the name of Sophie Volland's chambermaid. *Est-il bon? est-il méchant?* has been cited as a biographical piece ever since Baudelaire observed that all the characters were real people.

That Sterne favored imaginary people while Diderot was more intrigued by recreating real personalities in no way detracts from the skillfulness of their characterizations. But their respective preferences further reflect the tendencies exhibited by their realism. Sterne turns within himself and the world of his imagination for the essential materials for his characters. Diderot, penetrating the lives of men and women in the eighteenth century, finds the stimulus for his inspiration among the inhabitants of the world in which he lives.

NEW FICTIONAL DIRECTIONS

The similarities between *Tristram Shandy* and *Jacques le fataliste* do not end with aspects of the authors' investigations of realism or their treatment of characterization. Probably one of the main reasons for subsequent cries of plagiarism was that both works—often in very analogous ways—represented something quite new to the literary scene. Diderot and Sterne had intended the novelty, for they purposely introduced a number of devices that would help to make *Jacques* and *Tristram* the most experimental of all their fiction. As such, the two books can take their place in company with all experimental fiction, particularly novels that are written about how to write novels.

Both eighteenth-century writers assert the prerogative of a novelist to write as he pleases, unhampered by established rules. There is more to this than mere waywardness. They are conscious innovators who have found the reading public to be conditioned by popular modes of fiction. Diderot's ingenious techniques and especially his sharp admonitions to the Reader in *Jacques* clearly demonstrate his exasperation, but surely *Tristram* was written as a sly reproof to readers and writers. Sterne's *ab ovo* method, his disregard of propriety and chronology, his abrupt digressions and personal familiarity are all indications of his impatience with conventional novels. Even the modified *Sentimental Journey* was to be "something new, quite out of the beaten track." [55]

That their devices often coincide should be attributed more to mutual interests than to influence. In addition to the usual criticism that Diderot copied passages from *Tristram*—an accusation Diderot anticipated by admitting it—and the dubious charge that he attempted to imitate Sterne's humor, critics have frequently asserted that the manner and method of *Jacques* owe much to *Tristram*.[56] This view probably has been greatly exaggerated, for most of the devices which appear in *Jacques* have already been anticipated in Diderot's previous works—works which were written prior to Diderot's reading of *Tristram* in 1762. Sterne's use of pictorial effects may well have been stimulated by his earlier attempts at painting, but Diderot's predate both his readings in Sterne and his writing of the *Salons*—although his experience with the *Salons* doubtless sharpened his perception. He consciously utilized tableaux in *La Religieuse* (1760) and drew Meister's attention to this device many years later. He was also concerned with them in *Le Fils naturel* (1757) and *Le Père de famille* (1758), as his detailed stage directions indicate. Garrick's acting may have been instrumental in inspiring Sterne's dramatic devices; Diderot, however, was dependent neither on Sterne's treatment of pantomime nor on his own acquaintance with *cher Roscius,* as he called Garrick, for the theatrical elements in his fiction. His preoccupation with pantomime and detailed gesture is evident in chapters 37 and 38 of the *Bijoux indiscrets* (1748), in his *Lettre sur les sourds et muets* (1751), in his plays, in his *Entretiens sur le Fils naturel* (1757), in his essay *De la poésie dramatique* (1758), in his *Lettre à Mme*

Riccoboni (c. 1759), in the *Eloge de Richardson* (1761)—where he is "seduced" by Richardson's realistic details—and in the *Neveu de Rameau* (1761). And it is quite likely that keen observation, fortified, perhaps, by what they had learned from Locke, is responsible for Diderot's and Sterne's experiments with association and digressive interruptions. Even before Diderot's physiological investigations of the association of ideas in his *Entretien entre Diderot et D'Alembert* (1769), he had used digression in the *Neveu de Rameau,* in his earlier philosophical writings such as the *Lettre sur les sourds et muets,* in his own correspondence, and had brilliantly analyzed for Sophie Volland the associative progress of conversation in a letter of 20 October 1760.[57]

Furthermore, while Diderot is interested in trying out new techniques, his objective is not simply to be different and diverting. Once he had decided that fiction need not be useless, he sought additional measures for making it a poignant or meaningful experience for its readers. He admired Richardson's success in contriving to make the audience take an active role in his novels, and he refers, in the *Eloge,* to a French lady who was so impressed by *Charles Grandison*[58] that she requested a friend to visit Miss Emily, Mr. Belford, and Miss Howe when he arrived in London. In Diderot's own notes on the *conte historique,* he pictures the author as a man who is seated in the reader's chimney corner, spinning a true tale which he wants his audience to believe.

The result is a heightened emphasis on the author-audience relationship, which had marked Diderot's fiction even before the stories of the seventies. Suzanne of *La Religieuse,* in addressing her memoirs to the Marquis, does not talk *at* him; she solicits his help and often suspends her tale to speak to him more directly. It is Diderot himself who opens the *Neveu de Rameau* by casually chatting to the reader and revealing his own identity. There are really two audiences in the dialogue: one is Diderot, listening and talking to the Nephew; the other is the reader, to whom Diderot confides his reactions and describes the Nephew. Diderot frequently uses this dual technique. In addition to the reader, there will be an active audience within the framework of the tale, as in *Ceci n'est pas un conte, Sur l'inconséquence du jugement public, Les Deux amis de Bourbonne,* and *Jacques.* It is not unusual for Diderot to wind up conversing in one breath with a character in his story and in the next breath with the audience. In *Jacques,* he even has an arrangement of Chinese boxes: the audience joins the Reader in listening to a story one of the characters is telling someone else, and at any time, anyone, including Diderot, can break into the tale to state his opinion. Occasionally, this makes for rather confusing *reading,* but it is very clear as conversation, as if the book were *spoken* instead of read.[59]

The justification for this device, implicit in the notes to the *Deux amis,* is stated in the prologue to *Ceci n'est pas un conte.* When one tells a tale, Diderot says, one tells it to someone who is listening to it; and since the narrator can rarely avoid being interrupted sometimes by his listener, Diderot is introducing a special character who will play this role.[60] This is no idle whim; by subsequently protracting the preliminaries, Diderot is also teasing the reading audience and making it share the listener's impatience. *Jacques* appears to be a full-length expansion of the techniques set forth in *Ceci n'est pas un conte,* complete with curious listener, delaying tactics—the Master replaces Diderot as the snuff addict—and interruptions.

But here Diderot further elaborates on the relationship by

creating characters and roles for author and audience in the sallies which take place between them. The Reader, a foil for Diderot, is curious, literal, and conventional. He expects the novel to follow the lines of stories he has read, and he is often shocked by Diderot's frankness. Diderot is both ironic commentator and narrator. It is through the former role that he willfully teases and upbraids the Reader, comments on the stories, and makes his acid observations about how novels should and should not be written. Although he constantly reminds the Reader of his author's license, he makes it clear that he has no intention of using it in the way that the Reader expects. Time and again, he abruptly breaks the tale to confront the Reader with the possibilities afforded an author, and then refuses to exploit them. This gives Diderot the opportunity to criticize current fiction and to emphasize that he is doing something altogether different: he is writing a "history," he is telling the truth.

As narrator, Diderot is not always so detached. While he follows his usual practice of letting the characters do as much of the talking as possible, occasionally he acts as though he is a part of the story he is telling. Just as the "listener" of *Ceci n'est pas un conte* observes that Diderot interrupts his account of Mlle de La Chaux to weep over her misfortunes, so the Reader of *Jacques* catches Diderot in the process of confusing illusion with reality. Then the Reader, forgetting that he, too, has at times been carried away by the illusion, reprimands the author: "If *you* ever saw, indeed! You weren't even there. Say 'If *one* ever saw.' " [61] But these triumphs for the Reader come rarely. For the most part he is a captive audience at the same time that Diderot inextricably involves him in the novel.

Sterne is a good deal more considerate and establishes his

attitude in the sixth chapter of Book 1 by informing the reader that he wants his friendship and good will. He is, nonetheless, an extremely self-conscious writer like Diderot, and is intensely preoccupied with his audience. The reader to whom *Tristram* is addressed is indeterminate and general, for Sterne refrains from creating a specific character to act as a representative audience. As a result, he plays a role of minor activity in the novel. Occasionally inattentive and often curious and confused, he may interrupt the author, but his breaks are relatively infrequent because his major purpose is to listen. Sterne assuredly perplexes him, but he will not bedevil his victim or sharply emphasize the author-audience relationship to the advantage of the author: "But courage! gentle reader! —I scorn it—'tis enough to have thee in my power—but to make use of the advantage which the fortune of the pen has now gained over thee, would be too much—" [62] As a matter of fact, he deliberately avoids posing as an ironic commentator and buries his important statements about novel writing among the digressions which form such a basic part of his work.

The device of the personal narrator was nothing new in itself, as Diderot and Sterne would have agreed. Predecessors such as Cervantes and recent writers such as Fielding and Voltaire had all made a point of directly addressing an audience. But Diderot and Sterne do not restrict themselves to prefatory remarks or formal or precisely interpolated comments. They burst out of the story at completely unpredictable moments, thereby forcing the audience's attention to focus abruptly on the narrator instead of the narrative. They act like eccentric masters of ceremony who both direct and take part in their show. This may well be a reflection of their respective personalities. As irrepressible men, perhaps they could not avoid spilling over into their fiction in the most dynamic way possible.

Yet neither one would sacrifice his story to personal whim. They both see to it that the audience is able to visualize clearly what it is reading. As Diderot says, when he interrupts the Hostess to describe the story-telling scene in *Jacques,* "without this care you would have heard them talk, but you wouldn't have seen them at all; better late than never." His tendency often seems to be to think of visual effects in terms of painting. He says in the *Salon* of 1767 that he has the habit of arranging his characters in his head as if they were on canvas, that maybe he even transfers them there and that when he is writing, he is looking at a large wall.[63] He often sketches pictures of the D'Holbach group at Grandval for Sophie Volland. He consciously scatters pitiable scenes—*tableaux pathétiques,* he calls them—in *La Religieuse,* and years later he tells Meister that it is a work for painters to leaf through constantly. The visualized scenes in the *Neveu de Rameau* probably constitute the epitome of Diderot's talent for this kind of delineation, and what physical description there is in *Jacques* is vividly pictorial: Jacques, barefoot and in his shirttails, staggering around the room looking for his bed, or Jacques, his Master, and the Hostess, gathered about the table:

The Master, seated to the left in his nightcap and dressing gown, was carelessly sprawled out in a large upholstered armchair, his handkerchief tossed on the arm of the chair, his snuff box in his hand. The Hostess, towards the back of the room and facing the door, was by the table with her glass in front of her. Jacques, bareheaded, was to her right, his elbows propped on the table and his head sagging between two bottles; two more were on the floor beside him.[64]

Certainly the Master would have appreciated Diderot's effort, because he tells Jacques that he likes paintings only when they are described in a spoken account. Perhaps it is not coincidental that the "painting" Jacques proceeds to describe had appeared earlier as an interpolated anecdote in the *Salon* of 1765.

In a manner very similar to Diderot's, Sterne will carefully set the stage with a tableau before putting it into motion. As Walter prepares to read from the *Tristra-paedia,* Toby "lighted his pipe,—Yorick drew his chair closer to the table,—Trim snuffed the candle,—my father stirred up the fire,—took up the book,—coughed twice, and began." [65] Sterne intentionally holds up Trim's delivery of the "Abuses of Conscience" in order to give a very detailed picture of the corporal's physical attitude. He even burlesques his own stage directions—and Hogarth's *Analysis of Beauty*—by using mathematical exactitude. Yet Hogarth, whom he greatly respected, as well as Romney and Steele, with whom Sterne had studied painting in York, were probably very influential in determining Sterne's appreciation of pictorial effects.

Both writers may have found further stimulus in Locke, for their shorthand of looks and gestures constitutes a direct appeal to the senses. It is as close to a one-to-one relationship as can be achieved in an art form which is not constructed on immediately sensory materials. Diderot was well aware that a particular stance or an unconscious gesture could convey more than words, and Sterne interrupts the well-known pantomime of Trim's funeral oration to explain that he finds visual detail the most directly impressionable:

Let it suffice to affirm, that of all the senses, the eye (for I absolutely deny the touch, though most of your Barbati, I know are for it) has the quickest commerce with the soul,—gives a smarter stroke, and leaves something more inexpressible upon the fancy than words can either convey—or sometimes get rid of.[66]

Some of the finest examples of this occur during Trim's address, as, gazing on the weeping Susannah, he demands:

—are we not like a flower of the field—a tear of pride stole in betwixt every two tears of humiliation—else no tongue could have described Susannah's affliction—is not all flesh grass?—'Tis clay.— 'tis dirt.—They all looked directly at the scullion,—the scullion had just been scouring a fish-kettle.—It was not fair.—

—What is the finest face that ever man looked at!—I could hear Trim talk so for ever, cried Susannah,—what is it! (Susannah laid her hand upon Trim's shoulder)—but corruption?— Susannah took it off.[67]

Closely related to pictorial devices—indeed, Sterne often fuses them—is Diderot's and Sterne's use of theatrical effects. This is not surprising for Diderot; his preoccupation with drama is well known. In the *Lettre sur les sourds et muets,* he admits having had an early passion for the theatre; he knew the classic plays by heart, and there are hints that as a young man in Paris he considered becoming an actor. When, in his fiction, the characters move about and gesticulate, Diderot is activating his paintings by pantomime. He generally prefers scenes in motion because they make his pictures more dramatic. The tableaux set the stage—for, as Diderot has pointed out, one must see as well as hear—but they are rarely composed of frozen images. Even the beginnings of his stories are often marked by activity. Diderot is idling around the Café de la Régence when the curtain goes up on the *Neveu de Rameau.* The abrupt openings of *Ceci n'est pas un conte, Sur l'inconséquence du jugement public,* and *Jacques* give the impression of continuous action before the tale starts. It is as though one walked into a room where a conversation was already in progress, or into a theatre after the first act had begun. While Diderot rarely refers to the stage in his novels and stories, it is very likely that because of his reluctance to forsake the medium completely, he compromised by carrying it over into his fiction. His decision to work the moral and social material that he had initially tried to dramatize in his plays into a different genre, his use of dramatic selectivity for fictional realism suggest as much. And certainly for Diderot, nothing could be more valid, dramatically or psychologically, then the effects produced by his shorthand of looks and gestures.

It is less easy to account for Sterne's interest in theatrical devices, an interest which he takes care to underline frequently. He did admire Garrick and became his close friend, securing a pass to all Drury Lane productions. He had no experience in writing for the theatre, yet his first signed letter to Garrick, written before there is any evidence that Sterne had witnessed any of his performances, concludes with the suggestion of a "Cervantic Comedy" based on the first four volumes of *Tristram:* "Half a word of Encouragement would be enough to make me conceive, & bring forth something for the Stage (how good, or how bad is another Story)." [68] Counterbalancing this proposal is a report by one of Sterne's contemporaries who says that when *he* suggested that Sterne write a comedy for Garrick, Sterne regretfully confessed to a lack of talent and familiarity with "the business of the stage." [69] He had enough talent, however, to rely heavily on dramatic devices, and his frequent and self-conscious references to them would imply a confidence in their success. Actually he emphasizes far more than Diderot his role as author-dramatist.

Walter Shandy's comment on the "Abuses of Conscience"

probably reflects Sterne's own opinion: "I like the sermon well, replied my father,—'tis dramatic,—and there is something in that way of writing, when skilfully managed, which catches the attention." [70] Cross has indicated that this procedure is not restricted to Sterne's fiction: "His best sermons are embryonic dramas in which an effort is made to visualize scene and character, as though he were writing for the stage." [71] Sterne was admittedly eager to catch the attention of readers, and there is no doubt that he sought theatrical effects because they offered a lively means of presentation. Throughout *Tristram,* the narrator refers to it as a dramatic work or a whimsical theatre or farce, with the characters being introduced and activated upon its stage.

By using this frame of reference, Sterne can be the omniscient manipulator with perfect authority for any arbitrary change of scene. Referring to Toby's campaigns, he says that they "may make no uninteresting underplot in the epitasis and working up of this drama.—At present the scene must drop—and change for the parlour-side." [72] Shortly thereafter, he consciously prepares the reader "for the entrance of Dr. Slop upon the stage." When he wants to break into the novel, he often suspends the action by dropping a curtain over the scene, just as he will resolve an awkward transition by calling on the reader to help him wheel off the scenery, clear the theatre, and "that done, my dear friend Garrick, we'll snuff the candles bright,—sweep the stage with a new broom, —draw up the curtain, and exhibit my uncle Toby dressed in a new character." [73] Belying his admission to Cradock, he even interrupts a passage to exclaim, and perhaps again hint, "O Garrick!—what a rich scene of this would thy exquisite powers make! and how gladly would I write such another

to avail myself of thy immortality, and secure my own behind it." [74]

Visual and theatrical effects obviously help to orient the
audience in the worlds of Sterne's and Diderot's fiction. But
neither author was always willing to spoon-feed his readers.
Probably the most confusing device they both employ is their
use of associative interruptions and digressions. This is stimulated not only by their wish to break down popular concepts
of the novel, but also by their curiosity about man's inner
life, by their delight and fascination in the reflections of the
mind.

Diderot is intensely interested in mental activity and associations. If his audience has a tendency to think in fairly
rigid patterns, he takes care to break them. Much of the
amusement he derives from *Jacques,* for instance, is involved
with anticipating the Reader's assumptions and promptly
shattering them. Diderot's basic motivation is not altogether
humorous, however. It is an aspect of his serious attempts
to restore man to a more natural existence, to liberate him
from set, artificial modes of living and thinking. He is attracted to eccentrics, he says in the *Neveu de Rameau,* because they interrupt tiresome uniformity and act like cata-
lytic agents on society. The very form and content of the
satire are dependent on the presence of the uninhibited
Nephew whose thoughts, like Diderot's, are his doxies.

In *Jacques,* associative devices occur on two levels. One is
the author-Reader plane where a number of the interpolated stories have direct reference to the conversation Diderot
is carrying on with the Reader. The other is within the frame
of the story of Jacques and his Master. The most obvious example is Jacques's damning of the innkeeper because he is

associated in Jacques's mind with the chain of events that has led to Jacques's wound. But there are subtler variations of the same process. Frequently the Master and Jacques are either inattentive to each other or cause digressions from the main story of their respective mental flights. At one point, Diderot even explains that whenever the Master was in a bad mood, Jacques would fall silent, start dreaming, and only break the quiet by an observation "which was joined in his mind, but which was as disconnected in the conversation as reading a book by skipping pages." [75] Diderot's own sensitivity to such mental jumps, as he called them, is evident both in his own writings and in his well-known remarks to Sophie Volland about conversation. [76]

Sterne's characteristic digressions and interruptions are, as he has pointed out, essential to the very structure of the novel itself, and Sterne elaborates and stresses them considerably more than Diderot does. Thoroughly in keeping with Tristram's family traits, they are inspired by association of ideas. This makes for further confusion, because the narrator's associations are often so free that it is impossible to reconstruct the chain, and at times the transitions are deliberately effaced. Digressions, as Sterne has stated, are part of the Shandean sunshine, and Sterne uses them to provide the sort of variety that so fascinated Diderot in conversation.

They likewise serve as devices for other important elements in the novel. Characterization is one, as previously indicated, and suspense is another. For example, at a most crucial moment in Captain Shandy's suit for the widow Wadman, the narrator purposely suspends the action to go off on a digressive mock invocation which leads him, by association, to the story of Maria. A more formal treatment would have placed the tale in Book VII with the rest of Tristram's continental adventures, but Sterne deliberately saves it for Book ix. Digressive interruptions also help Sterne solve technical problems that arise. Just as Diderot will engage the Reader in conversation while waiting for Jacques and his Master to be reunited, so Sterne uses digression as a transitional device. Interpolating what appears to be material from the *Fragment,* he bridges the Shandy entourage's journey from Shandy Hall to the meeting which is to review the question of Tristram's christening.

But for experimental fiction the most significant operation of both brief and extended digressions is their function to provide useful hints about the course of the novel. As early as the sixth chapter of Book i, Sterne requests the audience to give him credit for more wisdom than may seem apparent. Later, in chapter twenty, he makes the reader go back over the previous chapter as a lesson that the "mind should be accustomed to make wise reflections, and draw curious conclusions as it goes along." Evidently, Sterne has no great faith that his advice has been effective, for well toward the end of Book iii he is admonishing his "unlearned reader" to read carefully or "I tell you beforehand, you had better throw down the book at once." He adds that without much reading—and by this, he explains, he means knowledge—the audience will be completely baffled. Inasmuch as "wise reflections" constitute an integral step in the process of gaining knowledge, as any disciple of Locke would agree, the whole matter depends on the reader's studiously following the directions outlined in the twentieth chapter of Book i. By paying heed to passing—indeed, digressive—clues, the reader will find that his familiarity with different themes in the novel is gradually developed.

For instance, in chapter seven of Book ii, there is a brief

reference to "a shock" that Toby has experienced in his affair with the widow Wadman. At the end of Book IV, Sterne is impatient, he says, to begin the amours. A little more information is revealed in the last chapter of Book VI with Susannah's report that the captain has fallen in love. Having spent an entire volume in digression, Sterne concludes Book VII with the hope of proceeding at once with the story of Toby's courtship. Throughout Book VIII, he improvises a number of little sallies in that direction. Finally, toward the end of Book IX, he correctly exclaims that he has "anticipated what it was a dozen times; but there is still fire in the subject—allons." At last, shortly before the conclusion of the novel, he explains what caused Captain Shandy's innocent amazement which he first mentioned early in Book II. It has taken him, intermittently, eight volumes to come to the heart of the matter, and the dénouement should be no surprise to the audience. But by assorted digressions, Sterne has managed to imbue it with enough fire so that the reader is still curious to learn Toby's reaction.

Sterne, of course, develops a fundamental method out of digressions, whereas Diderot seems content to hint at their possibilities. But Diderot does use those interruptions which so plague the Reader who is trying to follow the "story" for a very interesting and advanced manipulation of time. In *La Religieuse,* he is always careful to keep a distinction between the time past of Suzanne's account and the time present of her interpolated comments. In *Jacques,* however, he goes a step beyond this. He differentiates between experience on two levels—the italicized interruptions of the Hostess' tale or the breaks and hesitations in Jacques's recital as he shows concern over his unruly mount—and he also mingles layers of time. By the latter practice, he reinforces the notion of the

simultaneity of experience. In the story of the poet of Pondi-
cherry, Diderot participates in time present with the Reader
and time past with the poet, and both have equal significance.
The Master, *now,* becomes violently moved by something that
happened to Jacques years ago, just as Jacques actively fears
Mme de La Pommeraye as he listens to the Hostess tell her
story. Characters are reliving and reacting to what has happened to others, and for the moment it becomes an integral
part of their lives. When this occurs—and for Diderot, unlike Sterne, it does not form a basic method—the concept of
time by the clock breaks down, the barriers between truth
and fiction are destroyed, and real and imaginary or vicarious
experience are fused into one. The audience can then better
appreciate Diderot's mocking advice to the Reader not to
confuse appearance with reality.

Actually, the most dramatic example of such a fusion is
to be found in Sterne, who began by making it a basis for
his entire novel, but eventually decided to employ it as a
device. Professor MacLean has convincingly demonstrated
that the time scheme of *Tristram Shandy,* a scheme Sterne
derived from Locke's theories of duration, is completely realistic. Indeed, its realism is so marked that the reader hardly
notices it and becomes an unwitting accomplice. Sterne's plan
was "to make his novel temporally realistic to the minute by
providing the reader with one hour's reading for every wak-
ing hour in the life of his hero, a program he completed with
considerable care and success through the first day." [77]

In chapter thirty of Book III,[78] Sterne leaves the brothers
Shandy for half an hour, he says, while he explains one of
Walter's eccentricities. Eight chapters later,[79] he stops to announce that he is five minutes overdue and still has not finished his explanation. Finally, after the interpolated story

of Slawkenbergius, he returns in the second chapter of Book
IV: "My father lay stretched across the bed as still as if the
hand of death had pushed him down, for a full hour and a
half before he began to play upon the floor with the toe of
that foot which hung." [80] Presumably, in the original edition one would have spent an hour and a half, from chapter
thirty of Book III to chapter two of Book IV, in reading and
reflection. Although after chapter thirteen of Book IV Sterne
discontinued this project, doubtless realizing the inordinate
complexity of his plan, he managed to apply a strikingly original device to the better part of four volumes.

It is clear that in keeping with the avowedly crack-brain
purpose of Sterne's book, some of his devices are simply amusing tricks which he plays on his "gentle reader": the inked-in
block of mourning for Yorick, for instance, the diagrams of
the sporadic progress of the novel, or the blank page for the
reader to fill in with his own impressions of the widow Wadman. Yet some of Sterne's unconventional measures are, like
his time scheme, attempts at graphic realism. A series of long
dashes represents Toby, humming over a letter; asterisks
broken by brief words render Walter's quasi-silent researches
or the whispered gossip that pervades the town after Tristram's latest misfortune. Simply because Sterne will use certain techniques even as a source of personal amusement at
the expense of readers and writers is not reason enough to
condemn him of trickery rather than artistry.[81] Both he and
Diderot find in such devices not only excellent vehicles for
conveying fictional realism but also a means for exploiting
their originality and individuality as writers. In their two
most experimental novels, they are seeking what Sterne calls
a reflective kind of book.

There is no denying that Sterne tends to be more volatile
than Diderot. The digressions of *Tristram,* for instance, are

less controlled than the flights of conversation in *Jacques* or the *Neveu de Rameau*. This does not mean that Sterne did not know what he was doing; that he could restrain himself if he thought it was to his advantage is proven by the *Sentimental Journey*. Diderot's digressions are tighter because there is usually a serious motivation for them in all his writings. He has an argument or a problem that can be woven into his work by this method. Consequently, the digressive interruptions of *Jacques* spring from more limited points of departure;[82] they are not so spontaneous as the wilder patterns of association in *Tristram*.

Yet Sterne, even at his maddest, has an underlying purpose behind his most whimsical tricks. Like Diderot, he proclaims his independence and asserts, in the fourth chapter of Book I, that he will write the way he wants, following nobody's rules. He is not above deliberately misplacing a couple of chapters as an object lesson to the world "to let people tell their stories their own way." Sterne's way perforce is Shandean, and by posing as a carefree, unpredictable narrator, he can hardly be accused of committing any errors. Diderot gives himself the same authority by emphasizing that he is not a "novelist" but an "historian." If Diderot deprecatingly mentions what he *could* do if he were writing a novel, Sterne goes him one better and Shandaically points out what he actually does. At the risk of appearing paradoxical, both writers would insist that they are being constructive, not contrary, and that their seemingly perplexing book are, as experimental fiction, truly representative of the empirical tradition.

FORM AND STRUCTURE

Although the experimental method constitutes a valid discipline, many of the past critics of Diderot's and Sterne's works, while agreeing that both men were experimental, state or imply that they were lacking in method. Twentieth-century critics have gone far to correct this judgment, but it is no easy matter to refute briefly a prejudice that has existed for more than a century. In all fairness to earlier critics, it should be pointed out that both Sterne and Diderot seem to have taken perverse pleasure in encouraging myths about their careless writing habits. Goethe, referring to Diderot, was one of the first to recognize what damage could be done, and acutely foresaw its results: "His contemporaries, even his friends, used to reproach him for knowing how to write fine pages without knowing how to write a fine book. This kind of talk is repeated, it takes root, and thus, without further scrutiny, the glory of an eminent man is weakened." [83]

Sterne deliberately fostered, throughout his correspondence and *Tristram,* a similar kind of talk by suggesting that disorder was the keynote to his work. He has planted assorted remarks in *Tristram,* declaring that he writes too hastily to check the sources of his quotations, that he writes the first sentence and trusts to God for the second, that his pen governs him, that he never blots out anything. Frequent echoes are to be found in his letters in assertions such as that he never speaks or writes a premeditated word; that his book has appeared "hot as it came from my Brain, without one Correction"; or, again, that his pen governs him, not he his pen. These comments, "substantiated" by the superficial chaos of *Tristram,* have led critics from his own time through the early part of the twentieth century to take him at face value and agree that he is generally slipshod.

Diderot was a hardly less Shandean accomplice. In his *Pensées sur l'interprétation de la nature* of 1754, he says that he will let his thoughts follow each other from his pen just as the subjects present themselves for his consideration. This, he says, is the best way of representing the activity and progress of his mind.[84] More than a decade later, in the *Essai sur la peinture* of 1765, he exclaims, "Who knows where the chain of ideas will lead me? not I!"[85] In 1780, Diderot tells Meister that *La Religieuse* was written "au courant de la plume," just as he confides to the reader of the *Neveu de Rameau* that he abandons his mind to its wantonness and lets it follow the first idea, wise or mad, that comes along.

This is all very spontaneous and there probably is a good deal of truth in it, but perhaps Diderot, like Sterne, is being a trifle too artless. They both elaborate roles for themselves, exaggerating yet cleverly maintaining a relationship to fact, so that they cannot be accused of lying completely. The concluding statements of Diderot's *Eloge,* for example, are disarming until one refers to Arnaud's preface to the work, where the identical lines appear as a quotation from Richardson himself. Sterne at the mercy of his hectic pen is a delightful image, but frequent repetitions make one suspect that he protests too much and is not to be trusted altogether.

Indeed, one of the inferences to be drawn from the preceding chapters of this study is that while Diderot and Sterne are self-conscious writers, they are anything but unconscious writers. The two states are mutually exclusive, and there is no doubt that both men were acutely aware of how they wrote and what they wrote. External evidence pertaining to their work as well as internal evidence in the form and structure of their writings shows that although they may not have been methodical men, they successfully developed appropriate methods. The parallels between them here are marked not so much by similarity in detail as by the fact that Diderot and Sterne, each in his own way, give the lie to accusations of irresponsible haphazardness.

Actually, Diderot's notes to Catherine of Russia on his manner of working provide a fairly clear definition of his own method. While he does not fail to mention the usual points about the celerity with which he composes—"the faster · I write, the better I write"—and insists that he rarely revises, he also tells her that *before* writing he absorbs himself completely in his material and after that he organizes the ideas which he has jotted down. This procedure would indicate that whereas Diderot did not carefully plan every detail in advance, he surely must have thought out fairly completely the major lines of the central arguments which he later developed with such rapidity. Moreover, if the discipline required for his duties as editor of the *Encyclopédie* was not indigenous to his nature—as the charming fable of the nightingale and the cuckoo would imply [86]—he certainly managed to impose it on himself successfully. And the unpublished Vandeul manuscripts, according to the preliminary report, constitute a telling refutation of Diderot's negligence.[87] It becomes increasingly likely that Diderot was not playing the game altogether fairly when he encouraged people to regard him as a disorganized enthusiast, and that some critics have been taking him too much at his word.

Professor Yvon Belaval is one of the recent scoffers at the "legend" of Diderot's blundering, and cites the careful organization of the revised and definitive version of the *Paradoxe sur le comédien*.[88] He could also have added such tightly constructed works as Diderot's *Réfutation suivie de l'ouvrage d'Helvétius intitulé "L'Homme"* or his article "Encyclopédie." Diderot's writings are no more diffuse than his aims require. Jean Pommier, examining the *Lettre sur les sourds et muets,* mentions Diderot's preference for the epistolary form because of its latitude for tangents and possible extraneous flights. He believes that Diderot used this genre because it gave him the most freedom until he found an even more fluid one, the dialogue.[89] This basic principle underlying Diderot's choice applies to all his works. Whenever possible, he always seeks and uses frames of reference that afford him much free-play—letters, dialogues, memoirs, *Salons,* interviews. The freedom of form of his literary endeavors is not an isolated characteristic, but part of this general tendency. He shows a conscious desire for easy, natural expression, and consequently there is no set or preestablished pattern. He uses whatever suits his themes and purpose, and it is important to note that he never sacrifices these themes to waywardness. Diderot was always too concerned with content to let his experiment get out of hand.

In *Ceci n'est pas un conte,* he develops the platitude that there are good men and bad women—and its reverse—into a neatly balanced contrast of characters and stories. The structure of the *Entretien d'un père avec ses enfants* is composed of three separate discussions, all variations on the main theme of the justness of laws and the advisability of submitting to them. In *La Religieuse,* he so constructs Suzanne's story that each of her experiences reveals new features of the cloistered life, and in this way the story emphasizes the thesis of the novel. For the *Neveu de Rameau,* Diderot needs an appropriate frame for the realistic delineation of his eccentric, for the analysis of his place in society, for the exposure and condemnation of his group, and for a discussion of aesthetics, ethics, and genius. All this must still have some relation to the protagonist because he and Diderot furnish the unity. Diderot resolves his problem by using the old Roman concept of satire, and to make it more convincing, the Nephew admits that his thoughts and speech are disordered. Conversation forms the basis for the structure of the dialogue, and it appears to be freely associative. But it is selective, not uncontrolled, for Diderot makes sure to air all the major themes.

The device of conversation also becomes a key to the organization of *Jacques*. There are conversations occurring on two major levels in the novel—that of Diderot and the Reader and that of Jacques and his Master. Jacques's narration of his love story is not only a burlesque of the current popular vogue; it also helps to unify the novel. Yet it is constantly broken into by the Master, by Diderot or the Reader, by odd happenings, by new tales, just as Diderot and the Reader interrupt each other. These seemingly arbitrary breaks in the continuity are not purposeless. One of the main aims of the novel is a satire of fatalism, that system so paradoxically defended by the hero. Lest anyone else espouse Jacques's view, Diderot takes care to demonstrate that there is no predestined arrangement. Chance, Jacques's true inscriber of the great scroll, under different guises upsets everything at any time. The audience, juggling the two levels, has no more security than Jacques or the Reader, the Master or Mme de La Pommeraye. Moreover, it has to contend with a confusing barrage of interpolated stories.

There are some fifteen of these interpolations, ranging from the polished, classical tale of Mme de La Pommeraye to brief incidents such as the adventures of the steward and the baker's wife. Actually, most of these diverse stories have a fairly clear connection with the novel, if one examines them closely. They are associated either with the level of Jacques and his Master, or with the level of Diderot and the Reader. The result seems to be a parallel and sometimes an interplay between the two planes. Diderot tells the story of Jacques and his Master to the Reader, and they both comment on it.

Jacques tells his stories to his Master; they also make comments and even exchange places. Breaks and suspensions occur on both planes of conversation. Often they are quite logical in relation to Diderot and the Reader, but are completely divorced from Jacques and his Master.

Is it not therefore possible that one level acts as a kind of reflection of the other? The Master is Jacques's audience, the Reader is Diderot's audience; both audiences ask questions, both comment and interrupt, both want to have stories told them; and the Master and the Reader are further associated because Diderot has pointedly remarked on the similarity: "He is a man, passionate like you, Reader; curious like you, Reader; troublesome like you, Reader; questioning like you, Reader. Why does he ask questions? That's a fine question! He asks so he can learn so he can repeat like you, Reader." [90]

The structure of *Jacques* is no more arbitrary than that of the *Neveu de Rameau*. Within the loose framework of an experimental novel, there is an interior organization of two parallel planes, sometimes complete in themselves, sometimes interacting on each other, which gives Diderot more liberty to manipulate his themes and materials. Far from subordinating these themes, the organization really points them up so that it is with considerable justification that J. Robert Loy has suggested that thematically the structure of *Jacques* revolves around three major subjects—an experiment in the realistic novel, a refutation of fatalism, and a discussion of morals.[91] One should bear in mind that it was *after* he had referred to *Jacques le fataliste* that Goethe said, "The *Neveu de Rameau* gives a new example of the art with which Diderot knew how to bring together in a harmonious whole the most heterogeneous details taken from reality." [92]

But in order for Diderot to achieve a "harmonious whole,"

he was often forced to rewrite, despite his disclaimers to Catherine that this was not part of his method. Naigeon says that the manuscript of *La Religieuse* which he received from Diderot was full of corrections,[93] and Grimm has emphasized the care Diderot applied to the preliminary letters to Croismare.[94] The *Deux amis de Bourbonne* and the *Entretien d'un père avec ses enfants* were also worked over. The *Deux amis* is not in itself a particularly good proof. Diderot does follow his notes to the tale by scattering natural traits and related circumstances, but he does not develop his characters and he really fails to utilize the eloquence which helps form the illusion. As a brief report it is adequate, but as a *conte historique* it requires considerable amplification. Nevertheless, Diderot revised and added to it even after it appeared in the *Correspondance littéraire,* reworked it for inclusion in a collection of Gessner's *New Idylls,* and corrected it further after the first German and French publications.[95]

Another illustration of Diderot's method of revision is to be found in his tendency to work additional material into his writing after he has already drawn up the major part. He does this with the *Deux amis,* for instance, and with the *Neveu de Rameau.*[96] He also tampered with *La Religieuse* many years after he had written it. He probably revised it considerably, for Naigeon says that the copy of the manuscript Diderot gave him shortly before his death included two important additions as well as numerous corrections.[97] It was sometime in 1780 or 1781 that Diderot added these passages, and one of them must have been the bulk of the first long letter which Suzanne writes to the Marquis. At the same time, he altered the letters constituting the *Préface-Annexe* so that it was transformed into an integral part of the story.[98]

Such apparent "afterthoughts" still remain within the framework Diderot has originally developed before he begins writing at all. He tells Catherine that it is his practice to scribble on bits of paper any ideas that may come to him while he is doing his preliminary thinking. He saves these, obviously with an eye to fitting them in at some appropriate place. It is plain that a number of the interpolated stories in *Jacques* come from this source, or from mental notes. Nicole and her suitor find their earlier counterparts in Taupin and Thisbé in a letter of 6 November 1760; Père Hudson's accident with the hackney-coach has already appeared in the *Salon* of 1765.

It seems to follow quite logically that while Diderot certainly did improvise spontaneously, he also revised, and did so a good deal more than he cared to admit. If his material requires a formal structure, he is capable of achieving it. When his method is experimental, it is deliberately so. Despite his comments to the contrary, one reaches the almost unavoidable conclusion that Diderot knew very well what he was about. He also knew what others were about. Possibly his delight in Sterne's wisest and maddest of books was increased by his ability to see through its author's hoax and by his recognition that here was a kindred spirit who could share Diderot's relish in occasionally duping his audience.

In retrospect, it seems singular that those Victorians who concentrated on pointing out Sterne's hypocrisy did not carry over their investigations to his pronouncements on his method. They would have found considerable evidence to further their condemnation, starting right with his prefatory quotations. Belying Sterne's comment that he is in too much of a hurry to check their origins, every quotation, from the lines from Epictetus to account for his interests to the passage

from Ozell's Rabelais to explain his procedures [99] and the
selection from Erasmus, via Burton, to state his position,[100]
is directly applicable to his book.

Most of Sterne's leading comments about his procedures
are to be found in the hints he has scattered throughout
Tristram. "My way is ever to point out to the curious, different tracts of investigation, to come at the first spring of the
events I tell," he announces in Book i. This is not a red her-
ring but a clue, as is his assertion that he so prides himself
that "my reader has never yet been able to guess at any thing"
that he will tear out a page rather than let the reader apprehend what is in it. He is, like Diderot, a very rapid writer,
and his fashion of working, appropriate to his speed, seems
to be a matter of thinking ahead constantly while simultaneously keeping in mind what has gone before. The ultimate
effect of Sterne's method is a psychological realism so marked
that it has led many people to agree with B. H. Lehman's
conclusion, "That the resulting imagined world has more
reality than a stripped and ordered account there is considerable evidence to show." [101] In a larger sense—and one equally
as important for Sterne as for Diderot, even though their
purposes differ—this method provides for much freedom.
This was what Sterne wanted, of course, for he had told
Dodsley that he intended to include everything he found
amusing. If he is to point out different tracts of investigation,
often with a maximum of spontaneity, he needs plenty of
latitude.

But Sterne watches himself closely and keeps track of what
is going on, although his manner purports to be devious.
When Toby commences a sentence in the twenty-first chapter of Book i, Sterne does not forget it. He assures the reader
in the fourth chapter of Book ii that when he has completed

the business at hand he will return to Toby and his sentence
—which he does in chapter six. He explains that he has de-
layed some information for a hundred and fifty pages because
it is more advantageous in a later place: "Writers had need
look before them, to keep up the spirit and connection of
what they have in mind." Later on, in Book III, he professes
to be in a quandary precisely because he has been looking
before himself. He can tell an anecdote at once, or save it for
two future situations, "—for it will do very well in either
place;—but then if I reserve it for either of those parts of
my story—I ruin the story I'm upon;—and if I tell it here—I
anticipate matters, and ruin it then." [102] Toward the end of
Book VI he advises the reader:

. . . when a man is telling a story in the strange way I do mine,
he is obliged continually to be going backwards and forwards to
keep all tight together in the reader's fancy—which, for my own
part, if I did not take heed to do more than at first, there is so much
unfixed and equivocal matter starting up, with so many breaks
and gaps in it. . . .[103]

Although he deliberately gets entangled in his sentence and
has to start the chapter again, it is evident that the clergyman
is not trusting to God for the next line; he is governing his
pen himself.

The need for this is obvious, and beneath the apparent
chaos of *Tristram* one can find evidence of much care and
planning. This is required particularly because of the structure and composition of the novel. Unlike the *Sentimental
Journey,* which was composed all at one period, *Tristram* was
written over eight years' time. From passing references [104] it
seems likely that Sterne regarded the novel as an experiment.
The structure is not worked out consistently from the beginning but goes through three major stages. The original

plan of one day's reading for each day in his hero's life carries into Book IV, as pointed out earlier.[105] There, in the last chapter, Sterne says, "From this moment I am to be considered as heir-apparent to the Shandy family—and it is from this point properly that the story of my Life and my Opinions sets out." From here to the twentieth chapter of Book VI, it is indeed Tristram's opinions and selected memories and adventures which generate the progress of the novel. But something is gradually crowding out the hero's dominating presence. Sterne indicates it at the end of Book IV when he apologizes to the reader: ". . . that I have not been able to get into that part of my work, toward which I have all the way looked forwards, with so much earnest desire; and that is the Campaigns, but especially the amours of my uncle Toby." [106]

The reason he was prevented from immediately developing this "Cervantic cast" was that Volumes III and IV appeared in January, 1761. By the following September, having completed Book V, he was working on Book VI and telling a correspondent, "These two volumes are, I think, the best.— I shall write as long as I live, 'tis, in fact, my hobbyhorse: and so much am I delighted with my uncle Toby's imaginary character, that I am become an enthusiast." [107] This is a leading confession because in chapter twenty of Book VI, Sterne abruptly announces a new scene of events, and from there until the end of the volume, Toby's campaigns and overtones of his amours hold the field. It has been suggested that this switch was the result of public disapproval of Sterne's indecencies.[108] But in view of Sterne's comments above, and his belief that the amours "are the choicest morsel of my whole story," it is more likely that he was carried away by Toby. Captain Shandy was an immediate favorite with his audience, a fact that the author could not fail to exploit, and Sterne appears to have had no advance reserve about the treatment of the amours. He advises his readers that when he reaches them, he will not be "at all nice" in the choice of his words.

Moreover, the change in emphasis is not wholly unprepared for. It has been noted above [109] that Sterne begins hinting about Toby's amours early in Book II and gradually builds up to the dénouement in Book IX. He was not so much the "enthusiast" that he was unable to appreciate the popularity of Toby while there was still time to develop the amours from a steadily growing underplot to a major subject.[110]

Sterne's labors were interrupted by an extended visit to France from January, 1762, to June, 1764. Even though he tried to write the next installment of *Tristram* once he and his family were settled in Toulouse, he really did not seriously take up work again until the fall of 1764, after he had returned alone to England. By then, he was desperate for both money and materials for his book, so he hit on the idea of making over some of his travel notes into a comic tour of France for Volume VII.

After the publication of Volumes VII and VIII in January, 1765, Sterne must have modified his pace. It was not until he had returned from another trip to the Continent, from October, 1765, to June, 1766, that he began the ninth volume. But his initial plan of two volumes a year—a plan which in itself reveals a definite method—had been altered. He tells a friend: ". . . at present I am in my peaceful retreat, writing the ninth volume of Tristram—I shall publish but one this year, and the next I shall begin a new work of four volumes, which when finish'd, I shall continue Tristram with fresh spirit." [111] Actually, he was eager to produce his *Sentimental Journey,* thereby hoping for a more favorable reputation. Far from being a repetition of Smollett's *Travels through France and Italy,* which had appeared in 1766, Sterne's book would present a wholly different and, he hoped, more laudable attitude. His last letter written in England before he left for his first trip in 1762 had expressed pleasure that his correspondent had been moved to tears by the story of Le Fever; he added that Garrick, too, had thought it sublime.[112] Comparing the reaction to this tale with the criticisms of Volumes vii and viii, Sterne could not help but note that while people admired the pathetic, they were growing weary of the Shandys. Sterne's own trouble in finding material for Volume vii suggests that he himself had had about enough. He finished off Volume ix in short order and set about gathering a list of subscribers for the *Sentimental Journey* in the winter of 1767.

The remarkable aspect of *Tristram,* of course, is that despite its spasmodic composition, the book really does have basic coherence. Much has been written in the past two generations to prove that *Tristram* has a planned structure. And indeed, to examine in detail its organization would be merely to repeat what numerous recent critics have said—for Sterne, perhaps even more than Diderot, has come into his own in the twentieth century as the darling of the moderns. Consequently, the discussion will be restricted to some major points.

It is necessary, however, to call attention to an article which has brought new insights to the form and themes of *Tristram.* D. W. Jefferson has contributed an excellent study of this subject. It is true that the book has many and various themes, and Sterne rarely chooses to limit himself by following closely a single line of thought. But Mr. Jefferson, in relating the major and more consistent elements of the comedy to the tradition of scholastic wit as Sterne found it in Rabelais,

Swift, and Pope, has provided a broad, unifying basis for both the content and form of the novel. His belief that Sterne is perhaps the last great writer in the tradition of learned wit and his development of this statement within the context of a historical pattern admirably demonstrate Sterne's skillful handling of variations on a common theme.[113]

What Sterne has done to keep up a further connection in his work is to rely on Locke, as he often admits. He thereby manages to maintain certain elements which are common at all times to the organization, even though the structure changes. The fundamental association of ideas helps to make his characters consistent and gives rise to his digressive method. By carrying over digressions from one book to another, Sterne links his novel together in a fluid but intellectually logical pattern. This is particularly successful for flashbacks and for the gradual development of a subject through a kind of musical or thematic construction. When the structural unity breaks down, he can still fall back on the familiar associations and digressions of characters and narrator.

Association of ideas also determines the concept of time. Sterne reminds the reader "that the idea of duration, and of its simple modes, is got merely from the train and succession of our ideas" [114] and later devotes an entire chapter to a Lockean lecture on this subject. It puzzles Captain Shandy to death, but Sterne understands it very well. In an unedited fragment, he includes some relevant particulars derived from Locke and Fontenelle:

The mind can in Idea multiply and increase any finite space or quantity infinitely, and also infinitely divide and subdivide it: nor can it find anywhere on either side any necessity of setting bounds to the works of creation, or fixing ye stage where ye scale of being must end. . . . By a different conformation of its senses a Creature might be made to apprehend any given Portion of space, as greater, or less in any Proportion, than it appears to us. . . . I doubt not also but that by a different conformation of ye Brain a Creature might be made to apprehend any given proportion of time as longer or shorter in any proportion than it appears to us.—I leave it to future ages to invent a method for making a minute seem a year.[115]

Sterne's modesty is touching, but he had already made a minute seem a year countless times, and he "invented" a perfectly good method himself which future ages have utilized in the stream-of-consciousness technique. Conventional chronology by the clock breaks down as Sterne emphasizes the equal immediacy of past and present.[116] Indeed, in the interior monologues of his characters, the past often dominates the present. It is no wonder that Virginia Woolf praises Sterne for stressing the interior life. He uses the very method which is characteristic of Mrs. Woolf's novels. His book either stands still in space and moves about in time, or stands still in time and moves about in space. For Locke's theories of duration Mrs. Woolf substitutes Bersonian time, but the basic treatment is quite similar. Even certain of Sterne's stylistic devices should have been familiar to her. When, on that fine day in June, Clarissa Dalloway walks across her room, her actions are parenthesized to separate them from her thoughts. Sterne sets the Shandy's actions and Dr. Slop's references to Obadiah in parentheses to distinguish physical movement and mental reaction from Slop's reading of the excommunication.

But while Sterne deliberately shatters his readers' expectations of traditional chronology, he also includes time by the calendar. Some of this refers to actual dates during the composition of the novel, but another feature supports the contention of most modern critics that Sterne has more method than madness. Theodore Baird has convincingly demonstrated that there is a specific background of calendar time against which the subjective or psychological time functions. The interweaving of these two frames and Sterne's use of Tindal's version of Rapin's *History of England* as the main source for historical details and allusions again reveal the author to be a careful planner, for the project is intricate.[117]

He has a less complex design in the *Sentimental Journey,* but in another way, perhaps, his problem is even more difficult. The author of *Tristram Shandy* had decided to write a book to convince people "that my feelings are from the heart, and that that heart is not of the worst molds." [118] Such an aim is clearly premeditated, and in view of Sterne's current reputation, it doubtless required a good deal of care in its execution. The framework of his travels gives him sufficient excuse for free-play, but Sterne refuses to exploit it—partly because he does not need to, since the book was composed without interruption, and partly because he does not want to. As a matter of fact, the *Sentimental Journey* only faintly echoes the organization of *Tristram.* Sterne does not set out to be willfully confusing here; he wants to be understood, and most of the novel does not bear out the Shandean beginning. When he saves material for later inclusion, he says so. Association of ideas still provides for digressions, like the tale of the Marquisina di F or Mme de Rambouliet, but they are short and controlled. He even apologizes for one brief digression because it has nothing to do with his tour, and begs permission to include another because it is appropriate. By subordinating physical action and clock time to the subjective, he achieves both conciseness and expansion. In the little World Classics edition, it takes him barely a page to get to Calais and fifty pages to get out of it, though he has spent only one hour by the clock there. Sterne deliberately wants this effect; and having often tested it out in an experimental novel, he can handle it with consummate skill.

Consequently, returning now to Sterne's claim that he does not correct or revise, one can see that his word is no more dependable than Diderot's. The manuscript copy of the *Sentimental Journey* bears evidence of extensive emendation. The publisher of *Tristram* was informed that "All locality is taken out of the book—the satire general; notes are added where wanted, and the whole made more saleable—about a hundred and fifty pages added." [119] Sterne tells a well-wisher that as he revises his book he will remove offending embellishments. His statement to another critic of *Tristram,* that he has "seen enough to shew me of the folly of an attempt of castrating my book to the prudish humours of particulars," [120] does not appear to be characteristic of a man incapable of forethought. [121]

Actually, Sterne provides a good deal of material, in addition to what can be inferred from his novels, to refute his Shandean protestations. For one thing, he went to the trouble of keeping a *Letter Book,* a practice Diderot never indulged in, and often entered in it first drafts which he later copied or revised. Frequently, the revision of the original copy could be dressed up a bit, as the situation demanded, and addressed to more than one correspondent. Toward the end of June, 1760, a copy of a letter appearing in the *Letter Book* was sent off to Mary Macartney. Sterne asks that "the Lord" defend him from people "who in lieu of sending me what I sat expecting—a Letter—surprize me with an Essay cut & clip'd at all corners. to me inconsiderate Soul that I am, who never yet knew what it was to speak or write one premeditated word." [122] It is to be hoped that Miss Macartney did not compare notes on premeditation with the "witty widow," Mrs. Fenton, who on the following August 3 received some lines from Sterne, including, "I promised to send you a fine set Essay in the Stile of your female Epistolizers, cut and trim'd at all points.—God defend me from such, who never yet knew what it was to say or write one premeditated word in my whole life." [123]

On June seventh, 1767, he gaily informs a male correspondent that he is "happy as a prince" at Coxwold: "I am in high spirits—care never enters this cottage—I take the air every day in my post chaise, with my two long tail'd horses." [124] Two days later, however, he sees fit to alter his material for inclusion in his *Journal to Eliza:* "I keep a post Chaise & a couple of fine horses, & take the Air every day in it—I go out —& return to my Cottage Eliza! alone—'tis melancholly, what shd be matter of enjoyment; & the more so for that reason—." [125]

There still remains a not wholly resolved controversy as to whether an early love letter Sterne addressed to Elizabeth Lumley, his future wife, was copied, with some changes, for his *Journal to Eliza.*[126] But there is no question at all about a letter of 18 June 1767 to Eliza Draper.[127] It is a literal transcription from Sterne's *Letter Book* of an earlier note to an unnamed countess. Sterne merely substitutes his "dear Bramine" for his "dear lady" or "countess" at the appropriate places.

On that day in early spring, when Sterne, flushed with his first success, told a correspondent that he was selling himself both inside and out,[128] he was being more truthful than he realized. Unlike Diderot, Sterne viewed practically everything he wrote in terms of remuneration. His memorandum of 28 December 1761 suggests that his wife go over various bundles of letters and publish them, in case Sterne died on the Continent, and sometime in 1767 he even jotted down in his *Letter Book* a list of people to whom Mrs. Sterne could apply for making up a collection of his correspondence.

Even that celebrated record of Sterne's feelings, the *Journal to Eliza,* gives rise to considerable speculation.[129] Hardly a page occurs in Professor Curtis's transcription of the *Journal* that does not have corrections and substitutions. These, as well as parts of its introduction, suggest that Sterne may have toyed with the idea of publishing it. Certainly it is not an altogether artlessly spontaneous document. It is difficult to believe that a man completely at the mercy of pathological emotions would stop to recall he had written a good line that he could use again and so copy it into the *Journal,* or copy material out of the *Journal* to use in other letters or in the *Sentimental Journey.* This was no private diary for two people, but an intimate journal written in the tone which Sterne had discovered was very gratifying to his audience. Throughout he seems to be very self-conscious, alert for any choice ideas and phrases. It may well be that a man in his weakened condition would want to preserve experience and sensations; but it also seems likely that Sterne wrote to his Eliza, as he wrote to everyone else, with more than a passing glance at the reading public.

Indeed, the facility with which Sterne could revise and shift material from one piece of writing to another reinforces one's suspicion that this procedure is as indigenous to his method as to Diderot's. Like Diderot, he delights in collecting assorted items for improvisation and allows himself room in both his novels for weaving in additional subject matter.

Interpolations of all kinds abound in *Tristram:* some, like the "Abuses of Conscience," are stolen from Sterne; others, like the tale of Slawkenbergius, are elaborated from another author; [130] and still others clearly manifest a debt to a previous source, such as the obvious relationship between the *Tristrapaedia* and the education of Martin Scriblerus. [131] He intersperses the *Sentimental Journey* with experienced or borrowed incidents and anecdotes, but for the most part he keeps his interpolations concise. As befits the title, the major number of these serve either to reveal sensibility and Sterne's goodwill or to provide little scenes and studies of French types.

The major difference between Diderot and Sterne as improvisers is that whereas the *philosophe* assuredly did borrow from others, he seems to take the most pleasure in elaborating his own ideas. Sterne rarely shows any preference, although if one is looking for the hearty guffaw of the curé of Meudon or the curious sidetracks of the *Essais,* one must go to Rabelais and Montaigne; they are transmuted, not reproduced, by Sterne. Diderot and Sterne do agree, however, in using for extended and transformed innovation the material that they have lifted into their writings.

The respective methods of organization they employ also show that both writers deliberated over their choice of techniques. Here their orientation in empiricism is strongly evident. Form and structure do not so much appear to be superimposed on their work as to rise out of it, according to the demands of the material and the interests of the authors. And the fact that their interests are not always identical marks the differences in their methods but does not refute arguments in favor of an inner coherence. Chance, for instance, plays havoc in the Shandy world, but it is not the source of life-long speculation for Sterne that it is for Diderot. Sterne explicitly states—with some justification, when one compares *Tristram* to *Jacques*—that his book is not written against chance. Accident is part of the amusing incongruity of life, for him; he gives no indication of sharing Diderot's interest in its further implications for the universe and evolution, for scientific discovery and artistic creation.

Indeed, the element that gives Diderot the core of his method is usually an intellectual concept: some idea or series of ideas, a moral argument, an aesthetic theory. Precisely for this reason, he is conscious of the need for some degree of control; the idea must be expressed, not sacrificed to either too formal or too formless a treatment. For Sterne, the preoccupation is not so much intellectual as almost purely creative. There is an intellectual justification for the form—Locke, for example—or an underlying idea like sensibility or Shandeism. But Sterne is perhaps more directly concerned with practice than with putting intellectual ideas into practice.

This contrast in emphasis does not prevent Diderot and Sterne from carrying their respective experiments to a successful conclusion. The interest that their work holds for recent generations disproves both Walter Bagehot's contention of 1864 that *Tristram,* "being, indeed, a book without plan or order, it is in every generation unfit for analysis," [132] and Diderot's mocking suggestion that *Jacques* is "an insipid rhapsody of events, some real, others imaginary, written without grace and distributed without order." Neither Diderot nor Sterne would have been so presumptuous as to declare that the innovation ended with the last pages of their books. But in writing for fame and fortune, the parson succeeded in directing attention to fruitful possibilities for the treatment and expansion of the novel form; and Diderot, at first seeing no serious purpose in the fiction about him, came to associate certain fictional trends with a genre that would reveal new fields of exploitation for the *philosophe* and for the creative artist.

CHAPTER V

STYLE

BOTH Sterne and Diderot have suffered somewhat from the traditional view that "style is the man." Suard, referring to Sterne's writings, says that to read them or to see and hear Sterne is practically the same thing, and holds this resemblance to be "perfect." [1] Folkierski, although he does not share Suard's advantage of proximity, sums up a popular judgment of Diderot:

Diderot writes the way he talks. There is not the slightest possibility of distinguishing his written language from his spoken language; and if the former is sometimes bombastic, one knows very well that he is simply copying the latter in an excess of enthusiasm. [2]

The eighteenth century was, of course, a golden era for conversation and conversationalists, and Diderot and Sterne ranked high among their loquacious contemporaries. It is undeniably true of both writers that the volatility and spontaneity of their temperaments affect their prose. But the self-consciousness which plays so important a role in their methods of composition works against a completely haphazard style; and their characteristic sensibility makes for a heightened awareness not only of impressions, but also of the means of rendering them.

More recently, critics have taken a warier attitude toward these two men who so delighted in spreading tales about

their harum-scarum workmanship. M. Lefebvre warns against
unquestioning acceptance of the notion of Diderot's "spoken
style." It is rather, he says, a skillful, deliberate, and carefully
contrived effect, written in such a way as to preserve the
movement and vivacity of dialogue.[3] Cross agrees that to
"read Sterne was for those in the secret like listening to him,"
but the secret does not involve any unconscious scribbling on
Sterne's part:

Whether speaking or writing, Sterne might be heedless of conventional syntax; but he was always perfectly clear. His dashes
and stars were not mere tricks to puzzle the reader; they stood
for real pauses and suppression in a narrative that aimed to represent the illusion of his natural speech, with all its easy flow,
warmth, and color.[4]

In point of fact, there is a considerable background of material to explain and justify what some people have deemed
to be Diderot's and Sterne's "peculiar" treatment of language
and style. With Sterne, what theory there is must largely be
inferred from the written results, whereas with Diderot one
finds a life-long preoccupation with both theory and practice
that has direct reference to his own modes of expression. Yet
there is a common denominator which joins both men together, and again it turns on the position they occupied in
their own times.

During the eighteenth century in France, an "immense
revolution," in the words of Mary Lane Charles, took place
in the language.[5] The struggle, which reached its force during the second half of the century, has been characterized by
M. Gohin[6] as one between "purists" and "neologists"—the
former favoring the fixing and purifying of the language,
and their opponents championing the right to create new
terms which were often technical and special, and to intro-

duce popular words and expressions. As Professor Brunel has pointed out, it was the partisans of classicism, striving against the enlargement of the language, who complained of changes in usage and the "fantasies" of innovators, while the sympathizers with the spirit of the *philosophes* approved and abetted the intermingling of technical and scientific vocabulary with the literary vocabulary.[7] In its broader sense, the controversy was really a manifestation of the collision between two spirits—that of neoclassicism and that of the Enlightenment, which was exhibiting preromantic tendencies. The curious and unprecedented result of this conflict was

. . . the coexistence alongside each other in the works of the same author of two fundamentally different styles—the one a perpetuation of the classical period, ample, sonorous, swollen with circumlocution and heavily adorned with flat and colorless figures, the other lively, concrete, abrupt, replete with words and phrases gleaned from the everyday speech of peasant and artisan.[8]

Across the Channel, the contest was considerably less forceful because the neoclassic vogue no longer occupied so dominant a position in England as it did in France. According to Professor Baker, the Royal Society, even in its early years, was urging a reform and simplification of the language: "The gradual substitution of a style based on the native idiom and suitable for plain dealing with actualities was of inestimable value to fiction, or was to be in the long run." [9] But while the atmosphere in literate England may have been more favorable to stylistic liberties than in France, there were strong and articulate adherents of certain aspects of the neoclassic spirit. Swift's objection to the fluidity of the English language—although he was not completely opposed to the occasional introduction of new words—took the form of a proposal to establish an academy "for correcting and settling our language, that we may not be perpetually changing as we do." Commenting on this entry in Swift's *Journal to Stella* for June, 1711, Professor Kerby-Miller has said:

Swift had long held strong views on the constant change and continual vulgarization of the English language; he was deeply impressed, as were many writers of the time, with the fact that in contrast to the masterpieces of classical literature those written in English, such as the works of Chaucer, rapidly became unintelligible to the average reader. France had been at work on this problem for almost a century and its means of fixing and refining the language, the Académie française, had already begun to have an appreciable effect.[10]

Dr. Johnson's *Dictionary* was surely a masterful endeavor to fix and purify the language; and although in his Preface Johnson notes the inexorable tendencies—including the "fugitive cant" of the "laborious and mercantile part of the people"—of language toward "corruption" and "decay," his common-sense conclusion is:

It remains that we retard what we cannot repel, that we palliate what we cannot cure. Life may be lengthened by care, though death cannot be ultimately defeated: tongues, like governments, have a natural tendency to degeneration; we have long preserved our constitution, let us make some struggles for our language.[11]

Indeed, there is little doubt that when Johnson commented disparagingly on the oddity of *Tristram Shandy,* the great practitioner of the sonorous phrase had in mind Sterne's erratic style as well as the other perverse features of his book.

The roles that Diderot and Sterne play in this antagonism between the old and the new spirits are both consistent with their personalities and with their activities in other spheres. Rejecting restrictive and artificial rules in the interests of free and natural expression, they sought a living, spontaneous style that would give the writer liberty to revive old words or to introduce new ones as he created an energetic language. Their styles reflect both themselves and their opposition to neoclassic restraints. Nodier's remarks on Diderot's prose could be equally applicable to Sterne's: "spontaneous as the imagination, independent and infinite as the soul, a style which lives by itself. . . ." [12] With their interest in the inner life of man, it is wholly appropriate that they turn to concrete, dynamic expression to render the individual's impression of experience.

And it is also appropriate that they find a point of departure for their experiments with style in the third book of Locke's *Essay Concerning Human Understanding*. It is here that Locke—somewhat belatedly, in the view of Condillac—takes up the problem of the relationship between sensory experience and words. Words, he says, are the "sensible marks of ideas; and the ideas they stand for are their proper and immediate signification." [13] Locke is careful to emphasize the implied distinction, for he stresses the fact that words do not, as some people think, stand for the reality of things, but only for ideas in men's minds. The basic difficulty, of course, is that words are at best inexact marks of ideas. Locke had made the point that all things which exist are particulars, and had insisted on the unreality of universals as distinct from the reality of individual substances. But words, of necessity, belong to the category of universals: while there are proper names for certain specific particulars, the greatest number of words have to be general terms if communication is to be at all possible. Indeed, a major point of Book III is that abstraction is both necessary for and stands in the way of communication:

When it is considered what a pudder is made about *essences,* and how much all sorts of knowledge, discourse, and conversation are pestered and disordered by the careless and confused use and application of words, it will perhaps be thought worth while thoroughly to lay it open.[14]

His devoted follower, Sterne, was to signify his agreement in the very words of the master:

Gentle critic! when thou hast weighed all this, and considered within thyself how much of thy own knowledge, discourse, and conversation has been pestered and disordered, at one time or other, by this, and this only:—What a pudder and racket in Councils about οὐδία and ὑπόδταδις and in the schools of the learned about power and about spirit;—about essences, and about quintessences; —about substances, and about space.—What confusion in greater Theatres from words of little meaning, and as indeterminate a sense! when thou considerest this, thou wilt not wonder at my uncle Toby's perplexities, . . . 'Twas not by ideas,—by Heaven; his life was put in jeopardy by words.[15]

But Diderot was to go even farther. Whereas Locke says that without first experiencing a simple idea one cannot understand the words that convey it—that, for example, one must taste a pineapple before its definition has any meaning— Diderot's Jacques insists that all abstractions are utterly meaningless unless they are associated with a specific experience: "He tried to make his Master conceive that the word 'pain' had no idea attached to it, and that it only began to signify something at the moment when it recalled to our memory a sensation which we had undergone." [16]

Actually, Diderot's researches on language owe more to Condillac's advances on Locke than to Locke himself. Condillac had planned the second part of his *Essai sur l'origine des connaissances humaines* as a supplement and addition to Book III of the *Essay Concerning Human Understanding*. Condillac's contention was that language deserves much study and emphasis because it is the principle which develops and communicates the germ of all ideas. Utilizing what he considered to be a more empirical process, he traced the growth of language from its inception as words of "action"—half cries, half gestures—to its more sophisticated stages. He thereby laid stress on its original emotive values, which Diderot immediately picked up. For literary purposes, Diderot favored an approximation of this first stage, agreeing with Condillac that the sound or tone which is the most appropriate for rendering emotion, or an emotive situation, is the one which imitates the natural cry of passion. In the evolution of languages, however, words gradually developed away from their originally close relationship with experience. At first, they were the names of sensible objects, but later they grew more abstract and the entire syntax became reversed from its natural order.

Sterne was content to dismiss abstractions simply because they interfere with direct communication:

I hate set dissertations—and above all things in the world, 'tis one of the silliest things in one of them, to darken your hypothesis by placing a number of tall, opaque words, one before another, in a right line, betwixt your own and your reader's conception—when in all likelihood, if you had looked about, you might have seen something standing, or hanging up, which would have cleared the point at once.[17]

Diderot, however, was much more specific in his attempts to restore a closer connection between words and what they stand for. The only good definitions, he says in his article "Encyclopédie," are those which gather together all the essential attributives of the object designated by the word.[18] He himself prefers attributives, and for a very good reason: he has a profound distrust of abstractions, which he finds are frequently more misleading than useful. It is all too easy, he explains, to fall into the habit of using them without carefully specifying what one means, to repeat simply what one has been hearing all one's life. This is bad enough for the *philosophe*, whose aim is always to be clearly understood, but it is even more discouraging for the creative artist. And a further reason for Diderot's aversion to abstractions is that they hinder the communication of sense impressions which constitute so vital a part of imaginative language.

Abstractions are lifeless, he believes, and are the farthest removed from sense experience. It is adjectives which carry the living qualities first perceived by sensory organs, he says in the *Lettre sur les sourds et muets* of 1751. Adjectives, ordinarily representing sensible qualities, are therefore first in the natural order of ideas.[19] Consequently, far from being the enemy of the noun, the adjective is really its vital support and justification:

Little by little, one became accustomed to believing that these nouns represented real objects [a danger Locke had earlier warned against]; one regarded sensible qualities as being simply accidents, and one imagined that the adjective was really subordinated to the substantive; whereas, properly speaking, the substantive is nothing and *the adjective is everything*.[20]

It is very possible that it is the adjective to which Diderot is referring when he suggests that he considers the word as an atom of the sensory perception of the whole, as an illumination which briefly reveals the total meaning of an experience: "I regard a certain spoken or written word as though it were a hole suddenly pierced through my door by which I see the inside of the suite; as though it were a ray which suddenly lights up the recesses of a cavern and then goes out." [21]

It is, of course, typical of Diderot's intellectual curiosity that he should examine more fully and even exemplify the two sides of the controversy waged about language during the second half of the eighteenth century. In this way he is representative of both conformist and rebel. The *Lettre sur les sourds et muets* shows that he conceives of two quite different roles of language, the one tending toward fixed precision, the other fluid and suggestive. The former, as Franco Venturi has indicated, is an institutional, analytic language, whereas the latter is artistic and synthetic, by which means the writer can express his emotions and transcend the formalizing rules of grammar.[22] Diderot even goes so far as to imply that one tongue cannot fulfill both purposes and establishes French as the language of reason: "French is made to instruct, clarify, convince; Greek, Latin, Italian, English are made to persuade, move, delude." [23]

As *philosophe,* concerned with elucidation, Diderot takes up the neoclassic interest in stabilizing language. Despite his emphasis in the *Lettre sur les sourds et muets* on the refinement and precision of French, a few years later in his article "Encyclopédie" (1754), he is seeking further exactitude. Agreeing with Condillac that the transmission of knowledge is dependent on words, he says that language must be fixed and transmitted in all its perfection to posterity.[24] He stresses the difficulty of defining words properly and brings considerable interest to the problem of fixing the meaning of words and imbuing them with a permanence that living languages work against.[25] It is as though he realized that in practice his theory in the *Lettre sur les sourds et muets* does not apply completely. It is noteworthy that in Diderot's *own* practice, he will often use quite a different language for his philosophical works from the ones he employs for his more creative and imaginative writings. Professor Brunot has said that Diderot the writer of the *Salons* has almost nothing in common with Diderot the writer of the *Encyclopédie*,[26] although one can occasionally find in Diderot's articles for the *Encyclopédie* the characteristic flights which mark his more creative works.

Stylistically, it is true that he often differentiates his expression, but in theory there is no fundamental contradiction. Diderot, as practitioner of both philosophic and imaginative language, shows a basic concern for communication and a basic dissatisfaction with the insufficiency of language. Actually, it is the artistic, synthetic language rather than the explicative which poses the greater problem for him—a problem he may have shared with Sterne, though Sterne gives little indication of being troubled by it. Diderot, however, is consistently articulate about this subject throughout his writings. As early as the *Lettre sur les aveugles* (1749), he says that language is generally indigent of words for the man with a lively imagination, and he compares the predicament of the writer to that of the perceptive foreigner who has to seek an out-of-the-way phraseology to express his new and original insights.[27] By this comment Diderot shows his awareness of the limitations language imposes on expression, of its tendency away from the direct rendering of experience. By suggesting that the common idiom is insufficient, Diderot is emphasizing the dilemma of the creative artist who finds a paucity of tools.

He takes up the cry again two years later in his *Lettre sur les sourds et muets,* where he is troubled because language is unable to grapple with the experience it undertakes to describe. It is here that he brilliantly sums up the difficulty of all writers who wish, like Diderot and Sterne, to convey the dynamic activity of the mind:

Our mind is a scene of moving tableaux which we ceaselessly pur-
sue in an effort to depict them; we take a great deal of time to
render a faithful portrait: but it exists simultaneously, as a whole:
the movement of the mind does not advance step by step like our
expression of it.[28]

He and Sterne were to solve this difficulty in a manner very
similar to a modern master of impressionistic language. A
recent critic, discussing the works of James Joyce, has made
some comments that are very applicable to his two eighteenth-
century predecessors:

Consciousness is a language for the self; thought is an interior
speech. What is this language? Not a series of arranged and connected propositions, but a rumination which expresses itself in-
completely, which jumps effortlessly from one term to another,
which says only the indispensable. What are the elements of this
expression? Rarely abstract words, for the normal man in normal
situations; but concrete words clothing concrete impressions—
sensations, images—gathered together according to a silent intuition of the force which animates them, an intuition of their import
and their interest for us, without defining these relationships or
marking them either by the rhetoric of style or the categories of
grammar.[29]

Diderot continually returns to this problem of the language
for the self. "One retains practically nothing without the
help of words," he says in the *Pensées détachées sur la peinture,*
"and words practically never suffice to render precisely what
one feels." [30] He even complains in a letter of September,
1766, to Falconet about language, the palette of the poet who
paints with words:

Consider how often it happens that this palette is poor, even for the
genius, who is powerless to enrich it. The poet feels the effect, and
it is impossible for him to render it. His idiom condemns him to

monotony. . . . Nature has endowed him with the soul and the ear; language denies him the instrument.[31]

The result of Diderot's consideration of the problems facing the creative artist is a constant preoccupation with and sensitivity to style. And his treatment of this topic becomes more dynamic through his realization that "each laborer, each science, each art, each subject, has its own language and style." [32] It is quite fitting that he carry over his interest in *idiotismes* into style itself. Just as he has stated that attributives bring vitality to substantives, so he believes that style, through the manipulation of words, rhythms, sounds, and nuances, is the quality that makes a subject live. "Color is to a painting," he says, "what style is to a piece of literature . . . and from all times, style and color have been rare and precious things." [33] Because style is the element that infuses a subject with life, it must remain elastic if it is to convey the great variety and *idiotismes* of experience. Consequently, for imaginative writing Diderot rejects the *grande phrase oratoire* and refuses to impose style on his subject matter. Indeed, Diderot infers, as does Sterne, that style grows out of the material the writer wants to express; it cannot follow the dictates of an artificial, *à priori* norm because its function is to be flexible and dynamic.

This naturally involves both a keen ear and a skillful handling of whatever tools are at the artist's disposal. "I would certainly like to talk to you about the accent appropriate for each passion," Diderot says in the *Second Entretien sur le Fils naturel*. "But this accent becomes modified in so many ways; it is a subject so fleeting and delicate, that I can think of no other which makes one feel so strongly the indigence of all languages which exist and which have ever existed." [34]

Assuredly, formalized and grammatical style cannot express the *cri animal* which is so vital a part of the emotive language of artistic creation. It cannot possibly convey the intimate, interior speech of the individual at the moments when he is most truly himself:

What is it that affects us in the spectacle of a man animated by some great passion? Is it his discourse? Sometimes. But what always excites us is the cries, the inarticulate words, the broken sounds, some monosyllables which escape at intervals, I know not what murmur in the throat, between the teeth.[35]

Sterne admittedly is not concerned with the *cri animal* and the great passions which fascinate Diderot, but in practice he appears to agree with Diderot that the only way to counterbalance the indigence of language is to engage in a kind of "deformalizing" process which results in a marked disorder and often flagrant abuse of conventional syntax and grammar. This is not, however, the product of carelessness or perverse whim. It is an impressionism which owes much to Diderot's and Sterne's sensibility, but which also owes an equal amount to their self-consciousness as writers, to their observation and experiences, and—strikingly, for Diderot—to intellectual theory. Their intention is to develop a style that will convey feeling and moods in such a way that the the experience is not so much described *to* the reader as it is felt and undergone *by* him. And as a result, one cannot find one basic style in their creative works but a series of different styles, each appropriate for the particular experience it is to suggest.

For example, at the conclusion of the *Premier entretien sur le Fils naturel,* Diderot conveys the growing tranquillity and slow movement which accompany the end of a day in the country:

Voyez comme les ombres particulières s'affaiblissent à mesure que l'ombre universelle se fortifie . . . Ces larges bandes de pourpre nous promettent une belle journée . . . Voilà toute la région du ciel opposée au soleil couchant, qui commence à se teindre de violet . . . On n'entend plus dans la forêt que quelques oiseaux, dont le ramage tardif égaye encore le crépuscule . . . Le bruit des eaux courantes qui commence à se séparer du bruit général, nous annonce que les travaux ont cessé dans plusieurs endroits, et qu'il se fait tard.[36]

The suspension points which Diderot places between the sentences emphasize the languid mood of both scene and speaker, and where other punctuation occurs, it serves to unite rather than disrupt. Practically every key noun is accompanied by an appropriate and specific attributive which both lengthens the rhythm and particularizes the description.

In contrast to this, there is the opening of the *Troisième Entretien sur le Fils naturel,* suggesting the agitation which acts as a prelude to an approaching storm:

Le lendemain, le ciel se troubla; une nue qui amenait l'orage, et qui portait le tonnerre, s'arrêta sur la colline, et la couvrit de ténèbres. A la distance où j'étais, les éclairs semblaient s'allumer et s'éteindre dans ces ténèbres. La cime des chênes était agitée; le bruit des vents se mêlait au murmure des eaux; le tonnerre, en grondant, se promenait entre les arbres.[37]

Instead of the easy, uninterrupted flow of the first passage, the sentences here are broken up into short phrases, making for disorder and a quickened rhythm. Again Diderot takes care to provide specific impressions, concluding with the menacing image of the rumbling thunder stalking among the trees, and he utilizes sounds effectively to render the mood.

Indeed, one of the most lyrical passages in all his writing

approaches the condition of music through his use of incantation:

. . . demeure en repos, demeure en repos, reste comme tout ce qui t'environne, dure comme tout ce qui t'environne, jouis doucement comme tout ce qui t'environne, laisse aller les heures, les journées, les années, comme tout ce qui t'environne, et passe comme tout ce qui t'environne.[38]

Here he is conveying the peace and comfort of remaining in tune with nature. The general cyclical movement of the universe is produced by the lulling repetition of "t'environne," while "demeure," "reste," "jouis," "laisse," and "passe"—all appearing at the same place and marking the same rhythm in their respective phrases—suggest the gentle, almost passive activity that harmonizes, hourly, daily, yearly (note the progression) with the greater revolving of the cosmos.

Diderot did not happen to achieve these appropriate effects simply by accident. In the *Essai sur les règnes de Claude et Néron,* at the end of his career, he again demonstrated his sensitivity to different modes of expression:

It is necessary to distinguish two kinds of harmony: one busies itself with caressing the ear by a felicitous choice of expressions and by their various arrangements; the other, much less common, finds its source in sensitive feelings and is inspired in the writer by the diverse passions which arouse him. The first is appropriate for tranquil accounts; the second is suitable for all those circumstances which convey the turmoil of ideas, of feelings, of discourse. The voice of sorrow is weak and plaintive; the voice of anger is vehement. The imitative style of disorder or deformity heaps up spondees and elisions.[39]

Imitative styles of the sort that Diderot and Sterne employ quite clearly imply a conscious effort; indeed, both writers frequently use that heaping process which Diderot mentions. They are, as a critic has said of Diderot, mainly concerned with preserving the artistic experience in an unformulated state, in maintaining a mental mobility that will create its own laws of formulation.[40] It becomes increasingly evident that the disorder of their prose is what Diderot calls the "imitative style of disorder," and that it is the result not of lack of control but of studied spontaneity. In taking language out of the hands of the methodically composing stylists,[41] they are deliberately contriving styles that will reproduce experience.

Sterne, for instance, enters into a prolonged description of Uncle Toby's researches on military science:

He proceeded next to Galileo and Torricellius, wherein, by certain Geometrical rules, infallibly laid down, he found the precise part to be a Parabola—or else an Hyperbola—and that the parameter, or *latus rectum,* of the conic section of the said path, was to the quantity and amplitude in a direct ratio, as the whole line to the sine of double the angle of incidence, formed by the breech upon an horizontal plane;—and that the semi-parameter,—stop! my dear uncle Toby—stop! go not one foot farther than this thorny and bewildered track,—intricate are the steps! intricate are the mazes of this labyrinth! intricate are the troubles which the pursuit of this bewitching phantom knowledge will bring upon thee.—O my uncle;—fly—fly, fly from it as from a serpent.[42]

By the time the reader has waded through this parody of military jargon, he is ready to share the breathlessness with which Sterne mercifully breaks into the account. The interruption is so well placed and so skillfully contrived that after the confused technicalities its freshness and desperation convey the very emotion of one driven nearly to distraction by the lengthy build-up. But Sterne does not stop there. His self-consciousness is such that in a third and more subdued style, he promptly reflects on what he has just achieved:

I would not give a groat for that man's knowledge in pencraft, who does not understand this,—that the best plain narrative in the world, tacked very close to the last spirited apostrophe to my uncle Toby—would have felt both cold and vapid upon the reader's palate;—therefore I forthwith put an end to the chapter, though I was in the middle of my story.[43]

With the same aim of involving the reader in the activity of life itself, he renders a figurative gallop by broken sentences and phrases to achieve a fast rhythm like a helter-skelter ride: "So off I set—up one lane—down another, through this turnpike—over that, as if the arch-jockey of jockeys had got behind me." The pace increases and the style becomes further disjointed and spirited as Sterne uses the exclamations of a bystander to make the passage even more dynamic: "He's flung—he's off—he's lost his hat—he's down—he'll break his neck—see!" [44] In a completely different mood, Diderot uses a similar technique of piling on words to describe the unhappy confusion of Suzanne in *La Religieuse* when she is apprised that her efforts to leave the convent have failed:

Je me remis un peu, je pris la lettre, je la lus d'abord avec assez de fermeté; mais à mesure que j'avançais, la frayeur, l'indignation, la colère, le dépit, différentes passions se succédant en moi, j'avais différentes voix, je prenais différents visages et je faisais différents mouvements.[45]

The first part of the sentence follows, somewhat flatly, almost mechanical motions. Then the passage speeds up, words suggesting different feelings follow each other in quick succession. The reader himself feels the effect of the rushing emotions while they are in action, *before* Suzanne says that various passions are overcoming her. Even more deliberately chaotic is the disorder that characterizes the Nephew's imitation where everything breaks out of control. The words spill over in frenzied abundance as the style catches up the wildly disorganized personality of the performer:

Tantôt avec une voix de basse-taille, il descendait jusqu'aux enfers; tantôt s'égosillant et contrefaisant le fausset, il déchirait le haut des airs, imitant de la démarche, du maintien, du geste, les différents personnages chantants; successivement furieux, radouci, impérieux, ricaneur. Ici, c'est une jeune fille qui pleure, et il en rend toute la minauderie; là, il est prêtre, il est roi, il est tyran, il menace, il commande, il s'emporte, il est esclave, il obéit.[46]

In their desire to achieve a lifelike replica of experience in which the reader has to participate, both Sterne and Diderot often ignore rules of grammar and heap fragments to approximate a particular sensation. Broken, disconnected phrases, complaints and groans, render a graphically impressionistic account of a rough Channel crossing in *Tristram*.[47] Brief directions, terse commands, and carefully situated pauses are used by Diderot to describe the wounded Jacques's being carried to his cot by the officious surgeon and the reluctant hostess.[48] In two short passages, Diderot and Sterne both use the same method of balancing short phrases to evoke the illusion of continual motion. Sterne is dealing with the hectic life of soldiering, and Diderot is describing the compulsive fluttering about in the uneasy atmosphere of a convent:

—harassed, perhaps, in his rear today;—harassing others tomorrow;—detached here;—countermanded there;—resting this night out upon his arms;—beat up in his shirt the next;[49] . . . la journée se passait à sortir de chez soi et à y rentrer, à prendre son bréviaire et à le quitter, à monter et à descendre, à baisser son voile et à le relever.[50]

Common to both these passages is a juxtaposition of opposites in each pair of phrases which emphasizes the futility and frustration of the almost aimless activity.

All these varied effects are attained not by chance but through Diderot's and Sterne's concern for the precision of words that will reinforce the particular and the individual. Rather than using the more general *jupon*, Diderot will refer to the concrete "jupon celadon et or"; instead of an unspecified *canne*, he will write "la canne à pomme d'or." On that momentous occasion when Toby goes to his brother to seek an explanation of the widow Wadman's curiosity, he lays down his pipe "as gently upon the fender as if it had been spun from the unravelling of a spider's web." And when Tristram, having survived the Channel crossing, enters Paris, the reader is informed "that a man with a pale face and clad in black had the honor to be driven into Paris at nine o'clock at night, by a postillion in a tawny yellow jerkin, turned up with red calamanco."

Nowhere are Sterne's precision and control more in evidence than in the *Sentimental Journey,* where the words are carefully selected to enforce the brilliance of the description and, at the same time, to make it as concentrated as possible. The monk's character is particularized by his eyes "and that sort of fire which was in them, which seemed more temper'd by courtesy than years"; by his head, which reminds Sterne of a painting by Guido, "it look'd forwards; but look'd, as if it look'd at something beyond this world"; by his wordless reaction to Sterne's refusal of alms, "—a hectic of a moment pass'd across his cheek, but could not tarry— Nature seemed to have done with her resentments in him; he shewed none." [51] The beautiful Grisset has a "quick black eye"; the kindly old French officer puts his "large pair of spectacles" into a "shagreen case"; the fille de chambre pulls out "a little green sattin purse run round with a ribband of the same colour." Sterne did not seize on these little touches by accident. A manuscript copy of the *Sentimental Journey* in the British Museum gives evidence that when Sterne corrected it, his revisions were purely stylistic: the addition, alteration, or omission of words and phrases, all in the interest of exactitude.[52]

Very frequently in their search for the appropriate word, Diderot and Sterne turn to the old tradition of the language of common speech. They had, of course, read Rabelais and Cervantes, and doubtless marked the refreshing charm of the vernacular. But they also looked about them, as Sterne had suggested, and saw in the living, colloquial jargon—especially in that "fugitive cant" of Dr. Johnson's "laborious and mercantile part of the people"—the true vitality of speech. Despite—or perhaps, *to* spite—the current prejudice against the vernacular, Diderot and Sterne made marked and successful use of it.[53]

Tristram is full of vernacular expressions, many of them coming from the Yorkshire dialect. Characters "droll" rather than joke, Bridget falls "backward soss," animal spirits clutter away like "hey-go mad," love is "galligaskinish," "handy-dandy," or "ninny-hammering," and the cow pays a "pop-visit"—a word which Sterne himself may have introduced—to the bull. Sterne professed in a letter to his publisher to have cut locale out of *Tristram,* but he wisely allowed local speech to remain. It adds piquancy to the style by creating a more precise effect.

Diderot certainly had no objections to the use of archaic expressions, professional jargon—although he might have had some difficulty with Toby's scarps and counterscarps—or new words. Consistent with his belief that language should continue to be a living tongue, he says in the *Essai sur les règnes de Claude et Néron* that if we need a term and if it stirs the imagination and pleases the ear, we should risk it. Languages should always keep on enriching themselves, he adds, by the same channels which drew them out of their initial poverty.[54] He deplores the fact, in both his *Lettre sur les sourds et muets* and his article "Encyclopédie," that there has developed such a gap between the written and spoken word, and, like Sterne, he strives to keep a conversational ease in his writings. Sterne assures his reader that writing "is but a different name for conversation"; Diderot tells Sophie Volland, "I chat with you in writing as if I were sitting beside you."

One of the most important means Diderot uses to maintain a closer connection between written and spoken language is to introduce into his works the jargons of different trades, professions, and social strata. Diderot, like Sterne, had very close links with the common people; his father was an artisan, and it was Diderot who undertook the monumental task of writing the articles on trades and mechanical arts for the *Encyclopédie.* In his *Satire I,* he says that there are so many words from professions and trades that he would bore to death the most patient man in listing those terms which occur to him as he is writing. He consciously uses the technical terms which the classical style frowned upon, often drawing from philosophy, medicine, and music. Early in *Jacques,* he warns the Reader:

Ce qui reste de tabac le soir dans ma tabatière est en raison directe de l'amusement, ou inverse de l'ennui de ma journée. Je vous supplie, lecteur, de vous familiariser avec cette manière de dire empruntée de la géométrie, parce que je la trouve précise et que je m'en servirai souvent.[55]

In point of fact, he does not use it thereafter very often, but in at least one case jargon taken from geometry does indeed sum up the situation with admirable precision:

Un des professeurs, Prémontval, devint amoureux de son écolière, et tout à travers les propositions sur les solides inscrits à la sphère, il y eut un enfant de fait. Le père Pigeon n'était pas homme à entendre patiemment la vérité de ce corollaire.[56]

He is equally precise in his selection of words and expressions from colloquial language and popular speech.[57] He has the Nephew admit "il faut que chacun paye son écot"; he explains why Jacques would say "à la vue de l'eau, la rage me prend" instead of "hydrophobe"; he corrects himself when Dame Marguerite uses a phrase which is not part of the country vernacular: "D'accord, la mortelle heure est des dames de la ville; et la grande heure, de dame Marguerite." Realizing that the perceptive reader might wonder why a country innkeeper's wife talks so well, he has the Master comment that the Hostess speaks better than befits her station, and later makes the Hostess say that she was educated at Saint-Cyr, where she spent considerably more time reading novels than studying her Bible.

It is, then, the principle of conscious choice, not carefree abandon, which underlies the styles of Diderot and Sterne. And it is, perhaps, the very success of this choice which has fooled so many readers into believing that each writer recklessly dashed off whatever came into his head. Indeed, Sterne and Diderot are entitled to the last laugh at the disapproving purists, because for their own purposes, both writers were as deeply concerned with precision and exactitude as their more formal critics.

Yet why are they concerned? Why do they take pains to fix little details with such accuracy, to follow the sweep of experience? What motivation do they have for wanting concrete effects, for involving the reader in a mood or a series of moods? It is here that the divergences between the two writers' approach to style become apparent.

Diderot seems to be the intellectual man, the aesthetician, striving to overcome the limitations of language that were even more sharply defined by the restrictions of a current school of criticism. He feels the limitations personally, of course, but his personal problem is really the problem of all creative writers and of all intelligent readers. Referring to D'Holbach's translation in 1772 of Hobbes's treatise on *Human Nature,* he tells Sophie Volland:

Never before have I so strongly felt how essential is the manner of saying things. . . . A negligent, faulty style does not tarnish simply an isolated idea. It tires and bores the reader; it makes one throw down a book. . . . What a shame that the author has not united the elegance and clarity of his style with the clearness and force of the ideas.[58]

It is indeed the union of expression and subject to which Diderot keeps returning, but there is no particularly *subjective* note in his theories or in his efforts to find styles appropriate for different experiences. It is as though he were experimenting with style for the benefit of writers in general. Naturally, his own impressions of experiences must bear a personal stamp, and to that extent he is subjective. But as previously indicated, Diderot does not fuse *his* impressions and the expression of them with those of others. He appears to be engaged in a kind of intellectual exercise, exploring and exploiting materials that can be used by the writer who is trying to deal with impressions and reactions.

Sterne never provides any evidence that he faces a struggle with language. He ridicules abstract and obtuse writing as befits his heritage of the tradition of the learned wit,[59] but his parody does not mean that he necessarily feels any pressure on him to use a ponderous style. Actually, he feels free to break all rules because he *wants* to appear different. But the limitation that he does face and that he is doubtless aware of is that of his own existence. Unlike Diderot, whose boisterousness may often have been the excess energy of good health, Sterne was not a robust man; always keenly sensitive to experience, his perceptions may well have become more intensified as his health declined. It must be remembered that when he made his first trip to France, he was seeking a climate less harmful to consumptives than England's, and that when he consulted the doctors in Paris, they gave him little more than a month to live. He jokes about his "vile cough" in *Tristram,* but that is because he is determined to joke. When he wrote the first chapter of Book VII, he surely must have recognized that time was not on his side: "I have forty volumes to write, and forty thousand things to say and to do which no body in the world will say and do for me except thyself," he tells Eugenius. But Sterne did not fool himself into believing that there could be any substitute. Consequently, there is always the urgency for setting down his impressions and observations; such a process can at least crystallize experience, which flows faster for him than for most men.

Sterne is primarily concerned with the individual's reactions, and this interest gradually develops into a shift in emphasis. The impressions in his own mind were just as important as those which flooded his characters' minds, and this eventually leads to an alteration in his style. In *Tristram,* he is avowedly aiming to produce an original and eccentric work, filled with stylistic innovations. He is also seeking an appropriate expression that will both approximate the flow of life and involve the reader in it. He enjoys life, he relishes its paradoxes, he is delighted by contrasts in character and moods, and his gusto is preserved in an exuberance of style.

In the *Sentimental Journey,* the enjoyment is still there, but it centers much more exclusively on Sterne's personal impressions and emotions. There is a curious tempering of the style which suggests that Sterne, perhaps not fully consciously, is nearing the end. The gusto and the sense of continued activity that one finds in *Tristram* are gone—despite the Shandean start and abrupt breaking off. The very precision and polish of the style convey an air of finality. Each scene, each vignette, each shade of feeling is so minutely fixed that one cannot conceive of its going on endlessly. It is as though Sterne were establishing experiences that could not be continued. The reader is no longer so deeply implicated in the unpredictable flow of life nor, one suspects, is Sterne. Instead, one is witnessing selected *memories* that the author has carefully isolated and set down. They are described *to* the audience, but the audience is not in them. The *Sentimental Journey* is time past, rather than the eternal present of *Tristram.* Even the Shandy family, whom one expected to engage in confused conversations forever, is caught in this closing net. One of their greatest attractions lay in their timelessness, but Sterne, though "his eyes gush out with tears," improvidently announces that Uncle Toby "is no more." This conflicts with the kind of universe established in *Tristram,* but it also indicates that Sterne's thought—or perhaps his subconscious—is now oriented in the world of the *Sentimental Journey.* Mutability, generally unfamiliar to *Tristram* except as a source of laughter, is the dominant note here. The old monk dies, affording Sterne the opportunity to pull nettles off his grave and weep; Madame de L vanishes in the direction of Brussels, her mysterious sorrow unrevealed; Maria reappears only to retire, after Sterne has wept some more, into the crowd at Moulines as Sterne moistly takes his "last look and last farwel." The exquisite precision with which he describes these scenes also circumscribes and seals them.

Yet the simple fact that Sterne's attitude toward style is not so intellectually objective as Diderot's does not interfere with his achievements as a consummate stylist—of the two, perhaps one might argue with some justification that Sterne is the purer artist—or with his agreement with Diderot on a number of important points dealing with expression. Both share the belief that it is style which enlivens a subject, and although their reasons may differ, their techniques to achieve this end are often very similar. They give ample evidence that style grows out of its subject matter, that it is frequently most effective when it catches a subject in flight. They select a natural and informal idiom, thereby arriving at a spontaneity which appears irresponsible but which is really very deliberate. They are both writers who, contrary to superficial appearances, take real pains to accomplish a precision of effect which must not seem either forced or stilted. Reacting against the restrictions of "good taste," they turn to an earlier and more lively tradition of language to plunder it for their own experiments in dynamic prose. It has been pointed out that language "can never stand still and there can be no such thing as a 'return' to the style of an earlier age." [60] But Diderot and Sterne would not have disagreed; it is by their self-conscious efforts to keep language living, to make it *more* living, that they use aspects from an earlier tradition to restore vitality to imaginative expression.

Through all these achievements, these two men of the eighteenth century have rendered great services to future writers. Diderot speaks for both of them when he observes that "It is the style which assures a work of literature its immortality;

this is the quality which charms the author's contemporaries, and which will charm the centuries to come." [61] And certainly this quality should not be minimized in evaluating the appeal of both Diderot and Sterne nearly two centuries later.

CHAPTER VI

CONCLUSION

IT is only after the crosscurrents of literary and intellectual movements are separated into recognizable patterns that evaluation of the directions they take is possible. When criticism is in the position to benefit from both the physical and psychic distances Diderot mentions in his *Salons,* it is easier to see the true significance of literary figures whose achievements have remained somewhat obscured within the cultural ambiguities of their own era. The increased critical interest and acclaim that have marked the respective fortunes of Sterne and Diderot in the twentieth century suggest that in many ways we have reached this position. Nevertheless, at least one problem has continued to haunt their combined fortunes, and that is the question of the essential nature of their relationship.

Diderot, perhaps, has been as responsible as anyone for the confusion. By announcing that he plagiarized from Sterne, he has directed attention to an aspect of their association which has received undue emphasis. Actually, he has created a kind of posthumous joke which he would have enjoyed immensely, for in the very novel in which the borrowings occur, he is constantly enjoining his readers to beware of misunderstanding the author, to avoid mistaking the true for the false and the false for the true, to be careful lest they are misled by appearances. And since it has appeared to many critics that *Jacques* owes to Sterne even more than its author admits, Diderot's warnings have not been notably successful. Yet their connection cannot be reduced to so simple a matter as plagiarism. If two men are inspired, by common readings and sympathies, to develop independently similar ideas and practices, and if these developments themselves gradually and naturally bifurcate into different channels, then the entire subject of influence and imitation becomes singularly diminished in importance. That is not to say that the relationship thereby suffers. If anything, it becomes even more striking once the most superficial reason for it has been removed. And it is in their ultimate, historical significance that the affinities between Diderot and Sterne gain their fullest meaning.

As imaginative writers, they were not conventional eighteenth-century artists; moreover, their literary Bohemianism seems to reflect the lack of ceremony which marked their most genuine conduct in society. This individualism has great importance for their positions in relation to their times and is emphasized by a characteristic common to both men. Their contemporaries have described them as masters of conversation, but there is a curious scarcity of supporting examples. The fame of Diderot and Sterne as speakers did not rest on witty epigrams, on isolated, quotable gems or succinct verbalizing of universal standards of taste and belief. Conversation was for them an uninhibited revelation of their individuality—even Sterne admitted that he was bored by *marivaudage* as a steady diet—and it was completely personal. The spirited, polished comments of a Voltaire or a Fontenelle could be preserved and subsequently repeated by others, and still lose nothing by it. The success of Diderot and Sterne required their physical presence. Both were at their best in small groups where their temperaments stood out, so that their audiences carried away with them the impact of a total personality, the distinct impression of an individual.

Contemporary memoirs and reports give anecdotes about Sterne or Diderot, but for the most part they do not actually record the spoken words of their typical conversation. Diderot's letters to Sophie Volland probably represent the closest approximation, but his practice, generally, is to repeat for her the dialogue of others instead of writing his own spoken monologues. Suard failed to provide living statements of Sterne, such as Boswell did for Johnson or Eckermann for Goethe. He doubtless lacked the gifts of a Boswell, but he also lacked a cooperative subject. For in his truly natural moments, Sterne did not consider what he said; he just burst forth with it, and although Suard faithfully hung onto his words, his recollections of Sterne deal with the whole man— his voice, his gestures, his full effect. The young Garat met with the same difficulty in his encounter with Diderot. While certain allowances must be made for his report because it was a good-natured caricature of the voluble *philosophe,* even Diderot's intimates did not see it as too gross an exaggeration. It is plain that Garat was able to describe, despite his wrapt attention, only the general impressions of witnessing a brilliant mind in action.

Sterne and Diderot were very hard to quote in their most characteristic flights, for they were all improvisation and spontaneity. As both warmed to their subjects, there must have been a refreshing, if somewhat disconcerting rush about them, a completely personal informality. Because he was a thoroughgoing nonconformist, Diderot would forget that he was addressing an empress of Russia and slap her thighs as he emphasized a point or fling his wig on the floor in his excitement. Sterne would drop the formal rules of etiquette and social amenities and narrowly escape insulting some Irish beauties or a French gentleman as he elaborated a series of amusing stories on the spur of the moment. Suard's strongest impression of Sterne is his piquant originality—original, he adds, even for an Englishman. Certainly Sterne would not have objected. He would have agreed with Diderot's comment when the amused *philosophe* finished reading Garat's report in the *Mercure* of 1779 of the hectic, one-sided "interview" he had held with the voluble encyclopedist:

People will be tempted to take me for some sort of eccentric; but what matter? Is it such a great fault to have been able to conserve, while ceaselessly tossing about in society, a few vestiges of nature, and to distinguish oneself by a few angular characteristics from the mass of these uniform and well-rounded pebbles which abound on all shores? [1]

It is no wonder, then, that in their works Sterne and Diderot manifest a distrust, often scornful, of the standards and formulae which were widely accepted as the qualifications for good writing. The individualism that marked their personalities was also recognized in their written endeavors. Dr. Johnson's judgment that nothing odd will do long was a typical common-sense reaction, but rather premature. *Tristram's* popularity, as Sterne keenly surmised, rested on its originality, and when Sterne sought to prolong his fame by producing another novel, he again stated that it was to be something entirely new. A dominant theme throughout Diderot's work is his critical examination and rejection of generally unquestioned notions and precepts. It pervades his treatment of subjects ranging from science and sociology to morals and ethics, and it is reflected in his aesthetic theories and practices. As he notes in the *Salon* of 1769:

It is good to be able to paint easily, but one must conceal the practice which gives productions of all kinds an air of manufacture. It is not to Vernet alone that I address these remarks: it is to Saint-Lambert, to Voltaire, to D'Alembert, to Rousseau, to the abbé Morellet, to myself.[2]

Both he and Sterne admired works that did not bear the stamp of manufacture, and they strove to continue such performances in their own writings. They were not writing in a vacuum, for the very brazenness with which they often emphasized their nonconformity indicates that they were well acquainted with the prevailing taste. Recently a critic has again noted the contrast resulting from so deliberate a stand:

Sterne was still writing in the broad tradition of Rabelais, Cervantes, and Swift and, though he knew them well, flouted the rules of the dramatic and epic "kinds." In fact, he wrote with an experimental freedom of form which was not equalled, or even attempted, until the time of Joyce.[3]

Diderot, too, carried over the experimentalism he advocated in the sciences into his creative composition. As practicing literary individualists, both men would naturally appreciate Cervantes' satirical thrusts at conventional methods of writing, and they doubtless concurred in his "friend's" advice that "A writer has but to make his chosen medium his own; as he disciplines himself therein, so much the more perfect will his writing be." It is no accident that in the *Bijoux indiscrets* of 1748, Diderot's "conventional" novel, he suggests a recipe consisting of works by Marivaux, Crébillon *fils,* and Duclos, whereas in 1781 his recipe includes representatives of significantly different genres—*Le Roman comique, Don Quixote,* Rabelais, *Jacques le fataliste, Manon Lescaut.* For Diderot and Sterne, as they experimented with the media of their own choice, had before them the examples of other men who had preferred originality to mass production.

Actually, they were both proud of their "eccentricity," although they could not foresee its full implications. Underlying it was not merely personal whim but a kind of intellectual individualism. From their readings in the empirical tradition they gleaned authority for their antagonism to ready-made forms and *à priori* principles, for their belief in the efficacy of experimentation. They learned from Locke that a person's interpretation of reality was largely subjective and that thereby things of seeming insignificance could assume proportions of magnitude in the individual mind. The private, emotional life had deeper meaning than one's public conformity and was often revealed by almost imperceptible symptoms that could pass unnoticed if one chose to search out the general instead of the particular. Man was not everywhere the same, Diderot and Sterne believed, nor should he try to be, for the results could range from artificiality and monotony to warped natures and perversions. Instead of advocating a uniform sameness, they proclaimed the necessity of characteristic, personal differentness and put their faith in the validity of individual judgments. Without making such a fetish of it as Rousseau, they, too, recognized the value of uniqueness, of varied and idiosyncratic experience—and by doing so they crossed the threshold of romanticism.

This advance should be emphasized because it is as transitional figures that Diderot and Sterne assume their greatest historical importance. In a certain way, both these individualists are typical—not because they are illustrative of neoclassicism or of romanticism, but because they reflect the varied tendencies of their century, sometimes by rejecting them, sometimes by carrying them further. Their function in this role is brought out dramatically by their participation in one of the most significant intellectual developments of the eighteenth century.

In his discussion of the great chain of being, Professor A. O. Lovejoy suggests that "There have, in the entire history of thought, been few changes in standards of values more profound and more momentous" than the substitution of diversitarianism, "the one common factor in a number of otherwise diverse tendencies which . . . have been termed 'Romantic,'" for uniformitarianism, the dominant attitude of neoclassicism.[4] It has already been noted that neither Diderot nor Sterne believed that the universal appeal of a work of art depended on its dealing strictly with generalized subjects in a conventional manner. To them, this was flat. They rejected the neoclassic efforts at standardization. Because they viewed life and human beings as complex, they had little sympathy for false simplification. Assuredly, uniformitarianism as well as diversitarianism was implicit in Locke, but Diderot and Sterne were attracted by diversitarianism. Diderot was not misled into holding that the concept of the *tabula rasa* meant that all men were created with equal endowments, and he went to some pains to argue the point with Helvétius. Sterne's little lecture on Dolly and the sealing wax indicated that the nature and force of sense impressions were determined by the individual who received them, and that each person was conditioned by countless factors.

It is the principle of diverse and infinite variation which fascinated both writers. They were "local colorists" not only in creating the milieux against which their characters appear but also in particularizing the characters themselves by their "tics" and gestures, by the nuances of their moods. Each developed the art of suggestion, of the half-spoken word and the symptomatic reaction. Both agreed that nature was teeming with fresh subjects for the artist: Sterne admittedly seized the handle of whatever chance held out to him; Diderot warned writers that their most active imaginations could not possibly equal the bizarre in nature itself. Moreover, they believed that such a variety of material required new forms of expression and inspired new genres. Instead of sacrificing subjects to old formulae, one should develop new media: a bourgeois drama, a new lyric poetry, a fluid novel based on a natural rather than an artificial framework, a history instead of a romance, a story of men's minds instead of their deeds. And certain aspects of different genres could be combined or could be used to implement each other: music and poetry, painting and story-telling, dramatic gesture or dialogue and characterization. Anticipating a later impressionistic writer, Diderot and Sterne could agree that everything is the proper stuff of fiction and that rather than work within restrictive rules, the artist should experiment freely to do justice to his content.

Yet these tendencies, widely proclaimed by the romanticists, were not without roots in the tradition against which they rebelled. The principle of abundant diversity has been shown to have been frequently anticipated by the neoclassic discussions of plenitude. Although the emphasis on variety and differentness for their own sake and the exhortation to seek new vehicles to express them had not been stressed by neoclassic criticism, certainly the germ of these developments was to be found in the earlier spirit. It would be misrepresenting the positions of Sterne and Diderot to deny that they owed much to an influence which both positively and negatively affected their own thought. Yet they often exhibit these earlier manifestations in a curiously unorthodox fashion.

Diderot constantly voices the precept insisted upon by the neoclassicists, that art should imitate nature. He takes care, however, to distinguish between imitation and copy: a copyist is a faithful historian; an imitator improvises, using poetic license, and Diderot actually calls him a poet. Man, the creator, should not work in the same fashion as nature, the creatrix: illuminate your landscapes, Diderot says, according to *your* sunlight, which is not the sun of nature; be the *disciple* of the rainbow, not its slave. He recommends an ideal model, but it is educed from reality, not superimposed upon it. He advises artists to base their works on eternal phenomena—human nature, nature itself. Yet his fiction invariably breaks down the general concept, "human nature," into highly particularized individuals with the characteristic "scars" and "furrows" that alter the image of ideal beauty into the portrait of one's neighbor. And nature, for Diderot, is a dynamic, changing cosmos whose phenomena are constantly shifting and evolving and are never exactly alike. Consequently, as he interprets neoclassic principles, they take on new overtones, for he is stating them within a different frame of reference.

Sterne, on the other hand, clings to a modified neoclassical universe which seems to be frozen between unaltering plenitude and increasing change. It is filled with variety but is essentially static. It abounds with freakish happenings and chance occurrence, yet chance does not give rise to the transformism that Diderot perceived; it does not result in the notion of a world in the state of becoming. The inhabitants of Sterne's world, despite their disorganized lives and their personal peculiarities, remain stable. Even when mutability enters, as it does in the *Sentimental Journey,* it is not related to the larger cosmos. It has personal and perhaps not fully conscious meaning for Sterne; it conveys hints of a newer scheme of things which he might develop, but significantly he does not choose to dilate on its possibilities. So it remained for Diderot to anticipate "Le Lac" and "Tristesse d'Olympio" and "Souvenir" by his assertion that the first vow made by two creatures of flesh was sworn in the shadow of a crumbling crag beneath a visiting sky, while everything within and without these transient beings—who believed their hearts to be free from all change—was passing away.

Of even more interest for their transitional roles are their respective interpretations of diversitarianism. Professor Lovejoy has pointed out that this principle contains an important ambiguity: it can lead either to a preoccupation with the uniqueness of others or to the delight in the uniqueness of one's self. Now while both Diderot and Sterne uphold the necessity of differentness, a curious division grows out of their treatments of this concept. Diderot not only defends his own originality; he also takes great interest in the personalities, experiences, customs, and values of other people. He is an avid student of human nature and increases the meaning of his own life by penetrating other lives. And he is singularly gifted for this, as his fiction demonstrates. His characterizations, even in a sociological work like the *Supplément,* illustrate what Otis E. Fellows has described as Diderot's "remarkable ability for self-projection into the situation of another." Although the phenomenal world has its importance for Diderot, he also makes it serve for a concentration on individual reactions to those realities that a specific person reflects upon. One must see the variety and complexity of life in order to appreciate how it eats its way into a personality, making for individualized emotional reflections. The drama is an inner one, like the Nephew's, and by studying the transformation of the exterior world within the character, Diderot emphasizes the tension. He seems to get inside each figure in order to convey his argument that the thing one sees and that exists objectively has a mysteriously individual and subjective meaning. He thereby illuminates the striking disparities not merely between the outer and the inner world but between the interior lives of people. And it is essential to remember that for Diderot these multiple differences assume objective validity.

Certainly it would seem that Sterne is engaged in a similar process as he notes the idiosyncratic reactions of the Shandys to objective reality. But he really tends to externalize the drama by imposing subjectivity on the world without. Using glimpses of a "normal" world to highlight the hallucinatory lives of his characters, he projects private worlds clashing and producing frustrations. As the impressionism of *Tristram* is developed more fully in the *Sentimental Journey,* it becomes apparent that Sterne's interest in private experiences is leading him to a cultivation of the self. His tendency to twist diversity into exteriorized subjective reflection becomes increasingly centered on his own uniqueness and its personal value. Nor is this a completely new element; he had initially stated that the originality of his first book must resemble that of its author, and although he does not confuse fact with fiction, he seems to be working toward an interest in differentness not for its own sake or for what he can learn from it, but for how it can reflect himself.

By laying upon the neoclassic universe a very personal disorder, and by stressing its subjective validity, he anticipates two manifestations of the concern for personal uniqueness. The glorification of one's individuality—Schlegel's "divine egotism"—may naturally tend to an excessive interest in one's self and one's feelings, encouraging a delight in emotional experience for its own sake. From here it is an almost inevitable step to that degeneration of the emphasis on sensations that Mario Praz has studied in *The Romantic Agony*—erotic sensibility. In this way, Sterne exhibits tendencies that were to find their ultimate development in the psychological introversion of the decadent movement. And by exteriorizing subjective impressions, as he does in *Tristram,* he foreshadows expressionism, which is really another method for treating the same introversion. From Tristram's world of capricious chance and from Yorick's world of emotional contingencies, Sterne points to a newer world of disruption and chaos.

Diderot, too, anticipates the breakdown of the old order, but precisely because he recognizes that it has more than subjective meaning, he is led to seek something underlying the change and variety. It is an interesting commentary on Diderot's own personal complexity that as he approaches in time the era of the romantic critics, in certain ways he withdraws from them. It is true that there have always remained with him vestiges of neoclassic thought, but as he grows older they become more pronounced, even though he handles them in different contexts. For example, turning against his earlier contention that unbridled emotion gives rise to great works of art, he gradually undertakes to balance it by reason and judgment. Recognizing the action of the unconscious memory that was later to be "rediscovered" by Wordsworth, Chateaubriand, Nerval, and Proust, he declares that it is not in the first rush of passion that one creates. It is during unexpected moments that one relives experiences, and from these recollections one fashions, in calm, the work of art.

He substitutes, as Professor Belaval has suggested,[5] the dominion of reason for the uncertainties of emotions; conscious calculation and self-mastery are imposed on primordial enthusiasm. His intellectual development is marked by an increasing distrust of features in his preromanticism of the 1740s and 1750s. Analyzing the causes and effects of disorder in the feelings, he seeks to counteract it by advocating that men develop their faculty for organization, for this power is one of man's major links with nature. And the link is of greatest importance, because what Diderot is striving for is not artificial order, which he condemns in neoclassicism, but a new kind of order, a natural coherence. In this way, he is both classic and modern—classic in that he reacts against the chaos that he finds everywhere, modern in that he wants a basic and internal unity, as do Proust and Joyce and Woolf. These later writers will perceive it in mythic or archetypal patterns, in unity of experience, in the flux which mingles all consciousness. Diderot perceives his constant within that very nature whose dynamism is so impressed on his thought and work.

In the entry of their *Journal* for April 11, 1858, Edmond and Jules de Goncourt were chagrined that Voltaire was immortal while Diderot was only famous. Voltaire, they argued, was the last spirit of old France, but Diderot was the first genius of modern France. Sterne does not even win an honorable mention from these two latter-day eccentrics, although somewhat indirectly they might have traced their morbid preciosity to the "original Anglais." In retrospect, however, Sterne can lay claim to a position which more than compensates for the Goncourt brothers' neglect, and Diderot can justifiably demand from posterity a more extended evaluation. For the Anglican clergyman and the Parisian *philosophe* have ultimately transcended their native cultures and have emerged as prognosticators of trends in modern European literature. Granted, much of this judgment is based on suggestive tentatives in their works, on aspects of which they were unconscious or only partially aware. Yet these two men whose achievements were so germinative were not totally oblivious of the oddity of their place in their contemporary world. If they could not foresee that they stood in the *avant-garde* of the development of a new movement, they certainly realized that many essential features of what had been the dominant current did not satisfy them. If they instinctively utilized elements of this current, it was not for the conscious aim of appearing as traditionalists.

Chance largely determined their first meeting, but their subsequent and fuller relationship was not a matter of coincidence. Whether one can attribute this kinship, as would two of their most engaging heroes, to an "odd fatality" or to *le destin* may be open to question, but it is clear that time has sharpened the factors which initially determined a sympathetic union between an Englishman and a Frenchman of the eighteenth century. That combination of background, interest, and effort which encouraged compatibility during their encounters has served, since the eighteenth century, to bring them closer together in the historical perspective of their own age. And that age could both claim and reject them, for the two men were neither completely in nor completely out of their time. A final paradox, which both Denis Diderot and Laurence Sterne might have appreciated, is that notwithstanding their strong pleas for originality, individualism, and differentness, they functioned as representative men, typifying transition; that in spite of their insistence on particulars and their distrust of abstraction, they played a symbolic role in which echoes of the past were mingled with premonitions of the future.

NOTES

The following is a list of abbreviations and short titles used in the Notes and (in the case of titles of periodicals) also in the Bibliography. For fuller data, see the Bibliography.

A.-T. = Diderot, *Œuvres complètes*, ed. by J. Assézat and M. Tourneux
CL = *Comparative Literature*
EC = *Essays in Criticism*
ELH = *Journal of English Literary History*
FR = *French Review*
Grande R = *Grande revue*
JHI = *Journal of the History of Ideas*
Letters = *Letters of Laurence Sterne*
M.L.R. = *Modern Language Review*
MP = *Modern Philology*
Phil R = *Philosophical Review*
PMLA = *Publications of the Modern Language Association of America*
PQ = *Philological Quarterly*
QR = *Quarterly Review*
RCC = *Revue des cours et conférences*
RDM = *Revue des deux mondes*
RDSH = *Revue des sciences humaines*
RG = *Revue germanique*
Rhebd = *Revue hebdomadaire*
RHL = *Revue d'histoire littéraire de la France*
RHP = *Revue d'histoire de la philosophie*
RR = *Romanic Review*
R XVI S = *Revue du seizième siècle*
Sermons = Sterne, *The Sermons of Mr. Yorick*
SJ = Sterne, *A Sentimental Journey through France and Italy*
SP = *Studies in Philology*
Tr. = Sterne, *The Life and Opinions of Tristram Shandy, Gentleman*, Modern Library edition
VQ = *Virginia Quarterly*

NOTES

NOTES TO I: CONFRONTATIONS

1. Actually, more than one paragraph was involved. For a comparison of parallel passages, see Loy, *Determined Fatalist,* pp. 32–39.

2. The following is a selected list:

Andrieux, *Décade philosophique,* XI, 224; cited in A.-T., VI, 6.

Baldwin, Charles Sears, "The Literary Influence of Sterne in France," *PMLA,* XVII (1902), 226–29.

Barbey d'Aurevilly, Jules, *Goethe et Diderot* (Paris, 1880), pp. 166–68; cited in Loy, *Determined Fatalist,* p. 12.

Barton, Francis Brown, *Etude sur l'influence de Laurence Sterne en France au dix-huitième siècle* (Paris, 1911), pp. 98–126.

Brunel, Lucien, "Diderot et les encyclopédistes," in L. Petit de Juleville, ed., *Histoire de la langue et de la littérature française,* VI (Paris, 1909), 483.

Cross, Wilbur L., *The Life and Times of Laurence Sterne,* new ed. (New Haven, 1925), I, 274.

Cru, R. Loyalty, *Diderot as a Disciple of English Thought* (New York, 1913), pp. 97, 373–89, 451.

Ducros, Louis, *Diderot l'homme et l'écrivain* (Paris, 1894), pp. 220–23.

Ellis, Havelock, *The New Spirit* (London, 1890), p. 54.

Garat, Dominique-Joseph, *Clef du cabinet des souverains* (March 29, 1797); cited in Mary Lane Charles, *The Growth of Diderot's Fame in France from 1784 to 1875* (Bryn Mawr, Pennsylvania, 1942), p. 22.

Green, Frederick Charles, *Minuet* (London, 1935), pp. 457, 459–63.

Jasinski, René, *Histoire de la littérature française* (Paris, 1947), II, 209.

Lanson, Gustave, *Histoire de la littérature française,* 12e éd. (Paris, 1912), p. 743.

Le Breton, André, *Le Roman français au dix-huitième siècle* (Paris, 1925), pp. 321–22.

Loy, J. Robert, *Diderot's Determined Fatalist* (New York, 1950), pp. 32–50.

Monselet, Charles, *Catalogue d'une jolie collection de livres rares et curieux* (n.p., 1871); cited in A.-T., VI, 6.

Morley, John, *Diderot and the Encyclopaedists* (London, 1886), II, 36–41.

Mornet, Daniel, *Le Neveu de Rameau* (Paris, 1947/48), pp. 143–53.

Nitze, William, and E. Preston Dargan, *A History of French Literature,* rev. ed. (New York, 1930), pp. 480–81.

Reinach, Joseph, *Diderot* (Paris, 1894), pp. 94–97.

Rosenkranz, Karl, *Diderots Leben und Werke* (Leipzig, 1886), p. 324.

Saintsbury, George, *A History of the French Novel* (London, 1917), I, 404.

Schérer, Edmond, *Diderot: étude* (Paris, 1880), p. 68.

Texte, Joseph, *Jean-Jacques Rousseau and the Cosmopolitan Spirit in Literature,* tr. J. W. Matthews (New York, 1929), p. 284.

Wright, C. H. Conrad, *A History of French Literature* (New York, 1912), pp. 538–39.

3. See Hammond, *Laurence Sterne's "Sermons of Mr. Yorick,"* pp. 74–78.

4. *Ibid.,* p. 76. According to Diderot's daughter, Mme de Vandeul, Diderot himself as a young man sold a half dozen sermons to a Jesuit missionary for fifty écus apiece. See A.-T., I, xxxiii.

5. Letter of 2 July 1706 to Walsh in *The Works of Alexander Pope,* ed. Elwin and Courthope, VI, 52.

6. A.-T., X, 393.

7. *Letters*, p. 151.

8. *Letters*, p. 162.

9. Vol. XXVI (April, 1767), p. 206: "very affecting and sentimental."

10. Vol. XXXVI (April, 1767), p. 410: "This performance, which might more properly be called a dramatic novel than a comedy, is founded on a very tender and affecting story. The characters are all of the sublime cast, the sentiments philosophically refined, and the language pure and expressive. We recommend this pamphlet particularly to our fair Readers, as a work that will open and elevate their minds, without misleading their passions."

11. *Letters*, p. 166.

12. *Letters*, p. 162.

13. *Correspondance littéraire*, XII, 520–21.

14. Dieckmann, *Inventaire du fonds Vandeul*, p. 120.

15. *Ibid.*, p. 249.

16. See Dieckmann, "The Influence of Francis Bacon on Diderot's *Interprétation de la nature*," RR, XXXIV (1943), 303–30.

17. *Correspondance littéraire*, III, 116–17.

18. *Lettre à Mme Riccoboni*, in A.-T., VII, 402.

19. In the *Eloge*, he even ranks Richardson with Moses, Homer, Euripides, and Sophocles.

20. Legros, "Diderot et Shaftesbury," *M.L.R.*, XIX (1924), 188–89.

21. A.-T., VII, 111–12.

22. *Letters*, pp. 161–62.

23. *SJ*, "Character—Versailles," p. 166.

24. Cited in Hedgcock, *A Cosmopolitan Actor, David Garrick and His French Friends*, pp. 243–44.

25. *Lettres à Sophie Volland*, ed. Babelon, I, 161 (26 October 1760).

26. Foster, *History of the Pre-Romantic Novel*, p. 131.

27. *Lettres à Sophie Volland*, I, 36 (31 July 1759).

28. A.-T., XIV, 453.

NOTES TO II: SENSIBILITY

1. For some studies representing the skeptic's point of view, see Dilworth, *The Unsentimental Journey of Laurence Sterne* (New York, 1948); MacLean, "Imagination and Sympathy: Sterne and Adam Smith," *JHI*, X (1949), 399–410; Putney, "The Evolution of *A Sentimental Journey*," *PQ*, XIX (1940), 349–69, and "Laurence Sterne, Apostle of Laughter," in *The Age of Johnson*, pp. 159–70. See also Professor Putney's review in *PQ*, XXIX (1950), 300, of Professor MacLean's article.

2. Stephen, *History of English Thought*, II, 5. For more recent comments in the same vein, cf. Carré, *Phases of Thought in England*, p. 259: "Upon cultured opinion the impact of Hobbes' moral views was startling. The *Leviathan* provoked a storm in England comparable only to the ferment excited by the theories of Darwin in the nineteenth century." See also Bowle, *Hobbes and His Critics*, p. 13; Kyle, "British Ethical Theories: The Intuitionist Reaction against Hobbes," *The Australasian Journal of Psychology and Philosophy*, V (1927), 113; Souilhé, "Pourquoi Thomas Hobbes?" in *La Pensée et l'influence de Th. Hobbes*, p. 1. Summarizing the increasing anti-Hobbes sentiment in the late seventeenth century and its expansion into the eighteenth century, John Bowle remarks: "Hobbes' Machiavellian view of human nature was to be swamped [in the eighteenth century] by an outlook which erred to the other extreme" (*Hobbes and His Critics*, p. 194). A useful review of this reaction is to be found in Laird, *Hobbes*, in his chapter on "Influence in Ethics and Politics," especially pp. 273–89.

3. For a fuller discussion, see Crane, "Suggestions toward a Genealogy of the 'Man of Feeling,'" *ELH*, I (1934), 205–30.

4. For a recent summary of their opposition to Hobbes, see Chapter I in Brett, *Shaftesbury*, pp. 13–32. Ernest Tuveson has traced a more specialized aspect of the contribution of Cambridge Platonist thought to the "new theory of human nature" in his analysis of the Burnet-Locke controversy. See his "The Origins of the

'Moral Sense,'" *Huntington Library Quarterly*, XI (1947–48), 241–59.

5. Author's italics; cited in Crane, "Suggestions toward a Genealogy of the 'Man of Feeling,'" *ELH*, I (1934), 220. A more extensive study of this new attitude is to be found in Humphreys, " 'The Friend of Mankind' (1700–1760)—An Aspect of Eighteenth-Century Sensibility," *RES*, XXIV (1948), 203–18. For a general review, see Warner, " 'Education of the Heart': Observations on the Eighteenth-Century English Sentimental Movement," *Papers of the Michigan Academy of Science, Arts, and Letters*, XXIX (1943), 553–60.

6. Thielemann, "Tradition of Hobbes," p. 20. A similar position is suggested by Professor Willey's comment in *The Seventeenth Century Background*, p. 266: "The 'State of Nature,' in Locke, is so far from resembling the 'ill condition' described by Hobbes, that it approximates rather to the Eden of the religious tradition, or the golden age of the poets."

7. Paul Hazard has indicated its more dynamic effects in France in "Les Origines philosophiques de l'homme de sentiment," *RR*, XXVIII (1927), 318–41. See, for example, his contention, pp. 324 ff., that by exalting desire and dignifying sensation as the "sole point of departure for moral life," Locke brought about a "revolutionary change in values."

8. Shaftesbury, *Characteristics*, ed. Robertson, I, 295.

9. MacLean, *John Locke and English Literature*, p. 54.

10. Thielemann, "Tradition of Hobbes," p. 20.

11. Tuveson, "The Origins of the 'Moral Sense,'" *Huntington Library Quarterly*, XI (1947–48), p. 257, suggests that in his preface to these sermons, Shaftesbury appears as "an embryo Cambridge Platonist." Cf. Brett, *Shaftesbury*, p. 61: "Shaftesbury's endeavour was to rescue the philosophical tradition of the Cambridge Platonists from the dull and pedantic folio volumes in which it had been presented and to make it available to the man of culture and sensibility."

12. On Shaftesbury's divergence from Locke over the question of *à priori* ideas, see Brett, *Shaftesbury*, pp. 83 ff. He summarizes the major reason: "For Shaftesbury, Locke had played into the hands of the arch-enemy Hobbes" (*ibid.*, p. 83).

13. Shaftesbury, *Characteristics*, I, 292.

14. *Ibid.*, II, 129.

15. *Ibid.*, 174.

16. Cross, *Life*, I, 43–44.

17. See Thielemann, "Tradition of Hobbes," p. 194, note 2; Cru, *Diderot*, p. 153; Sterne, *Letters*, p. 166.

18. Locke, *An Essay Concerning Human Understanding*, ed. Fraser, I, lv.

19. *La Pensée européenne au dix-huitième siècle*, II, 123.

20. A.-T., I, 87.

21. A.-T., IV, 110–11.

22. For Sterne's use of the words "hobby" and "hobbyhorse," see pp. 121 ff.

23. Venturi, *Jeunesse de Diderot*, p. 55.

24. There has been some controversy about Diderot's authorship of these passages. Evidence in support of the contention that it was Diderot, not Rousseau, who wrote them can be found in both writers. In a letter of 26 February 1770 to Saint-Germain, Rousseau discusses the difficulty of distinguishing one man's style from another's: ". . . and this imitation of my style could be especially easy for Diderot, whose style I particularly studied when I began writing and who even included in my first works several bits which do not jar with the rest and which one would not be able to distinguish from the rest, at least so far as the style is concerned." Rousseau admits in a footnote that he appended to his personal copy of the letter that Diderot wrote some pages for the *Second Discourse*. I am citing the quotation exactly as it appears in the footnote, transcribed by Dufour: "Quant aux pensées, celles qu'il a eu la bonté de me prêter, et que j'ai eu la bêtise d'adopter, sont bien faciles à distinguer des miennes, comme on peut le voir

dans celle du philosophe qui argumente en enfonçant son bonnet sur ses oreilles (Disc. sur l'inég.), car ce morceau est de lui tout entier. Il est certain que M. Diderot abusa toujours de ma confiance et de ma facilité pour donner à mes écrits un ton dur et un air noir, qu'ils n'eurent plus sitôt qu'il cessa de me diriger et que je fus livré tout à fait à moi-même." See *Correspondance générale de J.-J. Rousseau,* XIX, 251–52. Rousseau includes similar remarks in Book VIII of his *Confessions,* where he specifically refers to material Diderot developed in the *Second Discourse:* see footnote to p. 401 of the Modern Library edition. Relevant comments by Diderot on his relationship with Rousseau appear in Diderot's *Tablettes,* written in 1758: "I have grown weary slaving over his writings. This he only partially admits. He says nothing about how much he owes to my attentions, my advice, our discussions, everything. . . . He would squeeze me dry, use my ideas, and yet he almost pretended to scorn me." See *Correspondance littéraire,* XVI, 221.

25. "Morceau de Diderot," A.-T., IV, 103–4.

26. A.-T., VII, 85.

27. "Maria-Moulines," p. 213.

28. *Letters,* p. 162.

29. See for more particulars, Bergmann, "David Garrick and 'The Clandestine Marriage,'" *PMLA,* LXVII (1952), 152 ff.

30. A.-T., VII, 103–4.

31. A.-T., VII, 108–15.

32. For a discussion of the role of sensibility in talent and genius, see Spitzer, "The Style of Diderot," in *Linguistics and Literary History,* pp. 155–56 ff.

33. For a penetrating study dealing with this relationship and its connection with the theme of genius in the *Neveu de Rameau,* see Fellows, "The Theme of Genius in Diderot's *Neveu de Rameau,*" in Fellows and Torrey, eds., *Diderot Studies II,* pp. 168–99.

34. A.-T., I, 408.

35. A.-T., II, 267.

36. *Lettres à Sophie Volland*, I, 195 (11 November 1760).

37. *SJ*, "The Bourbonnois," p. 318.

38. See May, "Diderot pessimiste," in *Les Quatre visages de Denis Diderot*, pp. 34–99.

39. For new insights into Diderot's self-appraisal in the early sixties, see Fellows, "The Theme of Genius in Diderot's *Neveu de Rameau*," in Fellows and Torrey, eds., *Diderot Studies II*, pp. 172–79 especially.

40. *Lettres à Sophie Volland*, I, 45 (10 August 1759).

41. See, for example, *Pensées sur l'interprétation de la nature* (1754; A.-T., II, 61); "Lettre à Landois" (1756; A.-T., XIX, 436); *Lettres à Sophie Volland*, I, 180 (6 November 1760); *Le Neveu de Rameau* (1761; A.-T., V, 469). This thought also is a major theme in his letters to Mlle Jodin, 1765–1769 (A.-T., XIX, 381–411); in *Jacques le fataliste* (c. 1773/74; A.T., VI, 181); and in "De la perfectibilité de l'homme," in *Eléments de physiologie* (1774–1780; A.-T., IX, 271).

42. A.-T., II, 323, 410–11.

43. See "Pensée VI," in *Pensées philosophiques* (A.-T., I, 129). Torrey's article, "Rousseau's Quarrel with Grimm and Diderot," in *Essays in Honor of Albert Feuillerat: Yale Romanic Studies*, XXII (1943), 163–82, should also be consulted.

44. See above, p. 20.

45. A.-T., XI, 25.

46. *Ibid.*

47. A.-T., XI, 11–12, 17.

48. He had also shown glimmerings of it in the *Essai sur le mérite et la vertu* (1745; A.-T., I, 35, footnote), and in his article "Beau" (1750; A.-T., X, 41).

49. A.-T., X, 123.

50. A.-T., X, 199–200.

51. A.-T., X, 469, 504.

52. A.-T., X, 520.

53. A.-T., VIII, 376.

54. *Lettres à Sophie Volland,* II, 280 (undated fragment).

55. For a most competent study, see Belaval, *L'Esthétique sans paradoxe de Diderot.*

56. Cross, *Life,* II, 219.

57. *Mrs. Montagu,* ed. Blunt (London, 1923), I, 187–89; cited in *Letters,* p. 238.

58. *Letters,* p. 163; the italics are Sterne's.

59. *Letters,* p. 305.

60. *Letters,* p. 395.

61. *Letters,* p. 330.

62. *Sermons,* I, 23.

63. *Sermons,* II, 245.

64. *Sermons,* I, 287.

65. *Sermons,* II, 175–76.

66. Bagehot, *Literary Studies,* ed. Hutton, II, 111.

67. *Life and Letters of the Late Reverend Henry Venn,* p. 71; cited in Cross, *Life,* I, 226.

68. Bagehot, *Literary Studies,* II, 110.

69. MacLean, *John Locke and English Literature,* p. 165.

70. These churchmen included Wollaston, Tillotson, Clarke, Hall, Stillingfleet, Norris, Whichcote, Cudworth, and Butler. For extensive illustrations of Sterne's borrowings, see the Appendix to Hammond, *Laurence Sterne's "Sermons of Mr. Yorick."*

71. *Sermons,* I, 113.

72. *Sermons,* I, 289–90.

73. See Dilworth, *Unsentimental Journey,* pp. 4–5.

74. *Tr.,* Book VIII, ch. 19, p. 590.

75. *Tr.,* Book V, ch. 6, pp. 373–74.

76. *Tr.,* Book IV, ch. 26, p. 327.

77. *Letters,* p. 401; italics are mine. Sterne repeats his remark, with slight modification, in *SJ,* "The Passport—Versailles," p. 156.

78. *Ibid.,* p. 160.

79. *SJ,* "The Conquest," p. 173.

80. *SJ*, "The Bourbonnois," p. 218.

81. *SJ*, "The Husband—Paris," pp. 299–300.

82. *Tr.*, Book VI, ch. 7, pp. 439–40.

83. Cf. Maria in *Tr.*, Book IX, ch. 24, p. 658; *SJ*, "The Gloves—Paris," p. 102; "Maria-Moulines," p. 213.

84. Dilworth, *Unsentimental Journey*, p. 23.

85. Condillac, *Essai sur l'origine des connaissances humaines*, première partie, p. 65.

86. A pertinent investigation of this problem will be found in Margaret Gilman's article, "Imagination and Creation in Diderot," in Fellows and Torrey, eds., *Diderot Studies II*, pp. 200–220. See also her earlier study, "The Poet According to Diderot," *RR*, XXXVII (1946), 37–54.

87. A.-T., VIII, 415.

88. A.-T., XVII, 335.

89. Putney, "Laurence Sterne, Apostle of Laughter," in *The Age of Johnson*, p. 159.

90. *SJ*, "Calais," p. 21.

91. *SJ*, "Calais," "The Monk—Calais," pp. 4–5.

92. *SJ*, "In the Street—Calais," p. 25.

93. See Garat's report in his *Mémoires historiques sur la vie de M. Suard*, II, 149. Sterne told Suard that he owed his originality to three factors: his imagination or sensibility, his reading of the Bible, and his study of Locke. Regarding the first, it should be noted that Sterne did not make such distinctions as Professor Gilman, in her latest article, has found in Diderot. He may, however, have furnished the suggestion for Garat's understanding of these terms as the capacity for both feeling and delineating all sensations. It is significant that "imagination or sensibility," with Garat's description of its function, heads the list.

94. Henry James, "Criticism," in Morton D. Zabel, ed., *Literary Opinion in America* (New York, 1951), p. 49.

95. *Letters*, p. 256; italics mine. He echoes this in *SJ*, "Montreuil," p. 199, in stating that he has always been in love "with one princess or other" almost all his life.

96. *Letters,* p. 394.

97. Note its subtitle: "Dialogue between A and B on the disadvantage of attaching moral ideas to certain physical actions devoid of moral import."

98. *Lettres à Sophie Volland,* I, 164 (26 October 1760).

99. In the *Pensées sur l'interprétation de la nature,* for example, he states the necessity of relating all ideas to things which exist externally; see "Pensées VII and VIII," A.-T., II, 13–14; see also repetitions in the *Rêve de D'Alembert,* A.-T., II, 179–80, and in *Eléments de physiologie,* A.-T., IX, 346, 354–55.

100. Yvon Belaval, for instance, has discovered five subdivisions that Diderot makes in his interpretation of *sensibilité*. See Belaval, *L'Esthétique sans paradoxe de Diderot,* pp. 90–92.

101. A.-T., III, 284.

NOTES TO III: HUMOR

1. *Letters,* pp. 183–84.

2. *Lettres à Sophie Volland,* II, 15 (7 October 1762).

3. *Correspondance littéraire,* V, 395.

4. *Lettres à Sophie Volland,* II, 239 (12 October 1770).

5. For his earliest discussion, see "Pourquoi nous ne pouvons pas définir l'humour," *RG,* II (1906), 601–34.

6. "The Solemn Romantics," *University of California Publications in English,* VIII (1941), 262–64.

7. A.-T., IV, 280–84.

8. *Tr.,* Book v, ch. 1, p. 355.

9. Stephen, *History of English Thought,* II, 441–42, admits this to be his own reaction.

10. "L'Humour en France au moyen âge," in *Essais en deux langues,* p. 109.

11. It is entirely possible that humor, forsaking the novel, took to the stage with the advent of Molière.

12. "An Essay on the Freedom of Wit and Humour," in *Characteristics,* I, 50.

13. On at least one occasion, Diderot was vastly amused to find

himself in this predicament. See his daughter's account of M. Rivière's visit, A.-T., I, xlix.

14. *Dialogues des morts modernes: Dialogue II, Paracelse, Molière,* tr. from Fellows and Torrey, eds., *The Age of Enlightenment,* p. 48.

15. "Pourquoi nous ne pouvons pas définir l'humour," *RG,* II (1906), 604.

16. *Letters,* p. 219.

17. *Letters,* p. 139.

18. See Cross's statement to this effect in *The Development of the English Novel,* pp. 75–76.

19. *Coleridge's Miscellaneous Criticism,* ed. Raysor, p. 111.

20. Worcester, *Art of Satire,* p. 8.

21. ". . . laughter is nothing else but sudden glory from some sudden conception of some eminency in ourselves by comparison with the infirmity of others, or with our own." *Human Nature,* in *The English Works of Thomas Hobbes,* IV, 46.

22. " 'Tis in reality a serious study to learn to temper and regulate that humour which nature has given us as a more lenitive remedy against vice, and a kind of specific against superstition and melancholy delusion. There is a great difference between seeking how to raise a laugh from everything, and seeking in everything what justly may be laughed at" ("An Essay on the Freedom of Wit and Humour," in *Characteristics,* I, 85).

23. *Cinqmars et Derville,* in A.-T., IV, 468–69.

24. A.-T., IV, 472.

25. A.-T., IV, 473.

26. A.-T., IV, 16.

27. A.-T., XIV, 466.

28. A.-T., VIII, 389.

29. *Dialogues des morts,* tr. from Fellows and Torrey, eds., *The Age of Enlightenment,* p. 48.

30. This difference has been summarized by Professor John F. Ross: "It is commonplace to distinguish between two modes of satire: the genial, laughing, urbane satire of Horace, and the

severe, lashing satire of Juvenal. Whatever hostility the first mode may contain, it nevertheless works largely in terms of laughter. For convenience, it may be termed comic satire. The second mode emphasizes a severely satiric attack in which laughter is at a minimum, or perhaps even lacking. This may be termed caustic or corrosive satire." "The Final Comedy of Lemuel Gulliver," *University of California Studies in English,* VIII (1941), 177.

31. For a recent discussion, see Dieckmann, "The Relationship between Diderot's *Satire I* and *Satire II,*" *RR,* XLII (1952), 12–26.

32. *Œuvres de Diderot,* Pléiade ed., p. 1435.

33. A.-T., V, 15–16.

34. In this change from the savage laughter of the *Political Romance* to the genial laughter of *Tristram,* Sterne seems to be representative of an important transformation in the English attitude toward "humours" which has been admirably studied by Edward N. Hooker, "Humour in the Age of Pope," *Huntington Library Quarterly,* XI (1948), 361–85. Professor Hooker shows how the condemnatory attitude toward "humours" as follies and vices to be excoriated in the Restoration changed to the growing tolerance of eccentrics in the eighteenth century and the new opinion of satiric laughter as being unpleasant. If Sterne at first followed Swift in condemning eccentrics, as he appears to in the *Political Romance,* he shortly exchanged this view for the benevolent sympathy he applies to Shandeism.

35. For information about the early years of Sterne's literary activity, see Curtis, *The Politicks of Laurence Sterne.*

36. See *ibid.,* pp. 69–70; or *Letters,* p. 20.

37. Cross, *Life,* I, 171.

38 *Letters,* p. 147. Appropriately, once Sterne had finished Book IV of *Tristram* in May, 1761, he excluded Didius-Phutatorius from the subsequent volumes.

39. *Letters,* p. 241.

40. *Tr.,* Book VI, ch. 22, p. 466.

41. "The Levite and his Concubine," in *Sermons,* I, 299–300.

42. *Letters,* p. 76.

43. See his description of Book VII of *Tristram* in *Letters*, p. 231: "—tis a laughing good temperd Satyr against Traveling (as puppies travel)—"

44. *Letters*, pp. 76–77.

45. *Letters*, pp. 120–21.

46. Which is the point stressed by Wayne Booth in "The Self-Conscious Narrator in Comic Fiction before *Tristram Shandy*," *PMLA*, LXVII (1952), 165–68.

47. *Letters*, p. 76.

48. *Letters*, p. 416.

49. With shrewd insight, he wrote in his last letter, three days before his death, "—my spirits are fled—'tis a bad omen—" (*Letters*, p. 419).

50. *Tr.*, Book VI, ch. 17, p. 455.

51. *Letters*, p. 411; Sterne's italics.

52. Worcester, *Art of Satire*, pp. 37–38.

53. See De Froe, *Laurence Sterne and His Novels;* De Froe's study probably could be amplified by a mid-century review of the subject.

54. For instance, the sermon on "Time and Chance": "Yet at the same time, in respect to God's providence overruling these [sundry] events, it were profane to call them chance, for they are pure designation, and though invisible, are still the regular dispensations of the superintending power of that Almighty Being" (*Sermons*, I, 133).

NOTES TO IV: FICTIONAL THEORIES AND PRACTICES

1. *Lettres à Sophie Volland*, II, 82 (10 November 1765).

2. *Letters*, p. 239.

3. A reference to Grimm.

4. *Letters*, p. 90; Sterne's italics.

5. *Letters*, p. 89.

6. *Letters*, p. 105.

7. *Letters*, p. 76.

8. For further information, see Taupin, "Richardson, Diderot et l'art de conter," *FR*, XII (1939), 181–94.

9. A.-T., IV, 500.

10. A.-T., XVIII, 98.

11. MacLean, *John Locke and English Literature*, p. 17.

12. For the importance of particularized detail for the realistic novel, see Watt, "Realism and the Novel," *EC*, II (1952), 383.

13. Richardson, *Clarissa* (Oxford, 1929–1931), p. xlv.

14. *Tr.*, Book IV, ch. 15, p. 300.

15. A.-T., V, 276–77.

16. A.-T., XI, 254.

17. Tourneux, *Diderot et Catherine II*, p. 452.

18. See May, "Le Modèle inconnu de *La Religieuse* de Diderot: Marguerite Delamarre," *RHL*, LI (1951), 273–87. See also, for a more expanded study, Chapter III of his *Diderot et "La Religieuse,"* pp. 47–76.

19. A.-T., V, 162.

20. He had also worked over the preliminary letters to Crois- mare. Revealing the plot later, Grimm said that Diderot would deliberately destroy anything in the letters which did not seem true, and consulted his wife, Grimm, and Mme d'Epinay about passages where the authenticity might be improved. A.-T., V, 204.

21 *Diderot Interpreter of Nature*, tr. by Jean Stewart and Jona- than Kemp, p. 250.

22. A.-T., V, 281.

23. May, *Quatre visages de Denis Diderot*, pp. 182–83.

24. *Ibid.*, p. 186.

25. *Tr.*, Book II, ch. 6, p. 101.

26. *Tr.*, Book V, ch. 5, p. 371.

27. Foster, *History of the Pre-Romantic Novel*, p. 132.

28. *Lettres à Sophie Volland*, I, 296 (16 September 1762).

29. A.-T., V, 213; tr. in Cru, *Diderot*, p. 348.

30. Professor Harry Levin has made some very applicable re- marks in a recent symposium on realism: ". . . looking backwards

from Gide, we can see how every great novel has attempted . . . to distinguish what is real from what is counterfeit. Defoe's narrations, he invariably assured his readers, are not fiction but fact; and Diderot pointedly entitled one of his stories *Ceci n'est pas un conte*. To convince us of his essential veracity, the novelist must always be disclaiming the fictitious and breaking through the encrustations of the literary" ("What Is Realism," *CL,* III [1951], 196).

31. Cited in Wellek and Warren, *Theory of Literature,* p. 223. For an interesting parallel, compare Diderot's statement and practices with Wellek's and Warren's discussion, pp. 223-24: "The novel is realistic; the romance is poetic or epic: we should now call it 'mythic.' Mrs. Radcliffe, Sir Walter Scott, Hawthorne are writers of 'romance.' Fanny Burney, Jane Austen, Anthony Trollope, George Gissing are novelists. The two types, which are polar, indicate the double descent of prose narrative: the novel develops from the lineage of non-fictitious narrative forms—the letter, the journal, the memoir or biography, the chronicle or history; it develops, so to speak, out of documents; stylistically, it stresses representative detail, 'mimesis' in its narrow sense. The romance, on the other hand, the continuator of the epic and the medieval romance, may neglect verisimilitude of detail (the reproduction of individuated speech in dialogue, for example), addressing itself to a higher reality, a deeper psychology."

32. *Letters,* pp. 89-90.

33. *Letters,* p. 76.

34. In *De la poésie dramatique,* Diderot had commented on this problem which has confronted innumerable writers: "Why search in an author for his characters? What has Racine in common with Athalie, Molière with Tartuffe? It is the men of genius who have known how to probe to the very depths of our feelings and to tear out the trait which impresses us. Let us judge the poems and leave the personalities aside" (A.-T., VII, 363).

35. *Letters,* pp. 402-3.

36. A.-T., XI, 254.

37. See above, p. 95.

38. *SJ*, "The Address—Versailles," p. 242. See also Sterne's reference to what he calls a "shorthand" of looks and gestures, *SJ*, "The Translation—Paris," p. 222.

39. *Letters*, p. 88; Sterne's italics.

40. MacLean, *John Locke and English Literature*, p. 47.

41. *Tr.*, Book viii, ch. 31, p. 608.

42. He does slip into common parlance while analyzing the character of Herod in a sermon, and he makes a passing reference to ruling passions in two other sermons. See "Evil-speaking," in *Sermons*, I, 175, and "Felix's Behaviour Towards Paul, Examined," in *Sermons*, I, 308.

43. *Tr.*, Book ii, ch. 5, p. 93.

44. For an excellent background for Sterne's place in the English tradition of "humours," see Edward N. Hooker, "Humor in the Age of Pope," *Huntington Library Quarterly*, XI (1948), 361–85.

45. See *Tr.*, Book iii, ch. 9, p. 171.

46. See *Tr.*, Book v, ch. 7.

47. *Tr.*, Book iii, ch. 39, p. 242.

48. *Tr.*, Book vi, ch. 39, p. 491.

49. *Tr.*, Book ii, ch. 12, p. 116.

50. See *Tr.*, Book i, ch. 22.

51. Actually, Suzanne, the one person whose story is intentionally developed over a period of years, is considerably altered by the end of *La Religieuse*.

52. A.-T., XII, 84.

53. His subsequent remarks are worth repeating: ". . . in case the character of parson Yorick, and this sample of his sermons is liked,—there are now in the possession of the Shandy family, as many as will make a handsome volume, at the world's service—" (*Tr.*, Book ii, ch. 17, pp. 147–48).

54. See Seiden, "Jean-François Rameau and Diderot's *Neveu*," in Fellows and Torrey, eds., *Diderot Studies*, pp. 143–91.

55. *Letters*, p. 301.

56. For example, in *Œuvres de Diderot*, Pléiade ed., p. 1442, the editor, André Billy, says that the digressions in *Jacques* derive from Sterne. Le Breton, *Le Roman français*, p. 322, believes that it was Sterne who taught Diderot to utilize little details, though he also adds Richardson, almost as an afterthought. Mornet, *Le Neveu de Rameau*, p. 153, makes the startling statement that Sterne's influence is evident not only in *Jacques* but also in the *Neveu de Rameau*—although the satire was written a year before Diderot had read the first six volumes of *Tristram*. Baldwin, "The Literary Influence of Sterne in France," *PMLA*, XVII (1902), p. 227, despite his belief that *Jacques* is only a superficial imitation of *Tristram*, itemizes the debt: pauses, digressions, interpolations, conversation between author and reader, gesture. Barton, *L'Influence de Laurence Sterne en France*, p. 113, says that Diderot copies, unsuccessfully, the "means Sterne uses to arouse our smile and laughter," although he does not clarify these means. He also states, p. 120, that Diderot did not use pantomime and gesture until after 1762, when he had read Sterne, and that therefore Diderot's treatment of these two devices from 1762 on is due to Sterne's influence. Ducros, *Diderot*, p. 221, says that Diderot owes both gesture and "tics" to Sterne.

57. See note 76 to this chapter.

58. Apparently, the lady had also read *Clarissa*, though Diderot fails to mention it.

59. This device, to be sure, is not original with Diderot. Leo Spitzer has pointed out Racine's use of a "multiplicity of planes" and has suggested that it is reminiscent of "the baroque 'mirror' technique of Velasquez" (*Linguistics and Literary History*, p. 107). Jean Hytier has gone on to prove that there is nothing either "specifically Racinian or baroque" in this preoccupation with the techniques of narrative realism. "La Méthode de M. Leo Spitzer," *RR*, XLI (1950), 57.

60. A.-T., V, 312.

61. A.-T., VI, 105; see also 91.

62. *Tr.*, Book VII, ch. 6, p. 503.

63. A.-T., X, 75.

64. A.-T., VI, 62.

65. *Tr.*, Book V, ch. 30, p. 406.

66. *Tr.*, Book V, ch. 7, p. 376.

67. *Tr.*, Book V, ch. 9, p. 379.

68. *Letters*, p. 87.

69. Cradock, *Literary and Miscellaneous Memoirs*, I, 207–8.

70. *Tr.*, Book II, ch. 17, p. 145.

71. Cross, *Life*, I, 226–27.

72. *Tr.*, Book II, ch. 5, p. 100.

73. *Tr.*, Book VI, ch. 29, p. 475.

74. *Tr.*, Book IV, ch. 7, p. 288.

75. A.-T., VI, 62.

76. See his letter of 20 October 1760, *Lettres à Sophie Volland*, I, 155: "What an odd thing conversations are, especially when the company is a bit varied. Note the circuits that we've made; dreams caused by delirium are no more anomalous; nevertheless, just as there is nothing disconnected either in the head of a man who dreams or of one who is mad, so everything also adheres in conversation; but sometimes it would be difficult to recover the imperceptible links which have drawn together so many disparate ideas. One man tosses out a word which he has detached from what has preceded and followed it in his head; another man does the same, and then it's every man for himself. A single physical quality can lead the mind which is preoccupied with it to an infinity of diverse things. Let's take a color, yellow, for example: gold is yellow, silk is yellow, bile is yellow, hay is yellow; how many other threads would not this thread respond to? Madness, the dream, the disorder of conversation all consist in passing from one thing to another through the mediation of a common quality."

77. MacLean, *John Locke and English Literature*, p. 87.

78. *Tr.*, Book III, ch. 30, p. 227.

79. *Tr.*, Book III, ch. 39, p. 242.

80. *Tr.*, Book IV, ch. 2, p. 283.

81. See Baldwin, "The Literary Influence of Sterne in France," *PMLA*, XVII (1902), 224.

82. J. Robert Loy has suggested that all the interpolated stories in *Jacques* may be seen as deriving from the theme of Diderot's short story, *Sur l'inconséquence du jugement public*. See Loy, *Determined Fatalist*, pp. 75 ff.

83. Cited in A.-T., V, 375.

84. A.-T., II, 9.

85. In his edition of Diderot's collected works, Naigeon was to continue the spirit of this comment by remarking on the typically brilliant disorder of the *Essai*.

86. See *Lettres à Sophie Volland*, I, 151–53 (20 October 1760).

87. See Dieckmann, *Inventaire du fonds Vandeul*, pp. xiii, xxvii, xlv.

88. Belaval, *L'Esthétique sans paradoxe de Diderot*, p. 289.

89. Pommier, "Autour de la *Lettre sur les sourds et muets*," *RHL*, LI (1951), 262.

90. A.-T., VI, 54.

91. See Loy on "The Composition and Structure of Jacques," in *Determined Fatalist*, pp. 54–78.

92. A.-T., V, 207.

93. A.-T., V, 207.

94. See note 20 to this chapter.

95. For an admirable and detailed reconstruction of Diderot's method here, see Geary, "The Composition and Publication of *Les Deux amis de Bourbonne*," in Fellows and Torrey, eds., *Diderot Studies*, pp. 27–45.

96. For a full analysis of its composition, see Schlösser, *Rameaus Neffe*. For an example, see the Nephew's account of the Jew of Utrecht, a story Diderot had picked up in Holland during his trip to Russia, 1773–74, and had included in his *Voyage en Hollande*, A.-T., XVII, 404–5.

97. A.-T., V, 207.

98. For detailed information about the latter, see Herbert Dieck-mann's study of "The Préface-Annexe of *La Religieuse*," in Fellows and Torrey, eds., *Diderot Studies II*, pp. 21–40.

99. "It has ever been my aim to run from the gay to the serious and backwards from the serious to the gay" (*Tr.*, Book II, ch. 1, p. 161).

100. "If anyone objects that my book is too light and fantastic for a divine or too satirical for a Christian, let him remember that 'tis not I but Democritus who spoke" (*Tr.*, Book V, ch. 1, p. 353).

101. Lehman, "Of Time, Personality and the Author," *University of California Studies in English*, VIII (1941), 245.

102. *Tr.*, Book III, ch. 23, p. 213.

103. *Tr.*, Book III, ch. 33, p. 482.

104. See, for example, Book IV, ch. 25, p. 323; Book VIII, ch. 6, p. 565.

105. See above, pp. 145–46.

106. Ch. 32, pp. 348–49.

107. *Letters*, p. 143.

108. See Putney, "Laurence Sterne, Apostle of Laughter," in *The Age of Johnson*, p. 164.

109. See pp. 143–44.

110. This point is also suggested in the introduction to James Work's edition of *Tristram Shandy*, and it is expanded more fully in an article by Booth, "Did Sterne Complete *Tristram Shandy?*" *MP*, XLVIII (1951), 172–83.

111. *Letters*, p. 284.

112. *Letters*, p. 150.

113. See Jefferson, "*Tristram Shandy* and the Tradition of Learned Wit," *EC*, I (1951), 225–48. For Sterne's refusal to be too restricted by this tradition, see the contrast between him and the Scriblerians, p. 78 above.

114. *Tr.*, Book II, ch. 8, p. 105.

115. Cited in Stapfer, *Laurence Sterne*, pp. xx–xxiii. For similar remarks in Diderot's works, see A.-T., I, 311: "You judge the successive existence of the world the way the ephemeral fly judges

yours. The world is eternal for you just as you are eternal for the being that lives but an instant." In the *Rêve de D'Alembert* (A.-T., II, 132), Diderot carries his perceptions even further: "Who knows what animal species have preceded us? what animal species will succeed our own? Everything changes, everything passes, only the whole remains. Ceaselessly, the world begins and ends; at each instant it is both at its beginning and its end."

116. Diderot's appreciation of this phenomenon is indicated not only in his devices—see above, pp. 144–45—but also in various comments such as his remark to Sophie Volland that place, time, and space are all suspended for the man in deep meditation, or his pre-Proustian observation that a certain sound, or object, or place can recall to immediacy a long interval of one's past. For a perceptive study, see Poulet, *Etudes sur le temps humain,* pp. 194–217. It should be noted, however, that whereas Diderot's concepts of time and their corollaries are considerably more developed than Sterne's, Sterne does give his an essential part in his novel. Diderot's theories appear elsewhere in his writings, for he exploits them relatively infrequently in his fiction. The situation is analogous to the place of the stream-of-consciousness technique in their writings. Diderot is surely aware of its possibilities, as his letter of 20 October 1760 to Sophie Volland shows, yet it is Sterne who deliberately employs it in his fiction.

117. Baird, "The Time-Scheme of 'Tristram Shandy,'" *PMLA,* LI (1936), 803–20.

118. *Letters,* p. 395.

119. *Letters,* p. 81.

120. *Letters,* pp. 90–91.

121. This entire letter is a carefully written defense which Sterne considered publishing as a preface to Book III.

122. *Letters,* p. 117.

123. *Letters,* p. 120.

124. *Letters,* p. 353.

125. *Letters,* p. 354.

126. *Letters,* pp. 12–15.

127. *Letters,* p. 360.

128. See above, p. 85.

129. See, for example, Cross, *Life,* II, 119.

130. Rabelais, in this instance.

131. Actually, once people had become used to it, nobody seems to have minded Sterne's gleeful pillagings. That audiences were aware of it in his own time is attested to by contemporary critics and letters, and in 1798 John Ferriar published an incomplete exposure entitled *Illustrations of Sterne* which ran into a second edition in two volumes.

132. Bagehot, *Literary Studies,* II, 294.

1. Garat, *Mémoires historiques sur la vie de M. Suard,* II, 136.

2. Folkierski, *Entre le classicisme et le romantisme,* p. 356.

3. Lefebvre, *Diderot,* p. 266. For an extended study, see Boutet de Monvel, "Diderot et la notion de style," *RHL,* LI (1951), 288–305.

4. Cross, *Life,* II, 215.

5. Charles, *Growth of Diderot's Fame,* p. 70.

6. See *Transformations de la langue française,* pp. 13–27.

7. Brunel, *Histoire de la langue et de la littérature française,* VI, 847–48.

8. Steel, *Diderot's Imagery,* p. 213.

9. Baker, *History of the English Novel,* III, 41–42.

10. *Memoirs of the Extraordinary Life, Works and Discoveries of Martinus Scriblerus,* ed. Kerby-Miller (New Haven, 1950), p. 8.

11. *The Works of Samuel Johnson* (Oxford, 1825), V, 49.

12. Cited in Charles, *Growth of Diderot's Fame,* pp. 70–71.

13. Locke, *Essay,* Book III, ch. ii, §1, p. 9.

14. *Ibid.,* ch. v, §16, p. 54; Locke's italics.

15. *Tr.,* Book II, ch. 2, pp. 87–88.

16. A.-T., VI, 25. Diderot held that men, for example, could never understand the pangs of childbirth.

17. *Tr.,* Book III, ch. 20, p. 205.

18. A.-T., XIV, 416.

19. A.-T., I, 350. Condillac had said that all abstract substantives were developed from adjectives, or from adverbs, which themselves had developed from adjectives.

20. *Ibid.;* Diderot's italics.

21. *Lettres à Sophie Volland,* II, 272 (undated fragment).

22. Venturi, *Jeunesse de Diderot,* pp. 257–58.

23. A.-T., I, 371–72.

24. A.-T., XIV, 429.

25. A.-T., XIV, 432, 433, 437–41.

26. Brunot, *Histoire de la langue française,* VI, 802. See also Gohin, *Transformations de la langue française,* p. 171.

27. A.-T., I, 301–2.

28. A.-T., I, 369.

29. Cazamian, *Essais en deux langues,* p. 56.

30. A.-T., XII, 77.

31. A.-T., XVIII, 207.

32. A.-T., XIV, 495.

33. A.-T., X, 127.

34. A.-T., VII, 107.

35. A.-T., V, 466.

36. A.-T., VII, 100–101.

37. A.-T., VII, 134.

38. *Lettres à Sophie Volland,* II, 275 (undated fragment).

39. A.-T., III, 398–99.

40. See Engelmayer, *Romantische Tendenzen im Werke Diderots,* p. 64.

41. *Ibid.,* p. 88.

42. *Tr.,* Book I, ch. 3, p. 90; Sterne's italics.

43. *Tr.,* Book I, ch. 4, p. 91.

44. *Tr.,* Book IV, ch. 20, p. 308.

45. A.-T., V, 18.

46. A.-T., V, 463.

47. Book VII, ch. 2, pp. 497–98.

48. A.-T., VI, 40.

49. *Tr.,* Book VI, ch. 7, p. 438.

50. A.-T., V, 154.

51. *SJ,* "The Monk—Calais," pp. 6 and 9.

52. See Cross's description in *Life,* II, 149 ff.

53. Cf. the following comments by Herbert Read and Otto Engelmayer:

"Sterne, more than any other writer of his age, reestablished the native tradition, returning to the original genius of the language and making the basis of his style an English idiom that had been lost almost since Milton's day" (Read, *The Sense of Glory,* p. 148).

"It can be said without exaggeration, that the vernacular in [Diderot's] later works—more in *Jacques* than in the *Neveu*—takes on a significance which was greater than any that had been met with since Rabelais, and which was, most important of all, unheard of in the eighteenth century" (Engelmayer, *Romantische Tendenzen im Werke Diderots,* p. 82).

54. A.-T., III, 384.

55. A.-T., VI, 33.

56. A.-T., VI, 70.

57. For lists of examples, see Engelmayer, *Romantische Tendenzen im Werke Diderots,* pp. 84–86; Gohin, *Transformations de la langue française,* p. 171; Steel, *Diderot's Imagery,* p. 214.

58. *Lettres à Sophie Volland,* II, 276 (undated fragment).

59. See above, pp. 160–61.

60. Turnell, *Novel in France,* p. 23.

61. A.-T., X, 127.

NOTES TO VI: CONCLUSION

1. A.-T., I, xxii.

2. A.-T., XI, 415.

3. Davis, "The Sense of the Real in English Fiction," *CL,* III (1951), 211.

4. *The Great Chain of Being,* pp. 293–94.

5. Belaval, *L'Esthétique sans paradoxe de Diderot,* pp. 286–87.

BIBLIOGRAPHY

WORKS OF DIDEROT

Œuvres complètes. Revues sur les éditions originales, notices, notes, table analytique, par J. Assézat et M. Tourneux. 20 vols. Paris, Garnier, 1875–1877.

Œuvres de Diderot. Texte établi et annoté par André Billy. Pléiade ed. Paris, Gallimard, 1946.

Correspondance inédite. Publiée d'après les manuscrits originaux, avec des introductions et des notes par André Babelon. 2 vols. Paris, Gallimard, 1931.

Correspondance littéraire, philosophique et critique, par Grimm, Diderot, Raynal, Meister, etc. Revue sur les textes originaux par Maurice Tourneux. 16 vols. Paris, Garnier, 1877–1882.

Lettres à Sophie Volland. Textes publiés d'après les manuscrits originaux, avec une introduction, des variantes et des notes par André Babelon. 2 vols. Paris, Gallimard, 1938.

Selected Writings, in Diderot, Interpreter of Nature. Tr. by Jean Stewart and Jonathan Kemp; ed. with introduction by Jonathan Kemp. New York, International Publishers, 1938.

WORKS OF STERNE

The Works of Laurence Sterne. Shakespeare Head edition. 7 vols. Oxford, Blackwell, 1926–1927.

A Facsimile Reproduction of a Unique Catalogue of Laurence Sterne's Library. Introduction by Charles Whibley. London, Tregaskis; New York, Wells, 1930.

Letters of Laurence Sterne. Ed. by Lewis Perry Curtis. Oxford, Clarendon Press, 1935.

The Life and Opinions of Tristram Shandy, Gentleman. New York, Modern Library, n.d.

The Life and Opinions of Tristram Shandy, Gent. Ed. with notes and introduction by James Aiken Work. New York, Odyssey, 1940.

A Sentimental Journey through France and Italy. World Classics edition. London, Oxford University Press, 1948.

The Sermons of Mr. Yorick. 2 vols. New York, Taylor, 1904.

SECONDARY SOURCES

Adam, Antoine. "Rousseau et Diderot," *RDSH,* LIII (1949), 21–34.

Arbuthnot, Pope, Swift, Gay, Parnell, Harley. Memoirs of the Extraordinary Life, Works, and Discoveries of Martinus Scriblerus. Ed. by Charles Kerby-Miller. New Haven, Yale University Press, 1950.

Bagehot, Walter. Literary Studies. Ed. by Richard Holt Hutton. Vol. II. London, Longmans, 1884.

Baird, Theodore. "The Time-Scheme of *Tristram Shandy,*" *PMLA,* LI (1936), 803–20.

Baker, Ernest A. The History of the English Novel. Vols. III and IV. New York, Barnes and Noble, 1950.

Baldensperger, Fernand. "Les Définitions de l'humour," in Etudes d'histoire littéraire (Paris, Hachette, 1907), pp. 176–222.

Baldwin, Charles Sears. "The Literary Influence of Sterne in France," *PMLA,* XVII (1902), 221–36.

Barton, Francis Brown. Etude sur l'influence de Laurence Sterne en France au dix-huitième siècle. Paris, Hachette, 1911.

Becker, Carl. "The Dilemma of Diderot," *Phil R,* XXIV (1915), 54–71.

Belaval, Yvon. L'Esthétique sans paradoxe de Diderot. Paris, Gallimard, 1950.

Bergmann, Frederick L. "David Garrick and *The Clandestine Marriage,*" *PMLA,* LXVII (1952), 148–62.

Billy, André. *Diderot.* Paris, Les Editions de France, 1932.

Birrell, Francis. "Things Diderot Could Do," *The Criterion,* XII (1933), 632–41.

Booth, Wayne. "Did Sterne Complete *Tristram Shandy?*" *MP,* XLVIII (1951), 172–83.

—— "The Self-Conscious Narrator in Comic Fiction before *Tristram Shandy,*" *PMLA,* LXVII (1952), 163–85.

Boutet de Monvel, A. "Diderot et la notion de style," *RHL,* LI (1951), 288–305.

Bowle, John. Hobbes and His Critics: A Study in Seventeenth Century Constitutionalism. London, Jonathan Cape, 1951.

Boys, Richard C. *"Tristram Shandy and the Conventional Novel," Papers of the Michigan Academy of Science, Arts and Letters,* XXXVII (1951), 423–36.

Brett, R. L. The Third Earl of Shaftesbury: A Study in Eighteenth Century Literary Theory. London, Hutchinson's University Library, 1951.

Brunel, Lucien. "Diderot et les encyclopédistes," in Vol. VI of L. Petit de Julleville, ed., Histoire de la langue et de la littérature française (Paris, Colin, 1909), pp. 316–85.

Brunetière, F. "Les *Salons* de Diderot," in Etudes critiques sur l'histoire de la littérature française, 2e sér. 3e éd. (Paris, Hachette, 1899), pp. 295–321.

Brunot, Ferdinand. Histoire de la langue française des origines à 1900. Vol. VI. Paris, Colin, 1930.

Butler, Joseph. The Works of Joseph Butler. 2 vols. Oxford, Oxford University Press, 1850.

Caldwell, James R. "The Solemn Romantics," *University of California Studies in English,* VIII (1941), 257–71.

Carlyle, Thomas. "Diderot," in Critical and Miscellaneous Essays, Vol. III (New York, Scribners, 1900), pp. 177–248.

Carré, Meyrick H. Phases of Thought in England. Oxford, Clarendon Press, 1949.

Cazamian, Louis. Essais en deux langues. Paris, Didier, 1938.

—— "Pourquoi nous ne pouvons pas définir l'humour," *RG,* II (1906), 601–34.

Charles, Mary Lane. The Growth of Diderot's Fame in France from 1784 to 1875. Thesis, Bryn Mawr, Pennsylvania, 1942.

Coleridge, Samuel Taylor. Coleridge's Miscellaneous Criticism. Ed. by Thomas Middleton Raysor. London, Constable, 1936.

Commaille, Anne-Marie de. "Diderot et le symbole littéraire," in Otis E. Fellows and Norman L. Torrey, eds., Diderot Studies (Syracuse, Syracuse University Press, 1949), pp. 94–120.

Condillac, Etienne Bonnot de. Essai sur l'origine des connaissances humaines. Paris, Colin, 1924.

Correspondance littéraire: see under Works of Diderot.

Cradock, Joseph. Literary and Miscellaneous Memoirs. Vol. I. London, Nichols, 1828.

Crane, Ronald S. "Suggestions toward a Genealogy of the 'Man of Feeling,'" *ELH,* I (1934), 205–30.

Cross, Wilbur L. The Development of the English Novel. New York, Macmillan, 1923.

—— The Life and Times of Laurence Sterne. New ed. 2 vols. New Haven, Yale University Press, 1925.

Cru, R. Loyalty. Diderot as a Disciple of English Thought. New York, Columbia University Press, 1913.

Curtis, Lewis Perry. "The First Printer of *Tristram Shandy,*" *PMLA,* XLVII (1930), 777–89.

—— The Politicks of Laurence Sterne. London, Oxford University Press, 1929.

Davis, Robert Gorham. "The Sense of the Real in English Fiction," *CL,* III (1951), 200–217.

Dieckmann, Herbert. "Bibliographical Data on Diderot," in Studies in Honor of Frederick W. Shipley (Washington University Studies, new series, Language and Literature, No. 14; St. Louis, 1942), pp. 181–220.

—— "Diderot's Conception of Genius," *JHI,* II (1941), 151–82.

Dieckmann, Herbert. "The Influence of Francis Bacon on Diderot's *Interprétation de la nature*," *RR*, XXXIV (1943), 303-30.

—— Inventaire du fonds Vandeul et inédits de Diderot. Geneva, Droz, 1951.

—— "The Préface-Annexe of *La Religieuse*," in Otis E. Fellows and Norman L. Torrey, eds., Diderot Studies II (Syracuse, Syracuse University Press, 1952), pp. 21-40.

—— "The Relationship between Diderot's *Satire I* and *Satire II*," *RR*, XLII (1952), 12-26.

Dilworth, Ernest Nevin. The Unsentimental Journey of Laurence Sterne. New York, King's Crown Press, 1948.

Ducros, Louis. Diderot l'homme et l'écrivain. Paris, Perrin, 1894.

Ellis, Havelock. "Diderot," in The New Spirit (London, Bell, 1890), pp. 34-67.

Engelmayer, Otto. Romantische Tendenzen im künstlerischen, kritischen und kunstphilosophischen Werke Denis Diderots. Memmingen, 1933.

Faguet, Emile. Dix-huitième siècle: Etudes littéraires. Paris, Boivin, n.d.

Fellows, Otis E. "The Theme of Genius in Diderot's *Neveu de Rameau*," in Otis E. Fellows and Norman L. Torrey, eds., Diderot Studies II (Syracuse, Syracuse University Press, 1952), pp. 168-99.

Fellows, Otis E., and Alice G. Green. "Diderot and the Abbé Dulaurens," in Otis E. Fellows and Norman L. Torrey, eds., Diderot Studies (Syracuse, Syracuse University Press, 1949), pp. 64-93.

Fellows, Otis E., and Norman L. Torrey, eds. The Age of Enlightenment. New York, Crofts, 1942.

—— Diderot Studies. Syracuse, Syracuse University Press, 1949.

—— Diderot Studies II. Syracuse, Syracuse University Press, 1952.

Ferriar, John. Illustrations of Sterne. 2d ed. 2 vols. London, Cadell and Davies, 1812.

Fitzgerald, Percy. The Life of Laurence Sterne. 2 vols. London, Downey, 1896.

Folkierski, Wladislaw. Entre le classicisme et le romantisme. Paris, Champion, 1925.

Foster, James R. The History of the Pre-Romantic Novel in England. New York, Modern Language Association, 1949.

Froe, Arie de. Laurence Sterne and His Novels Studied in the Light of Modern Psychology. Groningen, Noordhoff, 1925.

Garat, Dominique-Joseph. Mémoires historiques sur la vie de M. Suard, sur ses écrits et sur le XVIIIe siècle. 2 vols. Paris, Belin, 1820.

Geary, Edward J. "The Composition and Publication of Les Deux amis de Bourbonne," in Otis E. Fellows and Norman L. Torrey, eds., Diderot Studies (Syracuse, Syracuse University Press, 1949), pp. 27-45.

Gillot, H. Denis Diderot. Paris, Courville, 1937.

Gilman, Margaret. "Imagination and Creation in Diderot," in Otis E. Fellows and Norman L. Torrey, eds., Diderot Studies II (Syracuse, Syracuse University Press, 1952), pp. 200-220.

—— "The Poet According to Diderot," RR, XXXVII (1946), 37-54.

Gohin, F. Les Transformations de la langue française pendant la deuxième moitié du dix-huitième siècle. Paris, Belin, 1908.

Goncourt, Edmond, and Jules de Goncourt. Journal. Paris, Flammarion, 1935.

Gordon, Douglas H., and Norman L. Torrey. The Censoring of Diderot's Encyclopédie and the Re-established Text. New York, Columbia University Press, 1947.

Grappe, Georges. "Un Roman de Diderot: Jacques le fataliste," Rhebd, VIII (1922), 463-72.

Green, Frederick Charles. Eighteenth-Century France. New York, Appleton, 1931.

—— Minuet. London, Dent, 1935.

Greene, Graham, "Fielding and Sterne," in Bonamy Dobree, ed., From Anne to Victoria (London, Cassell, 1937), pp. 279-89.

Hammond, Lansing Van der Heyden. Laurence Sterne's *Sermons of Mr. Yorick*. New Haven, Yale University Press, 1948.

Hartley, Lodwick Charles. This Is Lorence. Chapel Hill, University of North Carolina Press, 1943.

—— "Tristram and the Angels," *College English,* IX (1947), 62–9.

Havens, George. "Diderot and the Composition of Rousseau's *First Discourse,*" *RR,* XXX (1939), 369–81.

Hazard, Paul. "Les Origines philosophiques de l'homme de sentiment," *RR,* XXVIII (1937), 318–41.

—— La Pensée européenne au dix-huitième siècle. 3 vols. Paris, Boivin, 1946.

Hedgcock, Frank A. A Cosmopolitan Actor, David Garrick and His French Friends. London, Paul, 1912.

Hobbes, Thomas. The English Works of Thomas Hobbes. Vol. IV. London, Bohn, 1840.

Hooker, Edward N. "Humour in the Age of Pope," *Huntington Library Quarterly,* XI (1948), 361–85.

Hubert, René. Les Sciences sociales dans l'*Encyclopédie*. Paris, Alcan, 1923.

Humphreys, A. R. " 'The Friend of Mankind' (1700–1760)—An Aspect of Eighteenth-Century Sensibility," *RES,* XXIV (1948), 203–18.

Hunt, H. J. "Logic and Linguistics: Diderot as 'Grammairien-Philosophe,' " *M.L.R.,* XXX (1938), 215–33.

Hytier, Jean. "La Méthode de M. Leo Spitzer," *RR,* XLI (1950), 42–59.

Jasinski, René. Histoire de la littérature française. Paris, Boivin, 1947.

Jefferson, D. W. *"Tristram Shandy* and the Tradition of Learned Wit," *EC,* I (1951), 225–48.

Johansson, J. Viktor. Etudes sur Denis Diderot. Paris, Champion, 1927.

Johnson, Samuel. The Works of Samuel Johnson. Vol. V. Oxford, Talboys and Wheeler, 1825.

Kyle, W. M. "British Ethical Theories: The Intuitionist Reaction against Hobbes," *The Australasian Journal of Psychology and Philosophy,* V (1927), 113–31.

Laird, John. *Hobbes.* London, Benn, 1934.

———"Shandyan Philosophy," in Philosophical Incursions into English Literature (Cambridge, Cambridge University Press, 1946), pp. 75–91.

Lanson, Gustave. Histoire de la littérature française. 12e éd. Paris, Hachette, 1912.

Le Breton, André. Le Roman français au dix-huitième siècle. Paris, Boivin, 1925.

Lefebvre, Henri. Diderot. Paris, Hier et Aujourd'hui, 1949.

Legras, Joseph. Diderot et l'*Encyclopédie.* 4e éd. Amiens, Malfère, 1928.

Legros, René P. "Diderot et Shaftesbury," *M.L.R.,* XIX (1924), 188–94.

Lehman, B. H. "Of Time, Personality and the Author," *University of California Studies in English,* VII (1941), 233–50.

Levin, Harry. "What Is Realism?" *CL,* III (1951), 193–99.

Locke, John. An Essay Concerning Human Understanding. Ed. by Alexander Campbell Fraser. 2 vols. Oxford, Clarendon Press, 1894.

Lovejoy, Arthur O. Essays in the History of Ideas. Baltimore, Johns Hopkins Press, 1948.

——— The Great Chain of Being. Cambridge, Mass., Harvard University Press, 1936.

Loy, J. Robert. Diderot's Determined Fatalist. New York, King's Crown Press, 1950.

MacLean, Kenneth. "Imagination and Sympathy: Sterne and Adam Smith," *JHI,* X (1949), 399–410.

——— John Locke and English Literature of the Eighteenth Century. New Haven, Yale University Press, 1936.

Martineau, James. Types of Ethical Theory. Vol. I. 3d ed., rev. Oxford, Clarendon Press, 1901.

May, Georges. Diderot et *La Religieuse*. Paris, Presses universitaires de France; New Haven, Yale University Press, 1954.

—— "Le Modèle inconnu de *La Religieuse* de Diderot: Marguerite Delamarre," *RHL*, LI (1951), 273–87.

—— Quatre visages de Denis Diderot. Paris, Boivin, 1951.

Mayoux, J. J. "Diderot and the Technique of Modern Literature," *M.L.R.*, XXXI (1936), 518–31.

Mesnard, Pierre. "Sophie Volland et la maturité de Diderot," *RDSH*, LIII (1949), 12–20.

Meyer, Eugène. "Diderot moraliste," *RCC*, XXVI, 1 (1924), 375–81, 469–80, 641–49; XXVI, 2 (1925), 521–37, 742–60.

Meyers, Walter L. "O, the Hobby-Horse," *VQ*, XIX (1943), 268–77.

Monglond, André. Le Préromantisme français. 2 vols. Grenoble, Arthaud, 1930.

Monro, D. H. Argument of Laughter. Melbourne, Melbourne University Press, 1951.

Morley, John. Diderot and the Encyclopaedists. 2 vols. London, Macmillan, 1886.

Mornet, Daniel. Diderot, l'homme et l'œuvre. Paris, Boivin, 1941.

—— Le Neveu de Rameau. Paris, Cours de Droit, 1947/48.

—— "La Véritable Signification du *Neveu de Rameau*," *RDM*, XL (1927), 881–908.

Muir, Edwin. The Structure of the Novel. London, Hogarth Press, 1928.

Naigeon, Jacques-André. Mémoires historiques et philosophiques sur la vie et les ouvrages de Diderot. Paris, Brière, 1821.

Nitze, William, and E. Preston Dargan. A History of French Literature. Rev. ed. New York, Holt, 1930.

Petit de Julleville, L., ed. Histoire de la langue et de la littérature française. Vol. VI. Paris, Colin, 1909.

Pommier, Jean. "Autour de la 'Lettre sur les sourds et muets,'" *RHL*, LI (1951), 261–72.

—— "Etudes sur Diderot," *RHP*, X (1942), 153–80.

Pommier, Jean. "Le Problème Naigeon," *RDSH*, LIII (1949), 2–11.

―――― "Les *Salons* de Diderot et leur influence au XIXe siècle: Baudelaire et le salon de 1846," *RCC*, XXXVII, 2 (1936), 289–306, 437–52.

Pope, Alexander. The Works of Alexander Pope. Vol. VI. Ed. by Whitwell Elwin and William J. Courthope. London, J. Murray, 1871–1889.

Pope-Hennessy, Una. "Laurence Sterne," *QR*, CCLXVI (1936), 81–101.

Pottle, Frederick A. "Bozzy and Yorick," *Blackwood's Magazine*, CCXVII (1925), 297–313.

Poulet, Georges. Etudes sur le temps humains. Paris, Plon, 1950.

Praz, Mario. "An English Imitation of Diderot's *La Religieuse:* C. R. Maturin's *Tale of the Spaniard,*" *R.E.S.,* VI (1930), 429–36.

―――― The Romantic Agony. Tr. by Angus Davidson. London, Oxford University Press, 1933.

Putney, Rufus S. D. "Alas, Poor Eliza!" *M.L.R.,* XLI (1946), 411–13.

―――― "The Evolution of *A Sentimental Journey,*" *PQ,* XIX (1940), 349–69.

―――― "Laurence Sterne, Apostle of Laughter," in The Age of Johnson (New Haven, Yale University Press, 1949), pp. 159–70.

Quennell, Peter. The Profane Virtues. New York, Viking, 1945.

Raleigh, Walter. The English Novel. New York, Scribner's, 1895.

Read, Herbert Edward. "Diderot's Love Letters," in In Defense of Shelley and Other Essays (London, Heinemann, 1936), pp. 183–203.

―――― "Sterne," in The Sense of Glory (Cambridge, Cambridge University Press, 1929), pp. 123–52.

Reinach, Joseph. Diderot. Paris, Hachette, 1894.

Richardson, Samuel. Clarissa; or the History of a Young Lady. Shakespeare Head edition. 8 vols. Oxford, Blackwell, 1929–1931.

Richardson, Samuel. Pamela; or Virtue Rewarded. Shakespeare Head edition. 4 vols. Oxford, Blackwell, 1929–1931.

Rosenkranz, Karl. Diderots Leben und Werke. Leipzig, Brockhaus, 1866.

Ross, John F. "The Final Comedy of Lemuel Gulliver," *University of California Studies in English,* VIII (1941), 175–97.

Rousseau, Jean-Jacques. Confessions. New York, Modern Library, n.d.

—— Correspondance générale de J.-J. Rousseau. Editée par Théophile Dufour. Vol. XIX. Paris, Colin, 1933.

Russell, H. K. "*Tristram Shandy* and the Technique of the Novel," *SP,* XLII (1945), 581–93.

Sainte-Beuve, Charles Augustin. "Diderot," in Causeries de lundi (Paris, Garnier, n.d.), III, 293–313.

—— "Diderot," in Portraits littéraires (Paris, Garnier, n.d.), I, 239–64.

—— "Diderot. Mémoires, correspondance et ouvrages," in Premiers lundis (Paris, Garnier, n.d.), I, 372–82, 383–93.

Saintsbury, George. A History of the French Novel. Vol. I. London, Macmillan, 1917.

Schérer, Edmond. Diderot; étude. Paris, Calmann-Levy, 1880.

Schlösser, Rudolf. Rameaus Neffe. Berlin, Dunker, 1900.

Seiden, Milton J. "Jean-François Rameau and Diderot's *Neveu,*" in Otis E. Fellows and Norman L. Torrey, eds., Diderot Studies (Syracuse, Syracuse University Press, 1949), pp. 143–91.

Selby-Bigge, L. A. British Moralists. Vol. I. Oxford, Clarendon Press, 1897.

Shaftesbury, Anthony Ashley Cooper, Third Earl of. Characteristics. Ed. by John M. Robertson. 2 vols. London, Richards, 1900.

Sherwood, Irma Z. "The Novelists as Commentators," in The Age of Johnson (New Haven, Yale University Press, 1949), pp. 113–26.

Sichel, Walter. Sterne, a Study. London, Williams, 1910.

Sidgwick, Henry. Outlines of the History of Ethics for English Readers. 3d ed. London, Macmillan, 1892.

Souilhé, J. "Pourquoi Thomas Hobbes?" in La Pensée et l'influence de Th. Hobbes (Archives de philosophie, Vol. XII [Paris, 1936], Cahier 2).

Spitzer, Leo. Linguistics and Literary History. Princeton, Princeton University Press, 1948.

Stapfer, Paul. Laurence Sterne, sa personne et ses œuvres. Paris Fischbacher, 1882.

Steel, Eric. Diderot's Imagery. New York, The Corporate Press, 1941.

Stephen, Leslie. The History of English Thought in the Eighteenth Century. 3d ed. 2 vols. New York, Putnam's, 1927.

Strachey, Lytton. Landmarks in French Literature. New York, Holt, 1927.

Taupin, René. "Richardson, Diderot et l'art de conter," FR, XII (1939), 181–94.

Terrin, Charles. "Diderot et la pensée moderne," Grande R, CXXXV (1931), 589–605.

Texte, Joseph. Jean-Jacques Rousseau and the Cosmopolitan Spirit in Literature. Tr. by J. W. Matthews. New York, Stechert, 1929.

Thackeray, William Makepeace. "The English Humorists of the Eighteenth Century," in Works (London, Smith, 1889–95), XXIII, 119–338.

Thayer, Harvey Waterman. Laurence Sterne in Germany. New York, Columbia University Press, 1905.

Thielemann, Leland James. "The Tradition of Hobbes in Eighteenth Century France." Thesis, Columbia University, Microfilm No. 2489, 1950.

Thomas, Jean. "Diderot et Baudelaire," Hippocrate (1938), 328–42.
—— L'Humanisme de Diderot. 2e éd. rev. Paris, Les Belles Lettres, 1938.

Torrey, Norman L. "Diderot's Atheism," The Literary Guide (1934), No. 457, pp. 117–18; No. 459, pp. 170–71; No. 460, pp. 182–3.

Torrey, Norman L. "Rousseau's Quarrel with Grimm and Diderot," in Essays in Honor of Albert Feuillerat, *Yale Romanic Studies,* XXII (1943), 163–82.

—— "Voltaire's Reaction to Diderot," *PMLA,* L (1935), 1107–43.

Tourneux, Maurice. Diderot et Catherine II. Paris, Calmann-Levy, 1899.

Trahard, Pierre. "Diderot," in Maîtres de la sensibilité française au XVIIIe siècle (Paris, Boivin, 1932), II, 49–286.

Trail, H. D. Sterne. London, Macmillan, 1882.

Trilling, Lionel. "The Legacy of Sigmund Freud—II: Literary and Aesthetic," *Kenyon Review,* II (1940), 152–73.

Turnell, Martin, The Novel in France. New York, New Directions, 1950.

Tuveson, Ernest. "The Origins of the 'Moral Sense,' " *Huntington Library Quarterly,* XI (1947–48), 241–59.

Vartanian, Aram. Diderot and Descartes: A Study of Scientific Naturalism in the Enlightenment. Princeton, Princeton University Press, 1953.

Venturi, Franco. Jeunesse de Diderot. Traduit de l'italien par Juliette Bertrand. Paris, Skira, 1939.

Walker, Eleanor. "Towards an Understanding of Diderot's Esthetic Theory," *RR,* XXXV (1944), 277–87.

Warner, James H. " 'Education of the Heart': Observations on the Eighteenth-Century English Sentimental Movement," *Papers of the Michigan Academy of Science, Arts and Letters,* XXIX (1943), 553–60.

Watkins, Walter Barker Critz. Perilous Balance. Princeton, Princeton University Press, 1939.

Watt, Ian. "Realism and the Novel," *EC,* II (1952), 376–96.

Wellek, René, and Austin Warren. *Theory of Literature.* New York, Harcourt Brace, 1942.

Willey, Basil. The Eighteenth Century Background. New York, Columbia University Press, 1950.

—— The Seventeenth Century Background. New York, Columbia University Press, 1952.

Worcester, David. The Art of Satire. Cambridge, Mass., Harvard University Press, 1940.

Wright, Arnold, and William Lutley Sclater. Sterne's Eliza. London, Heinemann, 1922.

Wright, C. H. Conrad. A History of French Literature. New York, Oxford University Press, 1912.

Yoseloff, Thomas. A Fellow of Infinite Jest. New York, Prentice-Hall, 1945.

Zabel, Morton D., ed. Literary Opinion in America. New York, Harper and Brothers, 1951.

INDEX